A Foreign Affair

A Foreign Affair

A Passionate Life in Four Languages

VALERIE BARNES

BANTAM
SYDNEY • AUCKLAND • TORONTO • NEW YORK • LONDON

A BANTAM BOOK

First published in Australia and New Zealand in 2004
by Bantam

National Library of Australia
Cataloguing-in-Publication Entry

Barnes, Valerie.
   A foreign affair : a passionate life in four languages.

   ISBN 1 86325 375 0.

   1. Barnes, Valerie – Journeys. 2. United Nations –
   Officials and employees – Biography. 3. Women translators –
   Biography. 4. Women travelers – Biography. I. Title.

910.92

Transworld Publishers,
a division of Random House Australia Pty Ltd
20 Alfred Street, Milsons Point, NSW 2061
http://www.randomhouse.com.au

Random House New Zealand Limited
18 Poland Road, Glenfield, Auckland

Transworld Publishers,
a division of The Random House Group Ltd
61-63 Uxbridge Road, London W5 5SA

Random House Inc
1745 Broadway, New York, New York 10036

Cover image: Getty Images/Lee Miller
Text designed and typeset in 13/16.5 pt Bembo by Midland Typesetters,
Maryborough, Victoria
Printed and bound by Griffin Press, Netley, South Australia

10 9 8 7 6 5 4 3 2 1

I dedicate this book to all those who contributed to my story.

Preface

When I first arrived at the Palais des Nations in Geneva, the United Nations was a young organisation trying to find ways of dealing fairly with never-before-experienced international problems. The leaders took their task very seriously and they were idealistic, hardworking and dedicated. Their vision was for a peaceful future for mankind; an end to all conflict. They were determined the fledgling UN would survive, grow, and make a real difference.

I, too, was young and inexperienced. As I entered the pristine white headquarters for the first time and wandered through its sunlit marble corridors, I felt insignificant and in awe. I had no idea that the rest of my life would be centred around what went on in this magnificent building and the ideals of the people in it. Or that, as the years went by, I would travel as a UN interpreter to most of the countries of the world and make my own small contribution to its achievements.

In fact it had all started long before that. It began in war-time Britain where, walking along the drab, grey London streets past bomb craters and piles of rubble, I daydreamed about a romantic world where people spoke exotic languages, played music, sang and danced with passion.

A career – and a life – I didn't even know existed awaited me. There would be lovers and husbands, babies, family and friends. And passion in all things.

Chapter 1

London in 1947 was drab and grey. The wonderful feeling of co-operation and solidarity that had prevailed during the war, when we willingly gave up our railings, saucepans and jewellery to the war effort, had come to an end. So, too, had the euphoria of victory. I had taken my place in the crowd in the sunshine in front of Buckingham Palace, shouting and waving with everyone else until members of the royal family came out one by one on to the balcony, smiling and waving back.

Now that the war was over, it was time for something exciting to happen, time for all the promises of the wartime songs to come true. I was twenty and waiting for my life to begin.

At Pinner County Secondary School I'd had the choice of studying Latin and Greek or French and Spanish, and had chosen modern languages. I took to French and Spanish like a duck takes to water. I enjoyed the music of the spoken languages and tried to speak them as if I were actually French or Spanish. I matriculated with distinctions in both (and Art) and I desperately wanted to keep studying languages at university. My three best friends were all going to university even though their results were not as good as mine. But, even though I passed the university entrance examinations with flying colours and won a scholarship, my parents were concerned about the financial aspects. They called a family council and my eldest uncle, head of the family, presided. My French teacher, Miss Jones, was present and while my mother busied herself with tea and cakes, it was decided that I would not be able to go to university but would have to go out into the big wide world instead to earn some money. My younger sister had always wanted to be a schoolteacher and would need to go to training college; my young brother had to be provided for. Even though the scholarship I had won would cover my tuition expenses, my parents were afraid they would not be able to afford my clothes, train fares and other expenses. It was a time of austerity and hardship and university seemed an unnecessary luxury. Miss Jones said she thought I would be able to find myself a good career even without a university degree and that clinched it. So it was decided I would do a nine-month commercial course including shorthand, typing and book-keeping. I was devastated – it seemed such a dreary prospect. To cheer me up, someone pointed out that the Pitman commercial course in central London included German. It hardly seemed a compensation.

However I threw myself into my new studies and happily found I could continue my language studies in the evenings. I discovered that I actually enjoyed shorthand and after a while my brain became so full of it that even while talking to people I would be mentally turning what they said into shorthand. At the final exams I passed the 250 words per minute test top of the class and became Miss Pitman of the Year – I still have the bump on my finger from holding the pencil tightly, to prove it!

When not reading during the one-hour train ride to and from London each day, I entertained myself by putting into shorthand all the advertisements in the train and on the platforms of the stations we passed through. They were some-times quite entertaining – the 'Bravington's Rings' ads were the wittiest. When I got bored with that, I tried adapting Pitman's shorthand into French and Spanish. This turned out to be useful. I had started keeping a diary by then and wrote it in shorthand. The really private bits I wrote in French or Spanish Pitman's shorthand.

Unfortunately, my boyfriend, Reg, was very serious and studious and there was never anything very exciting about him to put in my diary, in any language. He was five years older than me and already working in a London office as a French–English translator. He lived with his mother in St John's Wood. We had met at the Linguists Club, a club full of very earnest young men and women in corduroys. Reg had mousy hair but very kind dark grey eyes. We had never kissed but we did hold hands occasionally in the cinema when he took me to see French films. He also took me to poetry readings in Welsh – neither of us understood Welsh but we liked the sound of it. Reg never took me dancing and I never asked him to, thinking he'd find me frivolous.

I have always loved dancing and as a child went to a local dance school to learn ballet and Greek dancing (for which we swayed about, waving our arms around slowly with soulful expressions, draped in white). Later my younger sister and I learnt ballroom dancing, which we adored. I even won a bronze and later a silver medal for it, of which I was very proud. My favourite was the tango: the jerky steps and sudden dramatic head moves, as well as the deadpan, rather grim, tango face one pulls. You must not smile when dancing the tango. My sister and I felt very superior, knowing all about contra–body sway and the intricacies of the foxtrot and the fishtail. We still remember how to do the fishtail on dainty, pointed toes (with the appropriate bored expression).

It was heaven being swept off our feet by Bertram, the debonair teacher. The difficulty was finding dancing partners adept at the fishtail outside the dancing class. In fact, I don't remember ever finding one. It was demeaning for two women to dance together, but we sometimes did out of sheer desperation – at least if we danced together we could do the fishtail. With Pam, a friend from work, I sometimes went dancing on Saturday nights at Wembley Town Hall, or Hammersmith or Covent Garden dance halls. During the war there were always crowds of uniformed servicemen at all the nightspots and it was rare to sit out a dance if you didn't mind shuffling round the floor doing nothing in particular with your feet. I preferred Wembley because at the interval you could have coffee (at least, that's what they called it) and chocolate eclairs (with very sweet mock cream inside and fake chocolate on top). I once met a French airman there whose name was JoJo. He took me out to dinner in Soho which was a great excitement as we had steak and chips and I hadn't eaten red meat for ages. There was a lot of yellowish fat on the steak and it wasn't until I told my mother later about this that I learnt that what I had eaten was in fact horsemeat.

I was also a keen admirer of the famous flamenco dancer, Carmen Amaya. Flamenco was a flash of brilliant colour in grey austerity Britain. I never missed any of her performances in London, sometimes spending many hours in the queue on the pavement outside the theatre to get a seat in the gallery. That was quite an experience in itself because many of the students in the queue were dancers or singers themselves and entertained us with songs, conjuring tricks, clowning, mime or tap-dancing. When finally we got into the theatre and the show began, in true flamenco tradition we would call out in Spanish from the gallery, expressing our approval or disapproval, such as '¡*Viva la madre que te partió!*' ('Long live the mother who gave birth to you!') – the Spanish are serious about their compliments. The dancers would call back to us, answering our questions or making comments of their own. When the show was over we would join the stage door crowd, hoping to exchange a few words with the great Carmen Amaya herself or one of her family (most of the dancers, singers and guitarists as well as the seamstresses, hairdressers and make-up artists were her relatives) as they left. My mother seemed to understand my enthusiasm and to almost envy what I was doing. Both my parents were supportive and, having had a limited education themselves, they encouraged me in whatever I wanted to do (provided it was financially reasonable). However, I knew that if I told them that I was tempted to join Carmen Amaya and her gypsies, offering to sew costumes for them or cook or clean in exchange for a life of travel, adventure and dance, their support might not be forthcoming.

Immediately after the war, and indeed for some years to come, rationing remained in force in Britain and there were many shortages. We still needed clothing coupons. My sister, my mother and I shared many of our clothes; we had one warm llama winter coat we took it in turns to wear. Everyone was talking about the new synthetic material that had just been invented: it needed no ironing and felt silky, if a little stiff. Cotton and silk were all very well, but nothing could compare to the very latest nylon. I was given some sample squares of it and made myself a skirt and a drawstring blouse that I was very proud of.

I had heard about the new nylon stockings but had not yet seen any. Those of my friends who had some could only have got them by going out with an American soldier, but I had no GI boyfriend. We used to paint our legs with instant tanning lotion in the morning, to replace stockings. With a soft black pencil we drew a straight central line up the back to look like the seam.

My first lipstick was 'Tangee'; I shared a round box of Tokalon facepowder with my mother and sister. Toothpaste came as a round bright pink cake of some gritty substance with a distinctive smell, in a small tin – you rubbed your toothbrush on it before brushing your teeth. We used to put Melrose, solid hand cream in a tiny cardboard box, on our hands before we went to bed – and we waved our hair with curling tongs that had to be heated first on a gas ring.

Food was scarce and what we could get was unimaginative fare. The local 'British Restaurant' served waterlogged boiled cabbage. At home our occasional treat was bread and warm milk with sugar, or slices of bread with tinned condensed sweetened milk on top. On Sunday evenings we had slices of bread spread with lard and sprinkled with salt for supper.

I lived in Ruislip Manor, a suburb where the terraced houses and the streets all looked the same, with names like 'High Street', 'Station Road', 'Church Street' – just like all the streets in every other suburb. Ruislip Manor was just over an hour from central London on the Underground. It was always a rush to catch the last train home around midnight after my evening classes in London at the Instituto Español and the Linguists Club in Portman Square. Then I had an eerie fifteen-minute walk home from the station. The houses were dark, asleep – they could have been empty. My footsteps resounded on the grey pavements. Where trees might have been there were ugly brick air-raid shelters. At our street's Victory Party in 1945, these had been covered with bunting and long wooden benches had been propped up against them for people to sit on. In the middle of the road there had been two rows of trestle tables covered with red crêpe paper and laden with homemade yellow egg-powder cakes, currant buns, scones and endless cups of tea and Camp coffee in cracked cups.

There had been music and dancing but in the midst of it all a lean, khaki-uniformed figure had appeared, walking wearily down the street. He was the first man to come back, but we hardly recognised him because he was so thin. His toothless smile betrayed some of the tortures inflicted upon him in a Japanese prison camp. Later he told us how his finger- and toenails had been pulled out one by one, as well as his teeth, in the hope that he might divulge some useful information. It was impossible to imagine one human being doing that to another.

He had quietly gone into one of the houses, followed by a wife wondering, perhaps, whether she still knew him and really wanted him back after all this time. The joy had fallen out of our festivities, everything had gone quiet and we felt we should stay silent out of respect for our tired-looking returned soldier.

Now the air-raid shelters were silent and cast shadows as I walked past. They smelt of cat and human urine, and the odd shoe forgotten in the entrance betrayed the couples who had been grateful for the seclusion they offered. Cats darted out as I walked past, their eyes staring menacingly at me in the dark; sometimes a kitten would rub itself against my ankle, making me feel uneasy.

I walked down the middle of the road where I felt safer.

When I left for work in the mornings the houses had come to life, and as I hurried down the street to catch the 7.40, curtains twitched at every window. Everyone knew everything about everyone else – what you weren't told you could hear through the thin walls.

With my Miss Pitman award to bolster my confidence I answered an advertisement in the paper for a bilingual secretary (English and Spanish) and got the job on the strength of my Spanish and English shorthand speeds and an interview in Spanish. I worked on the editorial staff of a Fleet Street fashion magazine designed to promote the export of British fashions and textiles to Spain and South America.

I was soon covering London fashion shows together with my elderly, balding photographer – I believe we made quite an unusual pair. I was frequently given oddments of fabric from textile manufacturers who wanted a good 'write-up' and I made them into fashionable things to wear (hence the nylon windfall). Our Ruislip Manor neighbours, unfamiliar with the latest trends, must have gasped sometimes (understandably) as they watched me rushing to catch the train, dressed in my version of the latest Bond Street fashion.

On one occasion I was given a box containing a selection of knitting needles by a grateful client. Our advertising manager had come into my office in a flurry. 'I'd forgotten I promised a knitting-needle manufacturer that if he took a series of full-page advertisements I'd give him a few references in an editorial and perhaps slip in some photographs. Can you produce something? We've got exactly twenty-four hours.'

Knitting needles are not very inspiring to write about, or to photograph, and I was hard put to find an idea. Finally I went to the British Museum and wrote an article about the history of knitting with photographs of 'handknitted chain mail' that was the delight of the manufacturer – although I never did find out whether knitting needles had really been used for that purpose or whether I had created history.

Generally at lunchtime I walked to the National Gallery to visit Augustus John's smiling lady in red or Velásquez's Rokeby Venus and frizzy princesses in their wide skirts, attended by pale satin-clad princes. On the way there I would stop at Alf's Milk Bar and, leaning on the counter with my glass of milk in one hand and a sandwich in the other, would chat with him. Alf had a heart of gold and was a mine of Fleet Street gossip and precious tips.

One day I had hardly settled down to my sandwich when a hesitant figure appeared in the doorway. A tall, slim girl of about my age was struggling with two large suitcases, a bag that kept falling off her shoulder and a coat over one arm. She had fine features and looked French, with her fair hair piled on top of her head, wisps of it blowing over her face and at the nape of her neck. She wore elegant, foreign-looking clothes and high-heeled sandals. She seemed flustered and lost. Having stacked her belongings in the corner behind the door, she came to the counter and asked Alf in halting English with a strong accent: 'If you please, may I see the menu?'

I was afraid he might be rude to her in his straight-from-the-shoulder Cockney. He opened his mouth but I got in first and asked her in French if I could help.

A relieved smile spread over her face. '*Bonjour*. Please would you ask him to give me the same as you have?' she asked. Her name was Danielle, she said, and went on to explain: 'My English is not very good yet. I passed my written exams and I can read and write English but my ear is not good yet and I cannot understand well what people say. I fear I shall fail the orals so I managed to persuade my parents to let me come to England for two months. I have just arrived. I have a room booked with a family in Kent but first I thought I would spend a few days in London on my own to do some sightseeing. Now I am here I feel rather lost . . .'

There was a sweetness about her, especially her tiny mouth, which was the closest to a rosebud I have ever seen. Many years later I wondered whether the shape of people's mouths reflected the language they spoke and the sort of things they said. Danielle punctuated her speech with hand gestures.

We arranged to meet that afternoon when I had finished work and Danielle had checked into her modest hotel. Hoping to impress, I took her to the Shaftesbury Avenue Lyons' Salad

Bowl, which was the smartest place I had ever been to. It was hugely popular after the shortages of wartime and there was always a long queue. It was the first time for years we had seen such an array of food: two rows of bowls of different types of salad. It was also the first time we had experienced self-service and it was a thrill to be able to help yourself to whatever you fancied.

Later we went for a long walk, admiring the Law Courts, Westminster Abbey, Trafalgar Square and Tower Bridge and then I accompanied her back to her hotel. For the rest of her stay in England, several times a week she would come up from Kent on the train to meet me after work and we would explore all the London landmarks, stopping to pat the fat 'Archibald' fish on the iron lampstands along the Embankment. We day-dreamed as we watched the murky Thames and its lazy, grimy barges and photographed each other by the old cannons and pyramids of cannonballs. Dany came home with me for weekends and was amazed to see our rationbooks. 'How can you survive on so little butter?' she asked incredulously.

To me, Dany was a breath of fresh air. She represented the world I had glimpsed when learning French at school – a world of elegance, perfume, wine, finesse, courtesy. Gradually her English was improving. I told her which English books I had enjoyed most and she copied down a list of authors. One week-end we went to Hampton Court and got lost in the maze, the next we visited Windsor Castle and wandered along by the river afterwards in the weak spring sunshine. When we got home my parents had prepared the best dinner rationing would allow. We lay talking far into the night, Dany sleeping in my bed while I lay on a mattress on the floor in the bedroom that had always been mine, with its shabby wartime carpet and curtains.

'Do you have any sisters or brothers?' I asked her.

'One younger brother and an older sister, Marie. She was

married just before I left. There were many flowers, the *terrasse* was entirely decorated with white gladioli in tall vases. We decorated the barn with garlands of flowers and put up a wooden stage for the dance band.'

I imagined Deanna Durbin singing in the church and all the male wedding guests looking like Maurice Chevalier, Jean Sablon and Jean-Louis Barrault.

'It was at my sister's wedding that I met Bruno. We are going to get engaged. He is dark, kind and very intelligent. One day he will be a diplomat. He has a beautiful, deep, seductive voice. I think it's his voice that I fell in love with – that's what attracted me in the first place.'

I imagined Charles Boyer. I was enthralled. I felt I knew them all. Each person she described had, in my mind's eye, a magical golden aura.

'I live in the Loire valley, in a very old house in the country-side with many rooms and a cobbled courtyard with hens because of the war,' she continued. 'One wing of the house dates from 1734. There is a dovecote and a stream runs through the garden. There are apple and pear orchards, green lawns and weeping willow trees. We keep three dogs for hunting and many cats to keep away the mice.'

I could imagine it all, with Scarlett O'Hara as Dany on a garden swing, wearing a beautiful flower-sprigged, multi-layered skirt and a large flattering hat.

When the time came for Dany to go home, she was warm with her thanks and invited me to visit her in France a few months later. 'During the summer holidays my cousins come to stay as well and we put on plays and make music and go swimming in the Loire. My mother wants to meet you – I have written and told her how kind you and your family have been.'

I thanked her politely but she was talking about something I could not even imagine. I belonged to a world of treeless pavements and air-raid shelters, saving up to buy the wool to knit a new jumper or tickets to a concert at the Royal Albert Hall for my mother and me. I was not the sort of person who travelled abroad. France might as well have been on another planet.

I saw Dany off at Victoria Station and hurried off to my evening classes – there was a lot to catch up on.

When her letter arrived a week or two later I was pleased to think Dany still wanted me to visit her and flattered that her mother had added a note reiterating the invitation, but never thought of accepting. I showed the letters to my mother. She read them, then took off her glasses and laid them on her knee. Suddenly she looked up and said: 'And why *don't* you accept? You earn a good salary and if you keep it all for yourself for the next few weeks you should be able to afford the fare.'

Because my mother seemed to take the proposal seriously, I was forced to see that it could be arranged. Gradually we got more and more excited. My parents had been to France once on their honeymoon, had drunk wine and eaten Camembert and my father had bought my mother a cloche hat so elegant she had never dared wear it. She kept it on display in her bedroom and sometimes she would reach up to its special place above the corner wardrobe and put it into my hands. It was a little dusty but still very elegant.

In a dream I enquired in town next day about boat-trains and fares. After a month or two I had saved enough and reserved a seat.

The curtains at the windows twitched repeatedly as my father and I walked down the road in the direction of the station some weeks later. My father carried my suitcase with the expression of a man on an important mission. It was he who had packed. He worked for the Post Office so clearly he was an expert. I had passed the things to him and my mother had fluttered round us helpfully.

'What are all these white paper bags?' asked my father. 'Are you sure you need all these?'

'Yes, yes,' I said, too embarrassed to go into detail. My father stacked them among the underclothes and corsets, discreetly refraining from further questions. 'They may not have sanitary towels in France,' I had told myself, for they hardly fitted in with my image of open-air cafés, champagne and romance. French girls must be different!

I carried a brown paper bag containing two green apples and sandwiches for the journey. I was wearing the result of many hours' planning: a pale green dress and jacket I had made myself, shiny high-heeled black sandals and a precious pair of silk stockings given to me by a friend at work specially for the occasion. I had carefully adjusted the seams before leaving the house so that they ran straight down the centre of the back of my legs under my 'New Look' skirt. (It was the first time I had worn the 'New Look' and I felt rather conspicuous in the full, calf-length skirt after years of wartime straight, sensible ones.) I carried a pair of white gloves. Most important of all was the straw boater which was the epitome of London fashion at that time. I had decorated it with green velvet ribbon round the crown and a piece of green veiling along the front of the brim. As I stepped along beside my father, I felt particularly proud of my hat and knew how proud my father was of me. I pressed my new shoulderbag protectively to my side as Madame Bouvier had told me to. My mother had discovered there was a French lady living nearby and had taken me to see her for advice. She had given me many tips about travelling which I had taken to heart, although they dated from her youth and she was now quite old.

As we approached the railway station, we noticed a crowd outside milling around in front of a large blackboard. On it, chalked in hasty lettering, was BREAKDOWN ON THE LINE — NO TRAINS. There were no trains to London — what a disaster! We hurried to the bus stop where a bus was just pulling in, but the queue was already very long.

We looked at one another in stunned silence. It started to rain. I had no umbrella. I was afraid my boater would go limp or the veil stretch if they got wet. The people in the bus queue were muttering angrily. There were workmen in overalls and businessmen with rolled umbrellas. (Did they never open them, even when it rained?)

Suddenly my father jumped into action. I had never heard him raise his voice before. He addressed the queue in a tone of authority. 'My daughter has to go to Victoria to catch the boat-train to France. Does anybody mind if we go straight to the front of the queue?'

Nobody said anything. I hung back, feeling embarrassed, but my father bustled me forward, the queue meekly gave way before him and soon we were on the bus, luggage and all, balancing precariously just inside the door.

Chapter 2

The Channel was rough and most of the people on the deck of the ferry were being sick. I sat on my flimsy wartime suitcase, hoping it wouldn't collapse under my weight, though it was bulging ominously. I concentrated on the green apple I was eating: Mme Bouvier had assured me a sour green apple was a guarantee against seasickness. It seemed to work – or perhaps it was the excitement of my adventure. This was the most daring thing I had ever done in my life. I couldn't believe I was actually travelling to another country and that Danielle and her family really wanted me to visit them. Would my French be good enough? It had been adequate for school but real French people seemed to talk so fast.

Waiting for the train to leave Paris for Lyon, I was amazed to see people selling real oranges and bananas. I had forgotten what they looked like after the eight years of shortages. As far back as I could remember we'd had 'orange juice' that tasted of chemicals and came in flat bottles like medicine – 'The Tonic'.

As the train drew into Lyon station, I got my mirror out of my bag and anxiously touched up my hair and lipstick and rearranged my boater, drawing the green veil across my eyes. It came to the

15

tip of my nose so I would be able to kiss everyone on both cheeks without it getting in the way. My fashionable new shoulderbag, a wartime invention, kept falling off my shoulder.

Having checked that the seams of my stockings were straight, I stepped down on to the platform, suitcase in hand. My veil fluttered in the draught from the train. Looking back on it now I can imagine what an unusual sight I must have been for the French people waiting on the platform. I was trying to look like something from one of the London fashion shows and my new wasp-waister corsets were very tight.

Danielle was waiting for me, her blue eyes shining. Her father and brother were waiting outside, standing by a large black Citroën. After a brief introduction my case was stowed in the boot, I was bundled in the back with Dany and we were off. I noticed that, unlike me, they were all dressed in casual, comfortable summer clothes. 'It is good to have you here!' said Danielle warmly in English. 'But now we may speak French because I have just had my results. I passed my English orals with flying colours! We are going to have a champagne celebration with you tonight. We are preparing a special dinner.'

'I'm afraid I have forgotten all my French,' I apologised. 'In England it seemed OK but here I feel a bit overwhelmed.'

But from that moment on, not another word of English was spoken.

After a while we left the town and drove past farms and through little villages where there were just a handful of small houses grouped round a church. Peasant women dressed in black with black head-scarves crossed the road carrying long loaves. Children on bicycles carried breadsticks home, nibbling the end as they went past. There were scruffy dogs asleep in the middle of the road and cats darted in front of us. Wooden kitchen chairs had been squarely placed before the front doors of some of the houses with just enough room to sit and watch the world go by without getting in the way of the passing cars. The sun was shining and I could hardly contain my excitement.

'Here we are!' cried Danielle as the car slowed down and turned into an impressive entrance flanked by stone pillars. We drove slowly past a large barn containing several cars, a lorry, a tractor and a plough that I glimpsed inside in the shadows. We stopped and to our right was a staircase leading up to the glassed-in verandah of a large house. All around, hens and chicks pecked at the cobblestones.

'We're going in through the back entrance to surprise everyone,' explained Dany. 'My family are all so excited to meet you – they have never met an English person before!' I got out of the car, arranged my veil and gazed straight into the clear grey eyes of a lanky youth with thick black hair, who had been squatting with a pot of paint beside an old square black car. It was something like the shape of a London taxi – very high off the ground. The cool grey eyes looked at me in amazement as if they had never witnessed such an apparition, as well might have been the case.

'My cousin, Gérard,' said Dany impatiently.

He was wearing an old pair of brown shorts and a torn short-sleeved shirt. He continued to stare at me, paintbrush poised in his arrested hand, as I stood there in my white boater and green veil.

Dispelling my shyness with an effort, I bent forward to see that he was painting the three little Disney pigs, one on the rear of the car and one on each of the side doors.

Suddenly the whole family was around us and I was welcomed effusively, then hustled into the house and shown my room. Then Dany took me on a tour of the house.

It was enormous. There were three storeys and a high-ceilinged attic that had been turned into a theatre with rows of mismatched chairs, a stage and curtains.

'That is where my sister Marie lives with Pierre.' Danielle was pointing through the attic window to another tall grey and white house adjoining the one we were in at right angles. 'And over there is where we keep old furniture and cobwebs!' She laughed, indicating a derelict building with '1734' inscribed over the door, which completed the 'U' shape.

In the middle was a cobbled courtyard (which turned out to be impossible to walk on in high heels) and a dovecote. A lazy dog lay sunning himself.

'Dinner at eight,' said Dany, leaving me to unpack in my room.

When I entered the dining-room, having spent an eternity outside trying to pluck up courage, there were fourteen people sitting round a large wooden farmhouse table, which had been covered with a thick coarsely woven check tablecloth, and fifteen matching green and white check table napkins in silver rings. Each person had tied a special knot or marked their napkin in some way to distinguish it from the others; Dany's parents each had a little box of pills tucked into theirs.

I glanced desperately in Dany's direction and she indicated the empty chair she had been keeping for me next to hers. Opposite, cool grey eyes were studying my every move.

First came the champagne and the speeches, then an elaborate dinner and when everything was cleared away everyone remained seated, talking about the activities of the day and plans for the holidays. Finally, Danielle's father rose to his feet. 'You must be tired,' he said in my direction. 'Good night. Sleep well.' He shook my hand. There was a chorus of '*Bonne nuit!*' as each person rose and shook my hand, except for Dany and her mother who kissed me on both cheeks. I gratefully withdrew to the privacy of my room where I could think my own thoughts – in English.

The sheets were heavy starched linen with a swirling embroidered pattern of intertwined initials and pulled threads across the top sheet. There were no pillows but a thick bolster rolled inside the bottom sheet. I looked out of the window onto the slumbering lawn and willow trees, the lengthening shadows and the water of a stream glistening in the moonlight. Closing first the old-fashioned wooden shutters with heart-shapes cut out of them, then the windows and curtains, I climbed into bed. The mattress was twice as thick as any I had known, and what comfort there was in a bed you literally had to climb up to get into! It was like stretching out on a soft cloud.

At breakfast in the huge old-fashioned kitchen, Dany offered me tea. 'I will take tea also to keep you company,' she said, but I understood from the rest of the family, who came in one by one and poured themselves a bowl of coffee and hot milk from the two saucepans on the stove, that tea was something they drank only when ill. They observed my tea-drinking with wonder, and I understood why they didn't like tea when I saw the cook preparing mine. She boiled a saucepan of water, added a pinch of tea and then boiled it all up for a few minutes, stirring with a wooden spoon. It tasted very different from the tea I was used to and very soon I was a convert to the morning bowl of coffee. On the table was a long basket of breadsticks. They each cut off a long piece and dunked it in their coffee but Dany got some butter and home-made jam out of the pantry for me. There seemed to be unlimited butter in large oval cakes with a flower pattern stamped on top.

Indeed, all the meals were delicious and I really looked forward to them after the meagre fare in England. Here, there seemed to be no shortages, and certainly no rationing. There was never anything out of a tin. The womenfolk helped prepare the food and decided at breakfast what the menus for the day would be and who would prepare what. The two red-faced, silent women in sensible shoes and black dresses covered in voluminous black aprons were the maids who did the housework, washing and ironing, scrubbed the kitchen floor every evening, washed the dishes and peeled the vegetables according to Danielle's mother's instructions. They seemed to be at everyone's beck and call.

The fuel stove was enormous and homely; the coals glowed red when anyone opened the oven door or removed the heavy round lids from the top by means of a poker with a hook at one end.

The evening's soup was already cooking on top of one of these by the time we came down to breakfast each morning. The kitchen smelt of asparagus or leeks or carrots depending on the variety we would be having that evening.

The joints of meat were bigger than any I had ever seen, even at Christmas, and there were elaborate entrées with cold meats arranged artistically on large platters and decorated with gherkins, olives and small white onions, or eggs mimosa surrounded by rolled ham or boiled eggs in aspic. There were wire baskets of real eggs hanging in the kitchen. In England we used bright yellow egg powder and all the recipes I had seen my mother using referred to so many teaspoons of egg powder.

'Shall we make a fruit salad for tonight?' Dany asked me. I had never thought of it not coming out of a tin.

They were all as curious about me as I was about them. At first I could understand only a word here and there. When they spoke fast to one another and then suddenly everyone got up and went off, I was at a loss to understand what was happening and where we were going. Little by little, however, my ear became attuned to the language and my French improved. They delighted in teaching me French slang as we sat round the table at meals, and laughed good-heartedly when I made a mistake or mixed my metaphors.

On Sundays the family appeared at breakfast arrayed in their best clothes, ready for church. On the first Sunday, Dany stayed with me while the others went to Mass, coming home with white cardboard boxes of cakes for dessert.

'I generally manage to avoid Mass by getting to the church just as it is ending,' Gérard had explained to me airily as he sauntered out very late. 'The main thing is to be seen on the church steps as everyone comes out, and then go with them to the *pâtissier* to buy the cakes.' When I looked at him in surprise he added: 'I'm a communist, anyway!'

I questioned Dany about Gérard, who seemed to spend a lot of time at her house. It seemed that Dany, Gérard and I were roughly the same age although Gérard looked much younger. 'Since his mother died three years ago, he's been studying away from home. He gets very lonely during the long summer holidays so my parents make him welcome here and he often stays the night. So does his little sister. There are spare rooms and beds up in the attic.'

He seemed spoilt indeed, for his pockets were always full of money and he was the only one to have a car of his own.

A confusing jumble of uncles, aunts and cousins always arrived for Sunday lunch. At noon we all gathered in the salon for an apéritif and I was given a glass of milky-looking Pernod and water. Half an hour later we took our places round an even bigger table in the main dining room – this time there were twenty-six of us. Gérard's English was not very good and I was still too shy to speak to him in French but his older brother, a geologist, had come to lunch and was sitting beside me. I felt more at ease with him as he chatted to me in English. He had been to England once on holiday and told me about the modern ballet he had seen in London where the dancers had come on stage on bicycles.

Everyone drank wine, even the children, who had water added to theirs – except for the *vin vieux*, the old wine, which came later in smaller glasses and was too precious to have water added. The children were given this only as a special treat when they grew old enough to appreciate it.

There seemed to be endless courses. We ate each vegetable separately, serving ourselves from dishes passed round the table and the meat came at the end, also served on its own. Then the cheeseboard and they all helped themselves liberally to a large piece of each cheese with another long piece of bread (but no butter). The goat's cheese they all seemed to like so much was something I had never heard of and the smell was off-putting. Anyway, by this stage I was unable to eat another morsel so the family assumed I didn't like cheese. How could they know that in food-rationed England, if we were lucky enough to have cheese, it would be the mainstay of our meal?

After this came the *entremets*, the dessert course, which some-times was the French version of rice pudding (though it looked more like a cake), turned out on a dish and decorated with glacé fruit. Then came the cream cakes bought after church – gener-ally two apiece. They were twice as big as any I had ever seen and rich with dark chocolate and whipped cream. How did Dany keep such a trim figure, I wondered, and why was Gérard so slim?

Then baskets of fresh fruit were put on the table – peaches and apricots from the garden and *nefs*, strange small soft brown fruit. Finally coffee was served in tiny cups, accompanied by little almond-topped marzipan biscuits, marzipan-stuffed dates and a dish of luscious dark chocolates.

By this time I was yearning for an invigorating walk outside in the fresh air but one of the men opened the door of the elaborate *desserte* and produced bottles of liqueur which he placed in the centre of the table. We drank our liqueurs from the still-warm coffee cups and Dany's young brother introduced me to a *canard* (duck), a lump of sugar dipped into the liqueur. The conversation was very animated by now. At last the maid appeared with a large tray to take away the coffee cups and I glimpsed with relief the approaching end of the meal. But it was only an hour or two later that I could hear the rattling of soup plates as the table was laid again for supper . . .

The evening meal always started with soup, and they were all most amused at the English way of eating it. They taught me the French way and it is certainly more practical to spoon it towards you rather than away. I soon learnt, too, that in France it is considered rude to put your hands under the table, as you do in England, and that one should never take a knife to salad or a bread roll. In fact, the fork was used most, with a piece of bread in the left hand for pushing the food on to the fork.

I also learnt that the reason why so many French people could be seen carrying loaves of bread (something which had struck me more than once!) was that bread had to be eaten fresh at each meal. Three times a day the baker would deliver our baguettes. At dinner, anyone given a piece of bread that dated from breakfast or lunch would be outraged: bread had to be fresh.

Gérard, Danielle, her fiancé Bruno and I became a happy foursome and frequently went swimming together. Or rather, they swam and I watched for I had never learnt to swim. I hadn't seen much of the sea and had taken an instant dislike to public swimming pools in London because they reeked of chlorine and were always crowded.

'Quick, get your things before Pouche finds out where we're going!' whispered Dany. 'Once she hid in the boot of the car and was nearly suffocated by the time we found her.'

'But why don't we take her with us?' I asked.

'Oh, she's a nuisance. She tags along wherever we go – she clings like a limpet! We have to try all sorts of tricks to get rid of her.'

Pouche was Gérard's little sister. We called her 'Pouche' but her real name was Renée. She must have been about eleven years old and wore her hair with a central parting and a small round coil above each ear. Her face was full of mischief. She was very quick, and often when we got to the car to go somewhere we would find her already sitting in the back, waiting for us. Her favourite trick was to hide underneath the dining-room table where she could eavesdrop. She was growing up without much supervision since the death of her mother. Officially her grand-mother was responsible for her but Mémée was deaf and slow of movement and Pouche often skipped past her unnoticed and out of the door, shutting it soundlessly behind her.

One Sunday, Gérard's father, Monsieur Baumier, came to lunch and an extra-special festive meal was prepared, for he appreciated good food. He lived in a large apartment in nearby St Etienne with Pouche, Gérard (during the holidays), his mother-in-law Mémée and Antoinette the cook. M. Baumier was shaped like a barrel and was a kind, bon-vivant of a man. He had a small neat grey moustache, questioning eyebrows and arrived wearing a black béret and carrying a bundle of baguettes under one arm. He had only one eye, a legacy of *La Guerre de 14–18*. When he met me he stared unashamedly as I was the first English person he had ever encountered. After the usual cour-tesies, he asked: 'What religion do you have in England?'

I tied myself in knots trying to answer his impossible ques-tions about the Church of England, how it was the religion of the Kings and Queens, how the Protestants had protested, how the rules had been changed when Henry VIII wanted to divorce a wife and marry another. He made me feel like a savage from the jungle but he was just curious about those strange people who did not speak French and drank tea when they were not ill. He told me he had once seen a picture in the paper of a fire in London. The fire brigade and victims of the fire had been handed cups of tea instead of glasses of red wine to help them recover – '*Quel pays bizarre!*' He was also shocked when I asked if I could make tea in the middle of the afternoon. 'You eat and drink between meals in England?' he commented, shaking his head. 'That is very bad for your health.'

He and Danielle's father delighted in taking me for a stroll round the garden, stopping to tell me the French names of the plants and shrubs so that I would repeat them and they could laugh at my accent. I played up to them quite happily. They took me to the orchard and helped me pick peaches for I had never seen any growing before. We stopped near a willow tree by the stream.

'The English have always been our enemies, right through history,' said M. Baumier. 'You are so near to us, just across the Channel. Yet we have never been able to trust one another. You eat strange food, you have a strange religion. But you – you do not seem English,' he went on, in what was meant to be a compliment. 'English women are renowned in France for their projecting teeth and large feet!'

Funnily enough, M. Baumier himself exactly fitted the English concept of a Frenchman: a small, rotund gourmand complete with moustache and béret.

Next morning, Gérard arrived bursting with enthusiasm over his latest idea.

'Let us take Valérie on a sightseeing tour!'

'What a fabulous idea!' agreed Marie. 'We could take the two cars – I'm sure Papa will let us use his – and visit all the beauty spots. We could even take tents and camp!'

'Can I come too?' whined Pouche.

'I think that's a marvellous idea,' said Pierre, ignoring Pouche. 'We could take a week and really show her all the best places. But is your car safe?'

'My car goes just as well as yours!' retorted Gérard. Little did we realise how true his words would prove to be.

And so it was settled. Danielle's parents agreed, provided Marie and Pierre were in charge as they were the eldest. They were anxious that I be shown everything and well entertained. They helped prepare the sleeping bags and tents and the food supplies. They pored over maps with us and helped decide on the itinerary.

When finally we set off early one morning, the happy foursome climbed into the car with the three little pigs painted on it, while Marie announced good-naturedly that Pouche (who had prevailed) could have the back seat of their car all to herself.

Marie and Pierre drove off first, leading the way; we felt very excited as we followed them, hooting our farewells to the rest of the family grouped in the driveway. Gérard was at the wheel; his large competent hands commanded my respect for they seemed unhesitatingly confident. Bruno and Danielle sat close together in the back, full of anticipation about the joys that lay ahead. In the front next to Gérard, I felt like Queen Elizabeth during the Lord Mayor's Procession as I waved goodbye from my window. We chattered happily and Dany and Bruno taught me some French marching songs and a war song about having to eat nothing but potatoes. Judging by the meals I had seen, this did not apply to Danielle's part of the world.

We were beginning to feel stiff and hungry when at last the car in front pulled into the side of the road, then down a lane, and finally came to a halt by a lake.

We spread out a rug, sat down and enjoyed a picnic lunch of melon and ham, *saucisson en croûte*, baguette, peaches and apricots. We drank white wine Pierre had cooled in the water amid some rocks. We sat talking for some time and I was touched by Marie's solicitous care of me and the kindness of all of them. I felt a little bereft later when Marie, Pierre and Pouche were forced to abandon us when Pierre's car emitted a cloud of smoke and then broke down completely. Gérard drove to a nearby garage to get help. The mechanic repaired Pierre's car but explained that it was only temporary and the faulty carburettor needed to be replaced so reluctantly Marie, Pierre and Pouche returned home, promising to drive slowly and carefully.

Thus miraculously our happy foursome was finally left to continue our camping adventures unaccompanied and unchaperoned.

My three companions smoked a brand of cigarettes they called 'Heeg Leaf'. They told me it was English but I had never heard of a 'heeg'. It wasn't until I saw the cigarette packet that I realised they were in fact called 'High Life'. At that time it was very sophisticated in France to use English brand names.

When Gérard saw how impressed I was with his barefoot driving, he drove barefoot all the time. 'It's much safer,' he explained. 'I am at one with the car, sensitive to every reaction of the engine.'

We came to a river and decided to set up our tents. We cooked our supper over a campfire – everything tasted delicately smoked and delicious. Then we started to organise ourselves for the night. It seemed we had only two sleeping bags and two tents. Presumably I would be sleeping with Danielle in one, while the boys shared the other. I changed into my pyjamas and brushed my hair at length while I waited to see what would happen. After a while I saw that Dany was snuggling into Bruno's arms in his sleeping bag as if it weren't the first time. I looked hesitatingly at the remaining sleeping bag.

'It's for you,' Gérard said manfully. 'I shall roll myself up in this blanket. I'll be fine. We'll take the other tent.'

He lay next to me and put his arm under my head. I felt warm and relaxed. He kissed me but strangely there seemed to be very little contact. The kiss over, Gérard fell asleep.

After musing a little while about how things would have been if Marie and Pierre had still been with us and whose tent Pouche would have slept in, I must have fallen asleep too, because the next thing I knew someone was tugging open the top of the sleeping bag and climbing in.

'It's cold,' said Gérard as he settled himself in beside me.

I slept in his arms. It seemed the expected thing to do. I had never slept with anyone before and was fearful I might snore while asleep or that my stomach might rumble.

When he sat up in the middle of the night and fished about in the dark, I was curious.

'I have a packet of *lettres anglaises* somewhere. I think I tucked them under the sleeping bag. Where on earth can they be?'

Despite my inexperience I guessed what they were, for once I had gone into my parents' bedroom at home and caught my father with a mysterious packet in his hand. His surprise on seeing me and the guilty way he whipped them out of sight, muttering something about cigarettes, had aroused my interest. He must have mentioned it to my mother because the following morning she had explained to me about contraceptives, but I had never seen one close up.

'I shall wear one every night to save getting sticky,' Gérard explained.

'Oh, yes,' I replied in a matter-of-fact voice, trying to sound like a woman of the world whose sleeping partners always wore them.

I lay back thinking about it for some time but Gérard was already asleep again. Perhaps he was having sexy dreams. Apart from the goodnight kiss our relationship had been platonic so far.

'I respect you enormously,' he told me. 'Too much to touch you,' he added nobly.

I wouldn't have known what to expect even if he had. But I felt it was very gentlemanly to respect me so much.

Sometimes I thought Dany and Bruno were enjoying themselves more than we were, judging by the sighs and groans
coming from their tent. I would have liked our kissing to last a
little longer but Gérard seemed quite content so I concentrated
on going to sleep.

Some days later Dany asked 'How do you feel about Gérard?
I think he's falling in love with you.'

'He couldn't possibly fall in love with me! Anyway, he's more
or less unofficially engaged, he told me, to the daughter of a
friend of his father's. Her parents are very wealthy and their
business would combine well with Monsieur Baumier's.'

We were stirring a large pan of tinned soup (the first tin I'd
come across in France) over a camp fire while the boys struggled to put up the tents.

'She has a red sports car and she lets him drive it sometimes.
He said that if I ever see them together I must understand that
it's only because of the sports car . . .'

We visited countless cathedrals and churches and Bruno and
Gérard delighted in regaling me with details about the Catholic
religion, which I'd never come into contact with before. After a
day of ornate statues and golden decorations, pure virgins, adult-
faced baby Jesuses and Saint Anthonys with moneyboxes
underneath for those wishing to thank him for finding things
they had lost, we sat round our camp fire drinking 'grog' – a
mixture of rum, hot water, sugar and lemon juice – to keep out
the cold and damp.

'Tell Valérie about your convent school, Dany,' said Gérard.
'Isn't it true you had to wear a shift when you took a bath to
avoid sinning by seeing your own naked body?'

We were now quite at home with one another and they all
enjoyed my horrified bewilderment at their stories.

Bruno, going one better, joked about the Jesuit college he and
Gérard had attended. He insinuated and skated over facts so

cleverly that nothing he said was offensive, as he talked about love affairs between some of the senior and junior boys. As the import of what he was saying began to penetrate, my eyes opened wide. Dany was quick to jump to my rescue and, afraid I had been shocked, changed the subject.

'Come on, the water's hot – time to do the washing up!'

Next day we were up early. We washed in the river. I found it difficult to keep my hair tidy and my make-up in order and was very glad I had not brought my corsets with me (which I had seriously considered). Dany obviously wasn't wearing any and I would have been embarrassed if Gérard had glimpsed them. In London the saleslady in Swan and Edgars had stressed that, even though I was slim and weighed only 104 pounds, one's clothes could not possibly hang properly unless one wore corsets. I was a slave to them for many years.

'We're going to take you to Puy-de-Dome today,' they announced.

From afar we could see the impressive terracotta statue of Virgin Mary, massive and awe-inspiring high above us on top of the hill. Endless steps approached the statue from all sides. Gérard stopped the car for me to get a better view.

'I hope you're good at walking on your knees,' Bruno said in a confidential tone. 'We have to go up all those steps on our knees.'

I gasped and looked at him incredulously but a few seconds later Dany gave the game away by bursting into laughter.

The confessionals in the churches intrigued me. I questioned Danielle and Gérard but the scraps of information they gave me only whetted my appetite for more.

'Will you confess that you kissed me?' I wanted to ask Gérard, but didn't dare.

'You see those angels up there?' he asked, putting his arm round my shoulders and pointing up to a frieze. 'Would you say they are male or female?'

I had never thought of such a question. I looked at Dany and Bruno for help but they burst out laughing.

'Have you noticed that baby Jesus has no navel? That's because his birth was immaculate.'

None of this had been taught at my Sunday school. I was amazed. So were some passers-by.

'The baby's real father wasn't Joseph anyhow. He was illegitimate. His father was a mysterious stranger who visited Mary exactly nine months before the baby's birth on 25 December. Storytellers called him St Gabriel to mask the truth and that is why St Gabriel's day is on 24 March. Have you noticed how tall and attractive Archangel Gabriel always is in the paintings? And how his visit is always shown to have taken place in her bedroom?'

I was speechless. When it came to the Catholic religion, which seemed bizarrely exotic to me, I never knew if they were teasing or absolutely serious.

As we came out of the church Gérard disappeared, returning with a bunch of flowers. He presented them to me with a click of the heels and a mock bow. Danielle and Bruno looked on with a smile.

No-one had ever given me flowers before. In London I was no different from the thousands crammed together in the rush-hour Underground bound for home. Here in France I was suddenly unique. I blushed and stammered, 'Thank you'. Desperately I started talking about something – anything – to hide my embarrassment and delight.

I had fallen in love. It was just like the novels I had read.

Our camping expedition finally came to an end and we returned to Danielle's house but our foursome was now accepted by all and we kept apart from the rest of the household as much as we could. Bruno invited us to spend my last evening at his home nearby. His parents were away but he refrained from telling Dany's parents this detail.

Once again, Dany and I spent the afternoon preparing food and chopping up fruit for a fruit salad which we generously anointed with a precious bottle of old port wine found in the cellar, while the boys sorted out a pile of 78 rpm records and moved the furniture and carpets in the lounge so that we could dance. We emptied three or four dusty bottles of red wine from the cellar and danced late into the night to the strains of Charles Trenet's *La Mer*, and Jean Sablon's *Boum, mon coeur fait boum-boum . . .*

Dany and Bruno disappeared for a long period but Gérard and I continued dancing, holding one another close. It would have been nice to dance cheek to cheek but Gérard was too tall and, in spite of my very high heels, my face rested on the widest part of his tie. But the lights were low, we had drunk far too much wine and we were happy.

When Dany came back we crept home, taking our shoes off before going into the house and not even daring to whisper.

My holiday was over. The family waved to me from the driveway as Dany and her father drove me to the station next morning, but Gérard was nowhere to be seen.

The lump in my throat turned to tears when he appeared on the platform just as the train started to pull out of the station. Running alongside, he held out a small box which I was just able to stretch out and take from his hand before the train went into the tunnel.

I sat back on the seat and opened the box. It contained a brooch with a white seagull on it and a *billet doux* which read:

'You are my seagull, flying off across the seas. If you do not fly back again soon I shall have to fly out to join you in Perfidious Albion.'

Tears streamed down my cheeks as I read the romantic note again and again. It was a perfect ending to a wonderful holiday. I had entered the glamorous world I had previously known only from books and films. But it was all over now. My dream world would carry on existing perfectly well without me. One thing was certain: I was not the same person as the one who had left England three weeks earlier. I was no longer 100 per cent English. Some part of me was now French.

Back in London, it was raining. At work, I had been promoted a few months before and was now responsible for all incoming and outgoing correspondence in Spanish. It wasn't difficult: there was a file of model letters which I just had to adapt. With the help of a Portuguese dictionary and grammarbook, I also handled the Portuguese correspondence. One morning, my boss, Señor Ramirez, called me into his office to say that a very important Spanish businessman was coming to London for a few weeks and needed an interpreter to accompany him to a series of meetings connected with the magazine.

Sr Hernández was tall and elegant. He moved in a cloud of expensive eau-de-cologne and always had a folded silk handkerchief in his top pocket which matched his beautiful silk tie. When we were introduced, he kissed my hand with a click of the heels, and presented me with a little gift from Spain: a beautiful beribboned black box containing six tablets of luxurious Maja soap, so highly perfumed that just taking the lid off the box made me light-headed. He spoke very flowery Spanish which I soon learnt could be shortened considerably when translated into English. He insisted upon my company at all the cocktail and dinner parties he had to attend, and even at dinner when he would otherwise have been alone. We went to the best restaurants in London, jumping in and out of taxis; he invariably presented me with flowers in the course of the evening (though more expensive, they were never as beautiful as those Gérard had given me). He told me about his wife and daughters in Barcelona and showed me their photographs. I invented a fiancé, just in case. I had found a use for poor old Reg at last! (He phoned and left messages but I was never there.) But I had no problems of any sort with Sr Hernández. He was a kind, generous man and when he left, he invited me to visit his family in Madrid. They would take me out to cafés in the evenings for sherry and tapas; he would love to take me to a bullfight and explain the meaning of all the steps and gestures. He would also like to teach me the language of flowers and the language of the fan. With a bow, he gave me a beribboned packet of three pairs of pure silk stockings – an untold luxury in London in 1947.

I was becoming a little Spanish.

Back at the office, the English secretary I shared with another member of the editorial staff was on holiday. Her replacement, a buxom blonde temp called Grace, was efficient and friendly and explained to me on her last day that she was doing this job to earn money to go on holiday to Switzerland. She had a pen friend in Geneva who had invited her there. When she left I thought I would never see her again. Little did I know the important role she was to play in my life.

Gérard wrote every day. Sometimes twice or even three times. He painted portraits of me from memory and sent photographs of them. He was at university in Paris but must have devoted a large part of each day to writing the long letters I received. I know because of the time I needed to answer them. All my lunchtimes were now spent in the office, replying to his letters. I had been swept off my feet – I was madly in love. My eyes shone and my face flushed with excitement each time the postman brought a letter. My mother looked on helplessly. She too was lost in wonderment at this passionate Frenchman who behaved in such an un-English way and wrote so many letters.

But I was still seeing Reg, who took me to the ballet, to concerts and to Welsh poetry readings. I knew I had to tell him about Gérard but it was difficult to find an opportunity. He was such a gentle, considerate person, patient and quietly-spoken, and I respected his well-read opinions. One day he said his mother wanted to meet me, and he would like to take me home to tea on Sunday afternoon. The time had come to say my piece, and nervously I began: 'I have met a French boy named Gérard and I am going to Paris to see him for Easter.'

'When?' he asked quietly.

I knew I had to hurt him. 'I plan to leave on Thursday.'

He turned quickly so that I wouldn't see his face and hurried off. I called out a faltering 'Goodbye . . .' to his departing back.

Reg must have been very persistent in his enquiries. When I sat down in my reserved seat in the boat-train at Victoria, who should be sitting calmly opposite me but Reg! He carried a small hold-all and a parcel of sandwiches. He sat back with a smile, enjoying my surprise.

'I thought I might as well see you are all right,' he said, 'Perhaps I shall succeed in entertaining you during the journey.'

It was an unusual way of trying to win someone back, but he tried his hardest. From the hold-all he produced books for me but I didn't get a chance to read them because he kept up an interesting flow of conversation. He bought me fruit and coffee. I felt more and more guilty; I knew Gérard would be waiting on the platform when we arrived in Paris. I felt like a pawn in someone's chess game.

'Don't worry, I shall get off first,' he said when the train pulled in, and disappeared.

I was grateful to him and knew that, were I being reasonable, he was the man I should choose. But though I felt warm towards him there was no physical attraction and certainly no passion.

Then I forgot poor Reg completely as I leant out of the open carriage door, scanning the people on the platform. Yes, there was Gérard, conspicuously head and shoulders above the crowd, several parcels under one arm, the other ready to encompass me, take hold of my case and guide me to a waiting taxi.

The week passed in a whirl of theatres, concerts, candlelit dinners in romantic restaurants, cabarets, museums, cathedrals and art galleries. He introduced me to the paintings of Chagall. Gérard had a wad of notes in his wallet – his father thought he was on a skiing holiday with the red-sports-car girl and her friends and had been unstinting in his financial encouragement.

Gérard also explained: 'I have to present an account book to my father each week for reimbursement. Knowing you were coming, I have been taking precautions for some time.' He grinned mischievously. 'I have had friends dying for weeks, and others getting married so there has been a series of items entitled "wreath", "wedding gift", "celebration dinner". Then my father came to Paris last week for business and invited me to join him and his business partners in an expensive restaurant for lunch. I went there and asked for the money instead; I sat outside on a bench and ate some bananas. So you see, thanks to all my preparations, we have plenty of money.'

We visited Versailles and sat at the tables in the gravel under the trees, drinking *citron pressé*. People walked dogs on leads, children played in the pond with model sailing boats on a piece of string. I mused that Renoir would have liked to paint the scene. He probably did. We visited Marie Antoinette's village with its waterlily-covered pond, cottages and watermill dating from 1783, just before the Revolution. I thought I saw figures moving in the shade of the trees, wearing the clothes of that period, but Gérard waved a hand. 'Just ghosts,' he said airily. 'A lot of people see them.'

It took my breath away. It was so different from my everyday world.

Coming down the Eiffel Tower in the lift, Gérard taught me to say *tu* instead of *vous*. One evening he took me to the theatre to see Gérard Philippe. It was a tiny theatre with gilt alcoves and as we sat down he placed in my lap a dainty pair of white opera glasses. I was wearing my hair up in a new French hairstyle and had on a low-cut dress and a velvet ribbon round my neck. As the lights went up for the interval I leaned towards him to say something and a strange, familiar feeling struck me. Someone sitting behind us was leaning forward, trying to catch my attention. It was Reg. He must have heard every word we exchanged.

I have never understood how it was possible for him to be there, sitting just behind us in that theatre. Perhaps it was coincidence. Perhaps Fate had been helped by a little bribery.

I introduced the two men and they were coldly polite. After commenting on the play, we left him and took a taxi to Montmartre. First we had an apéritif on La Butte, at a table with a red and white check tablecloth, and a very French-looking artist came up and drew a caricature of us both. When Gérard asked him how much we owed him, the 'French artist' revealed himself to be a London cockney who could hardly speak any French at all.

In St Germain-des-Prés we went to the Rose Rouge and saw the Frères Jacques who were very much in vogue and Juliette Gréco, dressed entirely in black, her long straight black hair framing her thin face with its beautiful bone structure. (In those days she still had her original nose.)

The fashionable underground cave felt exotic and slightly wicked. You could hardly see the stage through the cloud of cigarette smoke. Gérard was gallant and protective. On the way back to the hotel, he recited poetry to me in the taxi.

We slept in an ancient double bed with a dip in the middle so we had no choice but to stay close together. He put his arm under my head, I put an arm round his waist and we kissed a brief goodnight.

'Tell me, what did you think of Juliette Gréco?' he asked. 'I'll buy you one of her records tomorrow.'

For some time we lay discussing Prévert's poetry.

'Do you know the Impressionists, Renoir, Monet, Manet?'

'I've only seen one or two Renoirs,' I said.

'Then tomorrow I'll take you to the Orangerie.'

He turned over and fell asleep. He was Pygmalion; I was his Galatea.

When I returned home, the train had no sooner left Paris than a face peered through the corridor window and the door opened. Reg sat down heavily on the seat opposite me.

'Here are the programmes of everything I've seen, I kept them to show you,' he smiled. I had no time for sadness at leaving Paris and Gérard behind because Reg kept me constantly amused with tales of his doings in Paris. He even told me of a French girl he had spoken to in an art gallery. I wondered later whether he had invented her to ease my conscience or whether she was the reason why I never saw him again . . .

Gérard was coming to England for two weeks in the summer holidays and I booked two rooms for us in a Bed and Breakfast by the sea in Bexhill. I was very excited and not a little nervous, for it would be his first experience of England and I wondered if he would like the food (he didn't) and understand the language (he couldn't). I made myself two new summer dresses from some fabric my young brother (now in the Fleet Air Arm) sent me from Malta. I knew my appearance was very important to Gérard. He was always critical if my hair was blown out of place or my lipstick smudged and he hated what he called 'English colours' so I knew I must not wear pink or mauve or any other pastel shades.

When I told my parents the news they were delighted for at

last they would have a chance to meet the romantic Prince Charming I had told them so much about.

We spent a happy week in Bexhill among flowered chintz and soft cushions; our white-haired landlady was sweetness itself. She cooked for us painstakingly, she mothered us but thoughtfully refrained from bringing us early morning tea in bed. She would have been surprised to find us in fact sleeping each in our own room – until the last morning when blood on the sheets and quilt bore testimony to the end of my virginity. I wonder whether she noticed the scrambling to scrub the sheets and quilt when she was not looking, and to keep her from making the beds until they were dry. Did she see the shine in our eyes when we finally came down to breakfast? If she did, she tactfully said nothing.

The following week my mother too was swept off her feet by this tall handsome Frenchman with his charming accent, attractive smile and exaggerated politeness. He bowed to her and kissed her hand. She was overwhelmed and fluttered like a butterfly. My father put lanterns in the apple trees in the garden and carried the radiogram outside on to the lawn so I could invite friends from work and my cousins and we could all dance in the open air. My mother pulled faces of delight to me over Gérard's shoulder as they waltzed by. I felt I was living in a fairy story but the neighbours must have thought we had gone mad, behaving in such an un-English way!

My parents were overjoyed to see me so happy. They were also far too well-mannered to comment on the creaking floorboards as Gérard crept into my room at night.

As we lay in the dark, Gérard made fun of me for being 'too red 'ot'. 'Are all English girls red 'ot under the icy exterior?' he asked. 'It would be better if you would keep still and not move so much.' From then on, I lay motionless each time we made love until he had finished. It made me feel maternal. With both arms round his neck, I watched him huff and puff and then suddenly collapse, and I patted his back to comfort him after all the effort until he fell asleep.

The day before he left, he announced: 'Perhaps I should send a postcard to my father to tell him I am in England.'

I was amazed. My parents were always part of my plans.

'The holidays haven't begun yet officially in France. I am supposed to be in Paris, studying for my entrance exams. I pawned my bedlinen, my sportsjacket and my winter coat to pay the fare to London. I had to come because we may not see one another again. My father intends that I marry the girl with the red sports car this autumn.'

So we only had until autumn. Well, it had been good while it lasted. I had always known our love affair could not last for ever. We would just have to make the most of the short time we had left. It would be sad when we said our final goodbyes but I supposed I would get over it eventually. Letters from Gérard continued to arrive after his return to Paris, as well as small parcels containing tiny bottles of French perfume, a silk scarf or a book. They were manna in a glamour-starved London. Once he wrote to me: 'I have cut myself deliberately in order to write to you in my own blood to prove my love for you.' Even the envelope was addressed in blood but the writing was rather pale towards the end of the address – it had begun to turn yellow and I wondered what the postman had thought.

He also wrote me poetry – a new poem every week until I had a whole book of them. I typed them out at the office after work and thought they were better than anything Verlaine or Prévert had ever written, but I didn't show them to a soul.

I wrote back letters as passionate as his. I bared my heart to him.

'I am not clever,' I wrote in my diary in a fit of humility. 'I am just ordinary. I have no genius like he has. My role in life must be to help people with genius in small, humble ways. I must be grateful for knowing them and grateful if I can help them, however modestly.'

'We must never say we need one another,' wrote Gérard. 'Gide says that to need someone or something is a weakness. If this happens then you must cut yourself off from the needed thing or person, otherwise you can never be self-sufficient.'

He sent me books by Montherlant and Gide (both renowned French philosophers), and while I admired them, in the back of my mind was an uneasy feeling as they were both so obviously misogynists.

There was no more mention of the girl with the red sports car. He wrote that he had failed his first year exams in Paris; he would now be going to Lyon University when the summer holidays were over. There seemed no chance of us ever being together again.

Then, one day, a telegram arrived, out of the blue. My mother and I read it several times, trying to comprehend. When my father came home from work, we all three sat down at the table and read it again.

INTERNATIONAL TELECOMMUNICATIONS SIX-MONTH CONFERENCE STARTING NEXT MONTH IN GENEVA. TWO THOUSAND DELEGATES. ARE YOU AVAILABLE TRI-LINGUAL REPORTER? IF YOU ACCEPT, CONTRACT WILL ARRIVE NEXT FEW DAYS. AIR FARE HEATHROW—GENEVA WILL BE REIMBURSED AND ALL TRAVEL EXPENSES. PLEASE ARRIVE GENEVA 1ST OCTOBER.

The first of October was only two weeks away. The telegram was signed: 'Colonel Reynolds, International Telecommunications Union, United Nations, Geneva.' I looked Geneva up on the map: Lyon was quite close.

I had vaguely heard of the United Nations but knew very little about it. In the course of my work I frequently had to visit various banks to confirm the financial solidity of companies with whom clients of the magazine were about to do business. That morning I slipped in a request of my own. 'What can you tell me about the United Nations in Geneva?' I asked. 'Financially, safe as houses,' came the crisp reply. That settled it.

This was the adventure I had been waiting for. I was twenty-one and free to decide for myself; my parents supported me and were very proud.

'You'd better take the llama coat,' said my mother. 'It will be cold in Switzerland.'

Once again my father packed my shabby brown suitcase so that everything fitted tightly into its own space. Once again, I handed him several white paper parcels (not knowing whether they would have sanitary towels in Geneva). And once again I was on my way to Europe. Except to visit my parents, I never returned.

Chapter 3

It was in October 1948 that I arrived in Geneva Airport after my very first flight. I was wearing my new purple tweed suit, which felt just right as I stepped forward towards a tall, moustached, distinguished-looking man also dressed in tweed. He was waiting as I came out of the customs hall, brandishing a card with my name on it in one hand, and puffing on a pipe held in the other.

After a few words of welcome, Colonel Reynolds took my case and led me by the elbow out of the building, towards his car. As we drove through town I was dazzled by the displays in the boutique windows – so many luxury clothes – and the *boulangeries-pâtisseries* with wondrous window displays of cream cakes and meringues. Finally we arrived at rue Gauthier, and after climbing a flight of stairs, he took a key from his pocket and opened the door of a small furnished flat, deposited my suitcase inside and, handing me the key, said: 'See you Monday, then, 9 o'clock at the Palais Wilson. That's where you will be working. It's not far from here, along the lake. The conference is being held in the Maison des Congrès next door. Take a taxi the first day, until you know your way around the buses.'

I sat on the bed for a while to collect my thoughts. Then, as soon as I had finished unpacking, I wrote to Gérard: 'I have arrived. My telephone number is . . .' It was Saturday morning. I had a whole day and a half ahead of me to discover Geneva before starting work on Monday.

I went for a walk up the Avenue de France to have a look at the United Nations' main building: the Palais des Nations. It was quite majestic, on top of the hill, sparkling white against the sky, which always seems bluer in Switzerland, perhaps because of the altitude. I had to show my contract of employment to get inside the main gates. When you reached the top of the hill in those days you were faced with a dazzling white archway through which the sky seemed an even more intense blue. Since then, extensions to provide more office space have unfortunately done away with the archway. But at that time there was something significant about it, so white against the crisp blue Swiss sky – it gave me a metaphysical feeling of grandeur and hope for the world which rose above humankind and their petty squabbles and struggles for power.

Once through the archway, you were confronted by well-kept flowerbeds and manicured lawns where peacocks strutted proudly, some displaying their beautiful fantails. In the centre was the *Globe Armillaire*, a golden sculpture in the shape of a globe that glittered in the Swiss sunshine and looked particularly spectacular in winter when the lawns were covered with snow. In the distance was the lake: blue, still and dotted with sailing boats. Behind that, high above the horizon, if you were lucky you could see the sparkling, glistening white Mont Blanc. Visible only on certain special days, it sometimes turned a delicate shade of pink mid-afternoon.

A uniformed doorman stepped forward and opened the glass doors for me. When people open doors for me, I always feel obliged to go in, even if that had not been my intention. Many times in my life in Geneva I went through doors and wondered what I was doing inside when I got there, hesitating a few moments before going out again, out of politeness to the person who had opened the door. If someone is kind enough to open a door for me, how could I not go through?

In this case, however, I did want to go inside and have a look round. I walked along the corridors, visited the newspaper stand and bought an English newspaper, and admired the stained glass windows in the delegates' coffee lounge. Then I went through the Salle des Pas Perdus and peeped through the small square glass windows in the heavy doors at the solemn timber and gold meeting rooms. On the third floor, the enormous Assembly Hall, with its blue carpet and matching blue velvet curtains and rows of upholstered chairs, was very impressive. Up high on the equivalent of the seventh floor, I could see the glass of the interpreters' booths. A guide was leading a group of tourists round the building and I joined them, keeping to the back. All over the Palais were gifts from various countries, some of them beautiful, some truly ghastly. There were chairs, paintings, statues from the governments of many countries, paintings from children in India and Africa, gifts from farmers and from other ordinary people all over the world.

Later I got to know the Palais very well; we used to go there for lunch in the cafeteria and later when a staff association was created and a co-operative set up we went to buy English goods that weren't available in town. Even later than that, when I became a simultaneous interpreter, I worked in the seventh-floor booths of the Assembly Hall and it all became very normal and everyday.

On Monday morning, when Colonel Reynolds showed me round the Palais Wilson and Maison des Congrès, I asked him how on earth he had found out about me. Apparently he had met Grace, the 'temp' who had worked for me in London while my secretary was on holiday. I recalled that when I had taken her out to lunch on her last day, she had told me she was leaving shortly to go on holiday in Switzerland where she would be staying with her pen friend's family. They lent her a bicycle so she could get around Geneva more easily. One Saturday she was happily free-wheeling along the Quai du Mont Blanc when the lights at the intersection of the Quai and the Pont du Mont Blanc changed to red. She put the brakes on suddenly and went straight over the handlebars, landing on the pavement at the feet of an Englishman sitting drinking coffee and puffing on his pipe. It was Colonel Reynolds, watching the passers-by while his wife was shopping.

Being the kind man that he was, he had jumped to his feet to help her up and insisted upon buying her a coffee to help her recover. In the course of their conversation, he told her of the important international conference he was organising, due to start in two weeks. He was at his wits' end, he said. He had recruited the rest of the staff required but a verbatim minute-writer with high-speed shorthand in English, French and Spanish seemed impossible to find. 'I think I know just the person you need,' she had said, and gave him my address. Fate had stepped in.

It was a strange idea to have the minutes of discussions prepared in the language of the speaker (except for the USSR speaker, who of course spoke Russian and which I had to note down in English later from the simultaneous interpretation as at that time I had no Russian). When a French-, Spanish- or English-speaker took the floor I had to take down what they said in the appropriate language, so the final document had some paragraphs in English, some in French and some in Spanish, which were later translated by the Linguistic Service to form three separate language versions. Whoever decided that such an unwieldy system should be used for the preparation of the minutes obviously lacked multilingual experience, but in those early days of the United Nations many decision-makers lacked experience in international and multilingual matters.

Before I could start work, I had to sign a contract which included a secrecy clause and I learnt that I was now a 'custodian of an international public trust' and could receive no instructions from any country or government as to the carrying out of my duties, or divulge to the press or anyone else what was said in the course of meetings.

I should perhaps explain here that the International Telecommunication Union is a Specialized Agency of the United Nations, along with the International Labour Organization, the World Trade Organization (formerly GATT – General Agreement on Tariffs and Trade), the World Health Organization (WHO), and many others. They all hold international conferences at regular intervals.

I shared a pleasant sunny office in the Palais Wilson with Colonel Reynolds, where I had a large desk in a windowed corner and the very latest electric typewriter. The secretariat was next door and consisted of secretaries from England, France, Belgium, Cuba, Russia and Egypt, who would type the minutes I produced on to stencils for reproduction as conference documents. The White Russian secretary had an enormous old-fashioned typewriter with the Russian (cyrillic) alphabet on it. The Provisional Frequency Board, which was the official title of the conference, had been convened to prepare a Frequency Allocation Table covering the frequency requirements of all member countries of the United Nations. It was obvious from the start that most countries would have to give up some of their frequency requirements so that the spectrum could accommodate everybody. Some countries, to be on the safe side, had clearly inflated their requirements while others – the so-called 'developing countries' – would not have the funds to make use of the latest radio technology for many years but still wanted to reserve part of the spectrum for their future use.

The Maison des Congrès, where the conference took place, was a glass-fronted building which, in spite of the central heating, got very cold in winter when the *bise* was blowing from the lake. In summer it was extremely hot and if we opened the windows to let in some air, we were subjected to the noise of the traffic and that of the holidaymakers strolling along the Quai eating ice-creams and calling out to one another, children crying and playing. But the view of the lake was magnificent. Sometimes the Mont Blanc would appear, white and glistening, out of the mist; nobody who saw it could ever forget the majesty of that sight.

When you entered the Maison des Congrès, you were confronted by an entrance hall and a steep flight of steps almost as wide as the building, at the top of which, facing you on the left, was the coffee bar, run by Max and Germaine. However quietly you might order your lunch, Max would repeat it in a shout that echoed down the hall, to be sure that Germaine in the kitchen could hear. '*Un plat du jour qui MARCHE!*' and '*Un café crème qui MARCHE!*' On the right were the smaller meeting rooms and, straight in front, the enormous plenary hall looking out onto the lake.

The coffee bar was where all the important decisions were reached, which were then ratified in the plenary meeting. Groups of delegates would sit arguing about their radio frequency requirements for hours, sometimes late into the night after the coffee bar had closed down. The offices closed at six but Swiss staff members would start gathering around five o'clock for their first glass of white wine for the evening, generally a 'nice dry little Vaudois'.

Upon entering the building, before you went up the stairs, you had to walk past the concierge's glassed-in office on the right. Jacques, the concierge, was a portly Swiss aged about fifty with fair curly hair and a very loud voice. He made it his business to know everyone's name and as you came in the main door he would call out: '*Bonjour Mademoiselle Taylor!*', '*Bonjour Monsieur Sautier!*' If you were late, you could be sure that everyone in the building knew. Even the top-ranking secretariat officials, the Deputy Secretary General or the Secretary General himself, could not stop him telling the world what time they arrived.

At the top of the stairs on the right was the document distribution counter, where there was usually a crowd of delegates clamouring for documents in their chosen language. Behind the counter the document boys would be rushing backwards and forwards to the rows of pigeonholes covering two whole walls, where the sorted documents awaited the delegates.

An underground tunnel connected the Palais Wilson to the Maison des Congrès. It was very useful in the snowy Swiss winters, or when the *bise* was blowing. Because the Maison des Congrès was mainly glass, if you stopped to talk to anyone outside, you could be seen by all. The underground passage was therefore often put to use for unofficial discussions. It did not exist officially so anything that took place there hadn't really happened, which saved many difficult situations.

Something I noticed very quickly was that the USSR delegates spoke English in the tunnel. Their English was in fact excellent. But the moment they reached either end, they could speak only Russian and needed an interpreter. I found the USSR delegates and interpreters intriguing. Even at cocktail parties, they always remained together and were obviously ill at ease if separated. The Russian delegation, including the interpreters who came with them, always stayed at the same hotel: the Eden on the rue de Lausanne; I understood that on Wednesday evenings they had meetings and watched Russian films together.

I had the feeling that some of the USSR delegation were checking on others, that the lower grade officials were checking on the higher grades. This was during the time of Stalin; I was often told what an excellent representative of handsome Georgian manhood Stalin was.

The Russian language attracted me enormously so I enrolled for a lunchtime course held at the Palais and after a while was able to wallow in beautiful melancholy Russian poetry and the novels of Turgenev, Chekov and Dostoyevsky.

After studying Russian for several years I knew the grammar perfectly and could translate with ease. But I could not speak.

The difficulty was the declensions. Not only does the noun decline but other words in the sentence do, too. By the time I had worked out whether it was the nominative, genitive, dative, accusative, instrumental or prepositional case, in addition to whether it was masculine, feminine, neuter or plural, I had forgotten what it was I wanted to say. I realised that I really needed to learn the language by ear, just as a child learns.

I enquired around Geneva until I found a little old White Russian lady who had once been a schoolteacher in Moscow. Edwige sent to the USSR for reading books first for a five year old, then for a six year old and so on. I went to her twice a week and we read the pages until I knew them by heart. Then she asked me questions about the text until I could reply without thinking about grammar. What a difference! Thanks to Edwige, I could speak freely and hold a normal conversation in Russian. It became my fourth language.

During plenary assemblies and meetings of the main committees, I had to sit on the podium, to the right of the Chairman, facing the auditorium, and if a delegate wanted his statement or reservation to appear in the minutes, he had to bring it up and hand it to me in writing. (Sometimes the pieces of paper handed to me weren't statements at all – they were invitations to dinner.) All United Nations meetings were held in English, French, Spanish and Russian, with simultaneous inter-pretation in all of those languages. (Nowadays, Chinese and Arabic have been added.) So speakers from India, Norway, Pakistan, Sweden, Denmark and many others had to use English which, not being their native tongue, was sometimes far from perfect; often considerable imagination was needed to under-stand what they meant.

Fortunately the discussions were recorded on tape – both the floor (i.e. the original speaker) and the simultaneous interpreta-tion, as heard by the delegates in their earphones. With my Pitman's 250-words-a-minute I knew I had not made a mistake yet one of the delegates occasionally claimed that what I had put in the minutes was not what he had said. The problem often was that it was not what he had *meant* to say, or what he *wished* he had said. As far as the delegates were concerned, it was often very important for them to be able to send home copies of the minutes showing that they had followed their instructions to the letter. Sometimes checking what had actually been said took a whole day listening to tapes in the various languages and it was not easy to find a satisfactory solution. I had to remain firm: I could not change what was in the minutes to satisfy the speaker because the consequent discussion might then become skewed and meaningless. I had to report in the minutes what I and all the other delegates had actually heard.

At first I was doing this on my own and working half the night to keep up. As a minute-writer, I worked the longest hours of all. I had to be there first thing in the morning when the meetings started, I had to sit through the whole day taking notes and only when the meeting came to an end and everyone else went home could I begin writing my minutes. The translators worked in shifts; the late shift would come in after lunch and work until midnight, sometimes until 1 or 2 a.m. It was important to have each day's new documents printed and available in all languages at the document distribution desk by eight at the latest the following morning. Late at night I would still be puzzling over my notes, alone in the building, trying to make sense of a complicated discussion. If the meeting had an efficient Chairman, there would be no problem but when the Chairman was ineffectual and let the discussion get out of hand, the minutes were difficult to write. After some months I managed to convince Colonel Reynolds that I needed some help to speed up the process – minutes lose their value unless they are published immediately after the meeting. In the end, instead of doing the typing myself, six typists from the typing pool were made available and I dictated to each for ten minutes in turn so the draft minutes would be ready for stencilling the following morning. After some time, fortunately, I also managed to convince Colonel Reynolds that there should be more than one minute-writer, that the minutes should be written entirely in English or French and then translated into the other languages, and that minute-writers should also work in shifts.

A few months later it was decided that I should have a secretary of my own to run my office while I was in meetings and help me when I was not. When the time came for me to interview candidates, there were five young women and one man. The clear choice was an impeccable, dapper little man with grey wavy hair (à la Bob Hawke) and a dazzling white handkerchief in his breast pocket. His efficiency was obvious after talking with him for five minutes. He was appointed and soon ran my office with a hand of iron. He watched over me, fetched cups of tea and coffee when I needed them most – his timing was always perfect. He took my messages but it was some time before I realised that he was also filtering them. If he thought I looked tired, he gave me only nice messages and just threw away the others. If people wanted to see me and he thought I was too busy, he would say I was out of the office. He was a human watchdog and kept the files and my desk in perfect order. The men on the staff were tickled pink that a woman in her early twenties should have an older male secretary. This was most unusual in those days but in fact it worked very well; Mr Gardener was devoted to me and my wellbeing.

Whenever I could, I would have afternoon tea with the secretaries and many became good friends, especially Gaby, an Egyptian girl whose family I later stayed with in Egypt. The Russian secretary, Alexandra, was the eldest. She was tall and gaunt, with grey hair in a bun. She had irregular, discoloured teeth. I was fascinated by the way she drank her tea. In those days, sugar came in lumps – powdered sugar was only for cooking. Alexandra never put sugar in her black tea. She would break a sugar lump in half and place one piece between her upper and lower front teeth. Then she sucked the tea through it, making a disgusting noise which was, she explained, perfectly acceptable in Russia. Grace, through whom I had been recruited in the first place, had enjoyed her visit to Geneva so much that she now was working in the secretariat and we often had lunch together.

Miranda, the other English girl, was very attractive. She always wore pastel colours and loved smart hats. She had an amazing figure – a small waist and very high breasts, which pointed forward aggressively, level with her armpits. We all wore our breasts very high in those days and the cut of our clothes took this into account. Our bras contained stiff wire like scaffolding. But Miranda's breasts were particularly high and she wore tight-fitting angora jumpers to show them to advantage.

Miranda enjoyed sex but also suffered a lot from painful cracked ribs because her Dutch lover was heavily built and about the size of a wardrobe. When she started complaining at work of chest and back pains, we imagined the worst. Each morning she poked her head round my door to tell me how she was. The pain was getting worse. I advised her to see a doctor urgently. She could have gone to the nurse in the Medical Centre in the Palais Wilson but she was too embarrassed to do that and preferred to go to an unknown doctor. The good news was that it was not a serious disease she was suffering from. The bad news was that she had to change her bra and lengthen the shoulder straps.

We all sympathised – clothes were very important to us and I for one wouldn't have dreamt of going to work without my 'foundation garment', an all-in-one affair which had replaced corsets but served the same purpose. Unfortunately the bosom part was not exactly where my bosom was. It had whalebones, as did the lower half, and sometimes when I bent forward they would lock into one another, making it very difficult to sit up straight again without a few private acrobatics.

The French and Belgian typists in the secretariat were barely civil to one another. The Belgian girl was big and fat – behind her back we called her 'Maude-la-grosse'. The French girl, Marie Dupont, was small and thin and everyone called her 'la petite Dupont'. She always had something to complain about. 'It's not that I don't *like* wine,' she would say, 'it's just that wine doesn't like *me*.' Or: 'I suffer a lot from the cold. I don't have much fat to keep me warm, you understand.' If someone wanted to open the window in the summer, she would bleat: 'I cannot *stand* draughts. I'm sure to be ill the next day if I'm in a draught.' Everything always went wrong for her. People took advantage of her; often she was forgotten altogether.

La petite Dupont sat opposite Maude-la-grosse. Their desks were pushed together in front of one of the windows, so that they sat facing one another. When one went on holiday, the other edged her desk forward a few inches to get more light from the window, thinking that the other wouldn't notice when she came back. One time when la petite Dupont returned from leave and found her desk had been moved, she pushed it back plus a few extra inches. Maude-la-grosse was not going to have that, obviously, and being bigger and stronger, pushed her desk forward a little too energetically, knocking over the pencils on la petite Dupont's desk. Soon the two of them were rolling on the floor, pulling each other's hair until one banged her head on a desk and started to bleed. People gathered round, enjoying the unusual excitement. Fortunately Colonel Reynolds heard the commotion and put an end to it. He called an ambulance and eventually everyone calmed down.

In Geneva I could do all kinds of things I could never have done in England. Coming from the austerity of post-war Britain it all seemed impossibly glamorous, but I soon became used to dashing across the border into France to go shopping or have my hair set in the new style, with curls on top of my head, the back held up with combs. I would try out the latest perfumes and buy high-heeled shoes. My new salary seemed more appropriate to a fairy story than real life, compared to my earnings in England, and we were exempt from income tax because the money we received did not come from Switzerland or any one country, but from the more than one hundred countries that contributed to the United Nations' budget. I spent money as fast as I earnt it on unaccustomed luxuries such as the latest fashions from the best stores and sent large parcels of clothes, food and chocolates home to my parents each month. Twice when I flew home to visit them I smuggled a Swiss watch in the toe of each shoe to avoid paying ferocious customs duties. Winklepickers were very fashionable at that time and had a very useful empty space in the pointed front – just big enough for a watch. Fortunately the Customs officials at the airport didn't notice the awkward way I walked.

During weekends, if you were lonely you had only to go to the Perle du Lac café-restaurant, the old town or the outdoor café at the Hotel des Bergues and you were sure to meet someone you knew. In fact, with so many delegates about town, you were bound to find someone from the conference in any café or restaurant you went into.

I soon became part of a small group of friends who went out to dinner whenever we could to Au Fin Bec, rue de Berne, in Geneva or to one of several good restaurants in Ferney-Voltaire, across the border in France. (We had to remember to put our passports in our handbags of course.) The restaurant we frequented most was Au Capucin Gourmand. As usual, I was the youngest of the group.

Occasionally we went to nightclubs in the old town, such as Le Bataclan and Club 51, but the dance floors were so small you couldn't do the fishtail or the tango and no-one danced the way I had learnt in England. These nightclubs often had a risqué floorshow in which scantily-clad dancers mingled with the audience and sat on men's laps. Sometimes they removed the man's tie and passed it between their thighs with a sigh mid-song. (I can only assume they weren't locals; it was very un-Swiss to be so unhygienic!)

I joined the French United Nations staff dramatic society and was given a lovely part in their production of *L'Aimable Lingère*. I was the young seamstress, led astray by the master of the house and by his son. I enjoyed the rehearsals after work in the Palais des Nations enormously. I also joined the Operatic Society and took part in their Gilbert and Sullivan productions in English. We rehearsed in the American Library, which was part of the American Church in the rue de Monthoux, a lovely old timber building with mullioned windows.

My romance with Gérard continued. He still wrote twice a day and I replied whenever I could – generally at high speed on my electric typewriter during my lunch hour. He never mentioned his impending marriage to the red-sports-car girl, and neither did I: I'd hear about it soon enough. I just wanted to enjoy life while I could.

Gérard and I often spent weekends together in Lyon or in Geneva. I got to know Lyon well – the banks of the Rhône where we walked with Fourvières rising above us, out of the mist, in winter. Punch and Judy were originally created in Lyon and we often stopped in the park on a Sunday morning to watch Punch and Judy shows, the characters all in the traditional costumes.

Gérard had a room in an apartment belonging to a widow, Madame Martineau. The apartment had beautiful polished parquet floors, and inside the front door was a row of felt soles with a strip across the top, into which you stepped so that they were secure on top of your shoes. Every step you took helped polish the parquet. When I was in Lyon, we would go out on Saturday evenings and creep back into Gérard's room as quietly as we could in the hope that Madame Martineau wouldn't hear that I was there too. (She was fortunately rather deaf.) But I am sure she found traces of my presence in the bathroom, not to mention Gérard's bedroom. On Sunday mornings I had to be smuggled out noiselessly. The felt slippers were wonderful for getting about silently as well as for polishing the floor.

In those pre-Pill days, abortions were quite common among my friends. We heard dreadful stories of illegal 'pregnancy interruptions', as abortions were called in French, with haemorrhages, fever and complications resulting in sterility. There were all sorts of magic anti-pregnancy potions available that one could take, combined with a very hot bath, but they never seemed to work. Horseriding was also supposed to be helpful but I never heard of anyone actually rescued from pregnancy by a bumpy horseride. However we were all earning high salaries and could afford to have it done legally, with the help of a professional gynaecologist in a hospital on the basis of a medical certificate. I had a few on Friday afternoons; luckily there were never any complications so I didn't have to take any time off work. Abortions were legal in Switzerland (though not in France) as long as you followed the rules. All you had to do was visit three doctors and get their signature on a form. One of the three had to be a psychologist or psychiatrist; you just had to cry and say you couldn't cope with a baby at this point in your life. It wasn't until you got married that you felt entitled to consult a gynaecologist to be fitted for a diaphragm. (I never heard of a single woman daring enough to ask for a diaphragm back then.)

The Swiss in those days (and probably still today) attached great importance to freshness. I enjoyed walking to work in the mornings and on my way would see sheets, pillows and duvets hanging out of apartment windows to air, even in winter. There would also be suits, pullovers and dresses on wooden coat-hangers, and a few silver fox furs and trilby hats perched among the pots of geraniums on balcony railings enjoying the cleansing morning air.

But if they were keen on fresh air, they were positively obsessed with personal hygiene. The modern idea of just taking a shower was not enough; you also had to scrub yourself all over before getting into the shower and women were not clean unless they washed themselves inside as well as out every morning. This is why the bidet was so important. I bought a metal jug with hose attachment for everyday use (you filled it with warm water and hung it up at head height) and a rubber equivalent for travel.

It was also important to wash yourself internally after sex. In fact, once you were married and possessed a diaphragm, this would be the scenario. You and your partner feel amorous? Before you get too involved, you dash off to the bathroom to put your diaphragm in place. This was not as straight forward as it might sound. First it had to be covered with spermicide cream from the tube. Then it was no easy matter to get the diaphragm in the right place and involved much poking about. If it was not in exactly the right place, it would not fulfil its purpose. Once in place, you could continue where you left off – assuming you were still in the mood. Then, once it was all over, while your partner was relaxing and enjoying the comforting afterglow and you wanted to do the same, you instead had to dash off to the bathroom to remove the diaphragm and irrigate yourself, prefer- ably with strong soap or some disinfectant that would be abhorrent to any errant sperm that had been left behind.

There was also the Rhythm (or Catholic) method of birth control. For this you took your temperature every day to deter- mine your fertile period, but this seemed to work better in theory than in practice. I had a married friend who took her temperature every day; her husband knew when it was safe to make love because on those days there would be flowers in the bedroom. They ended up with five children.

Occasionally Danielle would come to spend the weekend with me and we'd talk half the night. My whole life had changed thanks to her and to Gérard, with a little help from Grace.

In the winter Gérard and Dany took me skiing and the first time I tried, I skied down the slope like an expert. 'It's easy,' I thought exultantly.

'Do it again and I'll wait at the bottom and take a picture.'

The second time started off all right. Gérard got into position and aimed, but just as he put his finger on the trigger, I fell. All that could be seen in the photograph was a dirty patch in the snow and a cross against the sky. The cross was my skis. The dirty patch was me. After that I went to ski-school at weekends as often as I could.

Gérard and I each wrote solemn statements which we stuck in our passports: 'If I should die, I want all my books and personal possessions to go to Gérard/Valérie.'

Then one weekend he came to Geneva and announced that this might be our last weekend together for some time. He would be leaving soon to do his compulsory two years' military service in Toulouse. It was Monday, we had just eaten a picnic lunch on a park bench by the lake in the warm autumn sun and soon I would hurry back to work and he would catch his train back to Lyon.

'How often will you get leave?' I asked, devastated.

'Not very often,' he replied. 'Only married men get regular leave.'

Suddenly he stood up, excited. 'Why don't we get married, then I'll get more leave!'

'What a marvellous idea!'

I grabbed his arm and we strode round the park humming the Wedding March. I tried to keep up with his long strides and we laughed as I scrambled to fit in two or three steps to his one, and still keep in time.

'But I thought you were going to marry the red sports car?' I suddenly remembered.

'We had an argument some weeks ago. Then our fathers got involved and had a big row too, so it's all over. Now there's nothing to stop us,' he assured me. 'Besides, I think my father has taken to you.'

'I wonder how long it takes to get all the papers and do all that has to be done?'

I took the next day off work – luckily no plenaries were scheduled. The first thing I wanted to do was telephone home to tell my parents the news and I needed plenty of time for it. In these days of mobile phones and instant STD calls, it's hard to imagine how complicated it was then to telephone England from Geneva. I had to go to the special international telephone exchange in Cornavin railway station and queue to book a call.

There was always a crowd of agitated people there, waiting for a call that didn't come or upset about some bad news. When finally my chance came, I'd hardly had time for the preliminaries before crackling interference on the line made it impossible to talk and we had to hang up. In the end I sent a telegram.

After cabling my family, I took taxis to the British Consulate, the French Consulate, the Town Hall and the nearest Catholic church to find out what was required. Gérard and I needed eleven pieces of paper in all which had to come from Paris, Lyon and London, certifying that we had been born, baptised, and never been in prison or committed any offence. It seemed doubtful they would all arrive in time, as all this had to be accomplished before Gérard left for Toulouse. He would first be spending one month training in Lyon and might be able to get some of that time free for a honeymoon.

Before we could start on any of the formalities, however, M. Baumier insisted on travelling to England to formally ask my father for my hand in marriage for his son. He also said he had to speak to my father about my dowry but fortunately that subject was not mentioned again. A hasty trip to London was organised for Monsieur Baumier, Gérard and me. My family was overwhelmed with excitement. We took our visitors to the Festival Hall to see a ballet and had a balcony box all to ourselves. We took 'Papa', as I was now expected to call him, to see all the London sights and immersed him in English history, showing him where battles had been fought between our two countries, in which we each thought we had been victorious . . . History can be very subjective.

On our last weekend we had an English engagement party in the garden at home. I remember serving ice-cream as dessert in my mother's special china lacework bowls. She insisted I use them because they were so precious. It was fine until the ice-cream started to melt.

A week or two later, we had a French engagement party in a big restaurant in Gérard's home town, St Etienne. Danielle and Bruno organised everything; there were white gladioli every-where in tall vases, and I was given a beautiful ring with an enormous diamond. 'It was one of my mother's earrings,' Gérard explained. 'My brother had the other when he got engaged; the matching ring is in the safe at the bank, waiting for Pouche to grow up and get engaged.' The main feature of the French engagement party was of course an enormous banquet with so many courses I lost count.

Everyone at work rejoiced when I announced the news for it was obvious to all that I was head-over-heels in love. They all told me later that I 'had stars in my eyes'. Whispering went on in corners as groups made collections to buy a wedding present that I was not supposed to know about. All the secretaries admired my diamond engagement ring and I realised how extraordinarily lucky I was. I was deeply immersed in the *Women's Weekly*-style dream of romantic love; swept off my feet, given a diamond ring – white lace and orange blossom and then the next part of my life would be the 'happily ever after'.

Getting everything ready in time for the wedding was a chal-lenge, a feat of organisation we were determined to achieve. I was far too busy to sit down and think. Life was a whirlwind. A restaurant had to be booked for about 100 people, the menu obtained and approved by my future father-in-law (who was likely to be difficult about Swiss cuisine). The church arrange-ments had to be made in Geneva – I was not a Catholic like Gérard and his family. I would have to swear to raise our children as Catholics. I also had to study the Catholic religion and promise to read all the religious papers, magazines and books I was sent. Later, when my children were born, I had to promise to help them learn their *catéchisme* by heart. When the time came several years later, the first sentence they had to repeat after me was: '*Un mariage mixte est un grand malheur.*' ('A mixed marriage is a great misfortune.')

Our fairytale honeymoon was to be in Mallorca.

29 September 1951: As I stood at the top of St Joseph's church steps in the Eaux-Vives, Geneva, posing for the wedding photograph in the cold drizzle, I hardly dared look sideways at the imposing figure standing beside me. Since his arrival at the church, Gérard had behaved impeccably and was being perfectly charming but I knew that he had a reputation in his family for being an ogre. I had heard many family anecdotes about dreadful things he had done and what a bad temper he had. I hoped he would continue to behave as he should on our wedding day. At our engagement party his grandmother, Mémée, had taken me aside and warned me that, as a baby, he had had such dreadful tantrums the only way they could calm him down and stop him screaming had been to remove his nappy and hold his bottom under the cold tap, so the cold water took him by surprise. 'Papa' had told me quietly that I was making a mistake to marry the son. 'It is the father you should be marrying,' he had said. I presumed it was meant as a joke.

I looked at my sister, who was my bridesmaid, and smiled at her but she was standing very rigidly with an improbable blue veil on her head put together the night before in my flat.

'You did bring a long blue dress, didn't you?' I had asked. 'Gérard's sister, Pouche, is wearing pale blue.'

'I managed to borrow one, I hope the two blues don't clash.'

We had been talking until after midnight, catching up on family news, forgetting the orange blossom we were supposed to be sewing on the blue veiling. My father's health had been precarious for some time. Now he was in hospital again after an operation to remove stomach ulcers and my mother felt she should not leave his side. My young brother was still overseas with the Fleet Air Arm. So my sister was the only representative of my family. The cosy feeling had come back now she had arrived and I decided not to tell her about my friend Miranda's visit a few evenings earlier, it would only spoil the atmosphere, and in fact I had been trying to shut it out of my own mind ever since Miranda had turned up on my doorstep, her face tense with pent-up drama.

'Come in and celebrate,' I had said, opening the door. 'Only two more days and I shall be a married woman.'

'No drink for me!' she had replied dramatically, holding up one white-gloved hand. 'You must not marry him. I have come to stop you while there is time. This is a mistake you will regret!'

She seemed to have rehearsed what to say and was getting it said quickly, before she lost courage.

'He's not the man for you. You are his plaything, his creation, his object, his possession. Can't you *see* you are making a mistake? I know you're in love with him, but you don't have to get *married*. Marriage is for life –'

Wise words. But they had no effect on me. I was still in my *Women's Weekly* daydream. Now I looked around and noted Miranda in the crowd at the foot of the church steps, looking disapproving in the kind of monstrous white sailor hat with veil and trimmings that only she could get away with.

'Now with the family,' said the photographer, beckoning people to join us on the steps.

Bruno, our best man, grabbed my sister by the elbow and pushed her to the fore. He had taken an instant liking to her, which is possibly why Danielle has such a disgruntled look on her face in the photograph. It was still raining and people were pulling their coats closer to keep out the wind and the damp. I hoped my gooseflesh wouldn't show in the photographs.

My parents would have loved to be there but in some ways it was a relief not to have them. Their sincerity and integrity would not have been considered smart or sophisticated by Gérard and they would have found it difficult to cope in French. Being perceptive and sensitive, they might have found the atmosphere lacking in warmth and worried about me. But it was going to be all right. I loved Gérard so much and I knew he loved me: he was bound to change and show more warmth when we lived together. He had been deprived of love ever since his mother died. My love was bound to change him.

The wedding photographs are so crowded it is difficult to pick out real family and friends from the many well-meaning but almost unknown faces of people from the conference. Grace, smiling, is well to the fore. Colonel Reynolds and his wife are also there in the front. He is holding his pipe and she is wearing an amazing navy blue and white creation of a hat with tufts of veiling all round it. Behind them, Gaby in her best hat can just be seen. There were so many delegates I hardly knew – how had they found out where my wedding was taking place? – and office staff, interpreters, translators, typists and even Germaine from the coffee bar dressed in her best and trying to edge herself into the photograph. The chief of the roneograph department, Mme Fix, is there smiling right in the centre of the crowd, wearing a red béret on her blonde curls, and a red jacket. Two of my English girlfriends who had both sobbed through-out the church ceremony are wearing one another's hats and dabbing at their eyes and noses. When they met outside the church they each realised that the other's hat would suit them better, so they had changed over. In one of the group photo-graphs a tall fat lady in mauve stands behind the bride and groom, wearing an imposing befeathered hat and displaying an extensive bosom and a beringed mittened hand, but I have never been able to work out who she is. It was fortunate so many people had come from the conference because otherwise my sister and friends would have been the only ones on my side of the church. Gérard's large family had come from all over France, including his brother Jean who flew over from Morocco where he worked as a geologist.

Everyone had had to wait a while in the cold drizzle for the ceremony to begin. When finally the Baumiers' black Peugeot arrived, muddy and dented, the family had emerged with hats pulled well down over their faces and upturned coat collars, to hide their bruises. Gérard's grandmother stubbornly refused to alight from the car. She sat back, a dignified octogenarian dressed entirely in black, pulling her hat firmly over her eyes and signalling with a black gloved hand to the others to alight and continue without her. Resilient in spite of a large purple bruise across her face, Mémée would not allow herself to be seen. Her vanity kept her solemnly ensconced in the Peugeot throughout the church ceremony and out of the wedding photographs.

It was Gérard who had insisted upon driving his father, grandmother, sister and aunt to Geneva for the wedding. He had always been a vindictive driver. If he took a dislike to another driver on the road, he would spare no effort to dispatch him into a ditch, overtaking and 'fishtailing' when he could take him by surprise. He believed that the highway code was designed for ordinary, unintelligent drivers, not for him. He knew all about traffic volume and flow and was of the opinion that the faster you drove, the safer it was because you spent less time in dangerous situations. Red lights, too, were for ordinary drivers, not for talented people who could zip across safely when nobody was looking, so fast that no-one had time to read the numberplate or catch up with them.

On this occasion, while explaining in typical Gérard fashion that good drivers do not need to brake in S-bends, he had mis-calculated one of them and projected his entire carload into a beetroot field, to the astonishment of the farmer and the donkey pulling the beetroot cart. As the elderly ladies clambered out of the upturned car their shiny patent leather shoes had sunk deep into the mud, their hats had gone awry and the rain had drenched their clothes. Their faces were bruised and there was no way of distinguishing bruise from beetroot juice. The hour spent extracting the car from the mud and the beetroots – with the help of the farmer and his donkey – had meant that there was no time to lose and they had been obliged to come straight to the church without stopping to compose themselves or change their clothes and shoes. It was not a joyful wedding scene, but everyone felt better after champagne. Miranda had had more than she should and tried to give Gérard a piece of her mind. There is a photograph of her exploding in his direction, mouthing words of disapproval, while he looks at the photographer with an amused expression because a crazy behatted Englishwoman like this can only be talking nonsense.

Finally Gérard and I left them all at the restaurant to enjoy themselves and hurried off to change and catch the night boat-train to Mallorca where we were booked into the luxurious Principe Alfonso hotel. As we waited on the railway platform we collapsed in relief that the pompous part was over.

'Did you notice Mme Leblanc's hat?'

'Where on earth can she have found it?'

As we clambered on board, my sister and Bruno appeared with a bag of peaches.

'Those bunks look rather narrow for two. Well, at least you'll both get a good night's sleep,' he said.

'Not very romantic for our wedding night but we'll make up for it on the boat,' I answered, feeling daring. I could picture us dancing to the sound of violins under the stars and the full moon on the boat to Mallorca.

But when the time came, as we reached the top of the

gangplank, Gérard ahead of me carrying the two cases, an official in a navy blue cap directed: 'Men to the right, ladies to the left.' I sent a desperate look in Gérard's direction, he bent to kiss me goodnight but the queue behind us was impatient and we parted hastily. So wedding night No. 2 was spent below deck in a large dormitory surrounded by rows of vomiting women. Unprepared for separation, we hadn't arranged a meeting place and I had no idea where Gérard might be. In any case, the atmosphere of sickness seemed to be affecting my stomach too and I thought it safer to stay where I was. By the time we reached our palatial hotel, I was feeling so ill it took two or three days in bed for me to recover.

On the third morning I felt obliged to make the effort to go down to breakfast and sat watching Gérard eat. We both looked interestingly tired, but how could our neighbours know that it wasn't because of a night of wild sex, but because Gérard had spent a large part of the night reading Verlaine to me, explaining Matisse and Manet's paintings, and discussing Gide. It is true that we generally ended up making love. I enjoyed the closeness and wished it would last longer, but Gérard usually moved away to sleep in the cool part of the bed. I could not understand why it was all right to put my arms round him when we were making love but not at any other times. I longed to sit on his lap, remembering how comfortable my mother had looked sitting on my father's lap in the old days. One evening as he sat in the armchair reading, I put on my nightgown, brushed my hair, scented myself and gently crept on to his lap.

'What on *earth* do you think you're doing?' he exclaimed crossly, promptly standing up so that I had to scramble off quickly before I fell on the floor.

'Can't you see I'm reading?' He brushed his clothes and patted his trousers where I had creased them. 'You know I can't stand that sort of thing.'

To punish me, he sat in the chair reading until I had fallen asleep on my own and that night we didn't make love.

I felt I must be very primitive, needing to be loved like that. He seemed so cool and superior. He could manage without. It was all part of his theory based on Gide and Montherlant's philosophy, not to need anything from anyone.

'How can I ever reach his high standard?' I pondered, overawed. 'He's half man and half god!'

The next time we made love I tried to keep as still as possible to avoid spoiling it for him. I closed my eyes and imagined I was on Mount Olympus and it was a Greek god lying on top of me. We were high above the world and I knew not why I had been chosen for this supreme privilege.

Everyone knows honeymoons never come up to expectation, I told myself. The happy-ever-after was bound to begin soon.

Chapter 4

Gérard went straight from our honeymoon in Mallorca to join the army in Toulouse and I went back to Geneva and work. Instead of ending after six months, the Provisional Frequency Board had been extended, two months at a time, until it finally lasted two years. It took that amount of time for all the countries represented to agree on a frequency allocations table, decide which parts of the spectrum would be reserved for mobile, broadcasting and fixed services and to establish the rules and arrangements applicable to the use of the bands concerned.

Our wedding had coincided with the end of the conference so I was returning to a new job. I had no wish to return to gloomy old England and my employers didn't want to let me go – I was too useful with my three UN languages. I was invited to join the permanent staff of the organisation as Administrative Assistant to the new Secretary General who had just arrived from America. Our offices were now in the Maison des Congrès: I was in the inner office next to the Secretary General's, while the outer office housed a secretary and a typist or two, depending on the work-load.

I oversaw the secretaries in the outer office, prepared agendas and took minutes of all meetings that occurred in the Secretary General's office. I also translated all his correspondence that was not received in English. I would have liked to become a translator officially and work in the Linguistic Service but I had seen the job descriptions and knew that a university degree in the languages concerned was a prerequisite.

Although American, the new Secretary General spoke excellent French. He was short and portly with grey hair in a trendy crew cut, and he always busy. He explained to me once that if you are in an important meeting and you need to go out for a minute, you should always take some papers under your arm to give the impression you are on a serious mission. Every morning when he arrived he turned on all the lights, even if the sun was shining brightly. He liked to have the telephones ringing, people waiting to see him and as many lights flashing as possible.

Once a year, the Administrative Council met and I had to sit behind the Secretary General on the podium. The meetings were not always pleasant because two or three members were very keen to find fault with the accounts and kept asking leading questions. This was probably because they felt they should have been elected Secretary General instead of the encumbent. I felt sorry for the Secretary General, who was constantly attacked and needed great resilience to survive the malicious criticism. The member of the council with most weight was the leader of the American delegation, an elderly gentleman who was almost bald, but had one long strand of white hair which he wound round his head to make the most of it. Fortunately he and the Secretary General were good friends.

I soon became aware, sitting in high-level policy meetings, of the importance of the order of items on the Agenda. Something placed towards the end of the meeting when everyone was tired could often be passed without discussion.

Now when I arrived at work in the mornings Jacques, the concierge, boomed '*Bonjour, Madame Baumier!*' I wore my engagement and wedding rings proudly but missed spending weekends with Gérard. He still wrote every day and occasionally had leave to come to Geneva for the weekend; sometimes I went to Toulouse but that was a much longer train journey than the one to Lyon had been.

The two years Gérard spent in the French army seemed to reinforce his innate sense of superiority. He often quoted an Arabian proverb: 'Beat your wife every day. If you don't know why, she does.' He thought it very funny but I found it rather irritating. He rapidly became an officer and cut an elegant figure in his uniform. He enjoyed the authority his new status gave him. He had a room of his own in the barracks and I made a curtain for him to take back to hang at his window. 'When any of my men are late for assembly and drill in the morning,' he wrote to me, 'the punishment I give them is to clean my room. It works quite well.'

After dinner, during a weekend in St Etienne with his father, Gérard tipped his chair back and, puffing out a cloud of cigar smoke in a deliberate fashion with eyes half-closed, told us about a visiting British colonel who had come to inspect the army installations in Toulouse.

'He was so ridiculous!' he explained. 'We decided what to do. It was the only way to have a quiet life: we got him drunk.

'We each went off and came back with a different bottle he had to taste and when he said he liked this or that we went off for more and kept filling his glass until he couldn't speak even English any more, let alone French! Someone drove him back to his hotel, he just collapsed on the back seat of the jeep. But the funniest thing of all: a man, a grown man and an army officer – he had a *white handkerchief* tucked inside the cuff of his jacket sleeve! Can you imagine?'

They all laughed, but I felt sorry for the poor British colonel with his polite manners at the mercy of such a cynical group. I often tucked a handkerchief inside my sleeve. I was glad I didn't have one there at that moment.

One of the filing clerks at work was a blonde Polish Baroness, now middle-aged but who had once been a great beauty, as witnessed by the photographs on her piano, on the walls, and on the antique furniture in her large apartment in the rue de Lausanne. Her name was Evelyn and she was one of those larger than life people you meet occasionally, with incredible stories to tell of her past, including her amorous adventures with various famous princes, counts and barons. She taught a lunchtime class in Russian poetry at the UN which I enjoyed enormously – her classes were extremely colourful. Several times she recounted the story of her escape from Poland with most of her family jewels hidden in her long hair (which was piled on top of her head) and an heirloom ring with an emerald the size of a walnut taped inside her navel.

Evelyn had several spare rooms in her apartment so I moved in with her to save money while Gérard was in Toulouse. Also staying with her was a piano student, studying at the conservatorium: Natuscia Calza from Milan. Natuscia and I became good friends and went to many concerts in Geneva's Victoria Hall. We went to one by Dinu Lipatti, the Romanian pianist who played Chopin so sensitively, and afterwards she took me backstage to meet him.

He looked very much like Gérard, tall and slim with thick black hair, but seemed much more gentle. Although he was in fact dying from leukaemia, this was during the period when he was taking cortisone and feeling on top of the world. Cortisone was entirely new then and very costly. The musicians Charles Münch, Paul Sacher, Yehudi Menuhin and Stravinsky, as well as other friends and admirers, each in turn paid for a day's supply. After that first meeting, Natuscia and I never missed one of his concerts, and always went to see him afterwards. His death when he was only thirty-three was an enormous shock to us both and we were sad for many months. We bought all his recordings and kept playing them.

While Gérard was away learning how to be a good officer, I decided to learn flamenco, something I'd always longed to do. There was a very good Spanish Dance school in Geneva on the Quai Gustave Ador. It was run by Señor and Señora Valverde. I had a lesson one evening a week and often there were performances by the students on Saturday evenings. Dancing flamenco became a passion and after a few years I was the Valverdes' prize pupil, taking part in competitions and performing in local theatres.

I found some precious handmade castanets made of the wood of the olive tree at an antique shop in Toulouse. They were very good ones and had been sold by a professional Spanish dancer who ran out of money when performing in Toulouse some years before. They were covered with dust and very dry, but after I had rubbed olive oil into them and left them to soak in it for a few days, they produced a beautiful rich sound. The Valverdes were enthusiastic about my find.

Having mastered the technique of the castanets and worked hard at *zapateado* (heel and foot tapping, gypsy style), I managed to persuade Gérard to come with me to Madrid one Easter, where I had costumes made and bought another pair of castanets, smaller with a more delicate sound, for classical music such as Albeniz and Granados. Also a pair of sturdy-heeled red leather dancing shoes with straps across the top of the instep to hold them firmly in place. After that I returned to Spain whenever I could and attended flamenco classes in Granada and

Sevilla, making friends with several students who later became famous dancers.

If I had a free weekend at home when I was not seeing Gérard I would dance the whole day. The music had to be so loud that it penetrated my bones. I had a pile of 78 rpm records of Seguidillas, Sevillanas, Jotas and Fandangos. I closed the doors and windows to spare the neighbours and gave myself up completely to the music. The castanets clicked, I stamped my heels and danced myself to exhaustion. When I could stand no more, I collapsed in a panting heap on a chair or lay flat on my back on the floor until my breath came back. Then I would start again. I usually slept very well after that.

When Gérard's military service finally ended he came to Geneva, we rented a brand new fifth-floor flat with a large balcony, and our married life at last began.

One evening Gérard and I were lying in bed, the lights out, and Gérard said: 'When I kiss you I can feel you getting aroused. Women have to be aroused. Men are ready immediately but women are slower. They require patience on the part of the man.'

He was explaining the situation to me like a professor lecturing a slow student. He went on: 'I have heard of men who kiss their wife once or twice and then just leave an arm round her while they read the paper or smoke a cigarette, waiting for her to get aroused. That's what I should do! But I'm not a patient man.'

I felt ashamed to be like all those women he talked about.

We usually made love in the dark just before going to sleep. It happened that one Sunday morning I awoke first and, throwing back the covers, I discovered that Gérard had fallen asleep without putting his pyjama trousers on again. For the first time I saw his penis. It hardly seems possible these days, but till then I had never seen Gérard completely naked.

'What a soft, vulnerable little thing,' I thought, looking at it curiously. It was like a tightly closed rosebud with crinkled petals, wrinkled like a newborn baby and I felt protective and maternal towards it. I wanted to bend down and kiss it but dared not – I knew that Gérard would be furious if I touched it. The French have a lovely nickname for the penis, affectionate and tender with no vulgar undertones: *le zizi*.

How hard-hearted English parents must be to have such a vulnerable little thing circumcised, I mused, becoming quite indignant. Why did they do it? Were there statistics to prove that there were more infected or diseased penises among French boys than English? I shuddered at the thought of such a tender part of a baby boy's body at the mercy of the surgeon. It was enough to give a man psychological problems for the rest of his life. No son of mine would be circumcised, I decided there and then.

Gérard took some time to find the right career but fortunately I earnt plenty to keep us both. Eventually he became a research engineer and the work suited him perfectly. He worked hard, made several influential friends, and worked his way up the corporate ladder to become a top executive. He had a very bad temper and a lot of people were afraid of him (though he also had admirers). After an episode when Gérard threatened to tip the director's desk out of the window, and him with it if his request wasn't granted, even the director was nervous of Gérard's angry outbursts.

Gérard often asked me to translate research proposals for him, which I did gladly. Sometimes we spent hours in the evening with diagrams and charts all over the floor while he tried to explain how some new technique would work, so that I could provide a clear translation.

After a while, we built a house in Versoix, a little village by the lakeside seven kilometres from the city. It was a beautiful house on the top of a hill, overlooking the lake. According to Swiss tradition, as soon as the roof was on, a small fir tree covered in multi-coloured ribbons that blew in all directions was attached to its highest point.

The curved oak staircase was what I liked best, leading up from the oak front door to form a balustrade in front of the upstairs bedrooms. The main living room had a magnificent view of the lake and the Mont Blanc. It was an enormous room with central heating under the clinker-tiled floor, ideal for flamenco dancing, yoga classes and parties. Attached to the side of the house was a boathouse which later housed our sailing boat.

Like all Swiss houses ours was built to last, with thick solid walls to keep out the winter's cold and the customary vast basement holding central heating furnace and laundry. The purpose of a basement was to help keep the house warm during the cold winters and cool in summer, but in those Cold War days they could also provide shelter in the event of a nuclear disaster. The famous 'little red book' all Swiss households received at that time prescribed exactly how much rice, flour, water, milk powder, cooking oil and other provisions, as well as first-aid supplies, we should keep there in case of emergency.

From the outside, the house looked like a traditional Swiss chalet. Although actually built of brick and reinforced concrete, it was clad in timber with ornate wooden balconies and bright red shutters at the windows. There was a level stretch of garden around the house which we called the terrace; beyond that the garden sloped away quite steeply. The view from the house and terrace on a clear day was breathtaking. You could see Lake Geneva stretching into the distance, and beyond it, France. On the horizon to the right the Salève Mountains and straight in front of you – if you were lucky – the dazzling, glistening white Mont Blanc. They were special days indeed when the Mont

Blanc gradually turned from white to pink in the late afternoon – all you could do was stand and marvel at the beauty and majesty of it.

Not only did we look at France across the lake, if you went for a fifteen-minute walk through the woods at the back of the house, you emerged in the French countryside. And if you took the car and drove for fifteen minutes down the country lanes you would come to Ferney-Voltaire in France, a picturesque village where Voltaire once lived. The open-air market there on Saturday mornings was a joy. As you walked past the stalls, you would be invited to try this cheese or that, this ham or that, and fruit would be handed to you to sample. We loved French bread and used to go into France to buy baguettes as often as we could. Also French butter, which was much tastier than Swiss. For good coffee we would drive into Italy. The Aoste valley was not far and there was no doubt that Italian coffee was the best. (Until I went to Brazil.)

We soon got to know the local people well. Versoix was a typical Swiss village with a village square complete with fountain. In summer, cheerful baskets of red geraniums adorned all the lamp-posts – a special truck went round at dawn each morning to water them. The Quai was bordered with flowerboxes of geraniums, the harbour and the jetty too. Big white paddlesteamers called in several times a day to unload passengers and take on new ones, often for lunch or dinner trips, or to cross to the French side of the lake. On Saturday nights there was a *bateau dansant* (dancing boat) decorated with fairy lights, where the Old School Band played jazz until the early hours – Gérard and I sometimes took it. Monsieur Bolomey, an elderly man on crutches wearing a naval cap, was responsible for tying the ropes for the paddlesteamers to the bollards and always managed to hobble about and do his job, even if he'd had too much white wine. He knew everybody but muttered to himself in a bad-tempered way if he had been drinking.

As in all Swiss villages there were two churches: one Protestant and one Catholic, the Protestant sparse and austere, the Catholic elaborately decorated. Their bells were distinctive so that you could recognise them easily from the nearby mountains on Sunday mornings.

Out walking in the early morning I would pass large metal milk churns outside the farms, waiting for the milkman to drive up in his green motorised cart to collect them. Other farmers drove down to the village to empty theirs into the stone trough at the dairy.

I enjoyed visiting the dairy to buy cheese. The milkman brought the milk and butter to the house but I preferred to choose the cheese myself. It was always colder inside than out, even in winter. The fat, pink milkman would be standing behind the counter, his triple chin proudly displayed for he was not ashamed of his enjoyment of good food. After all, he could hardly prepare all those tasty fat sausages hanging from the ceiling above the counter if he didn't enjoy good food himself. His wife, too, was plump and rosy in her starched white apron.

Behind them was the long grey trough of hewn stone. There were two entrances: customers carrying metal jugs with fitting lids came in from one side to be served with milk. The milkman would unhook one of the metal ladles from the side of the trough and ladle the frothing milk into their outheld jugs. Through the other entrance came the farmers' boys and wives, red-cheeked robust women with scarves on their heads. Jerking sideways they would empty the contents of the metal milk churns strapped to their backs into the trough where the milk foamed, rich, creamy and fresh. (Many years later we were outraged at the thought of our local milk being mixed together with that from other far-away farms to be pasteurised, homogenised and generally bland-ised. We wanted to keep our local milk from cows we knew and farmers we could trust.)

There was an array of cheeses on offer. With a piece of wire attached to wooden handles the milkman would cut me a sliver of this, a piece of that, to sample before choosing. Finally he would pat a cake of butter into shape with two wooden palettes, leaving it imprinted with a posy of gentian and edelweiss.

The butcher was a small, hardworking, quietly-spoken man. He wore a white-striped navy-blue apron as butchers do and a starched dazzling white jacket. He cut and chopped with hardly a word. His wife, on the other hand, was tall and solid. She had the most enormous bosom I had ever seen. It seemed to distance her from people – perhaps that was why she always spoke so loudly. She would stand in the doorway behind the counter leading into their private room and gossip or criticise what her husband said and did, her loud voice often embarrassing me when she boomed on private matters such as pregnancies or other people's marriages.

The butcher's wife was generally more affable early in the morning, which was when I preferred to call in. She had a jar of boiled sweets by the till to give any children that came into the shop so underneath her loud and voluminous exterior I felt there must surely be a heart of gold. After lunch, however, she was to be avoided at all costs. She was very fond of Swiss white wine – the dry kind with a bite in it – and started partaking just before lunch. By mid-afternoon she could be heard shouting two lanes away, accompanied by the ominous rattle of knives and cleavers. One wondered how the meek, hardworking butcher managed to survive. Then one day the shop was closed. The doorway was draped in black and a sign said 'Closed because of death'. The butcher's wife had apparently fallen down the stone steps into the basement one afternoon after too much *vin blanc*, and that was the end of her. The butcher was quieter and even more hard-working than ever after that.

But I'll always remember the butcher's wife as I owed her a debt of gratitude that began with my desire to get a driver's licence when we first moved into our new house.

The driving test in Switzerland at that time consisted of three parts. After a course of lessons I passed Theory satisfactorily and all that remained was the two-part Practical. Driving in Traffic was a triumph ('You drive like a Japanese empress,' said the examiner, 'with deft footwork and dignity') but the third part, Manoeuvres, was what I feared. It involved stopping and starting again on a steep slope, parking in various ways and finally backing in between two trees on a tree-lined road just out of town where the spaces between the trees on either side were only slightly greater than the length of a car.

There must have been about eight of us taking the test that morning. Two at a time, we had to park between the trees, one on each side of the road. I was surprised to see my partner was the butcher's wife! She appeared so confident that, in comparison, I felt bound to fail. I reminded myself that I had been practising and knew I could do it provided I could take my own time and not get flustered. But when I saw the examiners huddled together under the trees with frowning faces, notebook and pencil in hand, I felt very nervous indeed. My partner and I were the last to go; the examiners were already glancing at their watches impatiently, no doubt thinking what they would have for lunch.

Without hesitation, the butcher's wife went into action. Her fat, powerful arms turned the steering wheel with authority and it was obvious she was an expert. She began to swing the car round but there was one possibility that had not occurred to her. We were not driving our own familiar cars but those of the driving school. On these, the horn was operated by pressure on the centre of the steering wheel. Unfortunately for her, each time she turned to look out of the side or rear window to see how she was doing, her voluminous bosom sounded the horn. The wild hooting coming from her side of the road drew the attention of all on-lookers, examiners and examinees alike. While no-one was looking in my direction I was able quietly to get on with my reverse parking to the examiners' satisfaction.

I shall always be grateful to the butcher's wife and her bosom. I never told Gérard – who scorned any kind of incompetence – how many lessons I had needed.

Gérard was so proud of me for passing the driving test that he presented me with a pale blue 'bubblecar'. The Isetta had just come onto the market and he was attracted by its novelty: mine was the first one in Geneva. The only door was at the front of the car and the steering wheel and dashboard were attached to it so that when you opened it, the steering wheel went away with the door. Above the seat, a flat metal bar supported the soft plastic roof that could be rolled back and tied on sunny days. I felt like a queen driving along in my beautiful pale blue bubble.

Some people think the Isetta had only three wheels but in fact it had four – the two at the back were just very close together. Because the Isetta was so small, I could always find a parking spot – I used to park right outside the main entrance of the Maison des Congrès. When I opened the door and stepped down I felt like Boadicea descending from her chariot.

The main drawback of the Isetta was its poor suspension. Versoix is seven kilometres from Geneva along the lakeside. The highway was in good condition and well maintained but every little bump in the road seemed to be magnified in the Isetta: screws would fall out all round me. I never managed to work out where they had come from, but it didn't seem to matter – the car never fell apart.

Apart from this, the fifteen-minute drive to and from work was a pleasure and a joy that I longed to share since there was room for one passenger beside me, provided he could squeeze himself in. One morning on my way to work in the rain, I passed the leader of the US delegation striding as fast as he could go along the main road towards the Maison des Congrès, obviously afraid of being late. I knew him by sight but had never spoken to him. Dare I offer such an important person a lift? Well, it was raining and he was clearly in a hurry. So I pulled in beside him, opened the door and invited him in. He was first surprised, then amused, and sat down with a smile, tucking his billowing raincoat in around him. He was a tall man but managed to fit in, his knees doubled up to his chest.

We chatted amiably but I noticed the delegate's pale face was getting redder. Then his neck started reddening too. I hated to take my eyes off the road – driving the Isetta, with all the noise it made and the screws falling out, you had the impression you were going recklessly fast – but occasionally I glanced sideways and, although he was putting a brave face on it, I could see something was wrong. It wasn't until I pulled up with a jerk in front of the Maison des Congrès that I could take a proper look. It was then I noticed that the metal supporting bar, about five centimetres wide, crossed the roof exactly above where his head had been. As he climbed out, I noticed a red mark across the top of his bald head which looked quite painful. The one long strand of white hair wound round his head was clearly not thick enough to act as a cushion (nor was it in the right place). But he was gallant and said nothing, bowing his thanks with an old-world flourish. Throughout the day from my seat high on the podium I kept my eye on him, to make sure he was all right but he showed no sign of feeling faint or collapsing, so I assumed the red mark looked worse than it really was.

I had been driving the car for a few months when the door

handle fell off the first time. As I went over a slight bump in the road, there was a clatter and the inside handle fell beside my feet. I kicked it out of the way and carried on. When I reached my destination, there was of course no way of opening the door. There was nothing for it but to stand up, roll back the roof, tie the tapes and then climb out of the top in as dignified a manner as possible, with my gloves, handbag and documents under one arm. I paused to compose myself before entering the Maison des Congrès. No-one said a word.

The concierge, Jacques, was there as usual. I handed him the car keys and said: 'Jacques, do you think you could put the handle back on the inside of the door for me please? The screws must all be there, somewhere on the floor under the seat.'

He jumped to attention. 'Of course, Madame,' he replied, as if such requests were made every day and all part of his job description. It was one of the few times he forgot to announce my arrival in his characteristically loud voice.

I must confess that such requests were made quite often after that and putting the door handle back almost did become part of his job description.

The most embarrassing thing that happened when I was driving my beloved Isetta occurred when I was late for work one day. I was probably going as fast as the Isetta was able along the busy highway, trying to overtake buses and trucks, and darting in and out of the traffic. Suddenly some shaken-up wires must have touched and the horn started to sound. I tried everything I could think of to stop it, to no avail. I pushed the horn button, I tried pulling it, poking it, reasoning with it, cajoling, shouting, banging it with my clenched fist. But the hooting continued as loud as ever. The bus and truck drivers looked down at me from their superior positions with contempt but there was nothing I could do. I slowed down and tried to look humble but the insistent hooting made that difficult. When I arrived, hooting, outside the Maison des Congrès everyone was at the windows to see what was going on and witness my late arrival. Fortunately the door handle hadn't fallen off this time so I could at least exit from the car with dignity. It was a moment of blissful relief when I took the key out of the ignition and the hooting stopped.

'Please, Jacques —' I began, handing him the car keys. There was no need to say more.

Chapter 5

Sometimes we spent the weekend at Gérard's father's home in St Etienne and I could sense the Baumier family's relief that Gérard and I were now respectably married. They were all much more relaxed with me now that we were legal and there was no creeping about at night. Mémée, Gérard's grandmother, was very kind to me. She was an aristocratic old lady, well into her eighties, stiff as a rod and always dressed with great care in old-fashioned clothes with long skirts, high collars and much black lace. She wore her grey hair in an elegant bun. Mémée rarely left the apartment, except for Sunday morning when she attended Mass in one of her smart black feathered hats.

When Mémée died I missed her, for I had grown fond of her and admired her dignified imperturbability. When we went to visit the Baumiers after that, I was the 'mistress of the house'. At mealtimes, I was the one who had to ring the bell to summon Antoinette to take away our plates and cutlery at the end of each course, and bring fresh ones.

'Would Madame care to discuss the day's menus?' Antoinette would ask after breakfast. She spoke to us all in the third person, never presuming to address us directly.

'Perhaps Madame would care to come to the market this morning and choose the vegetables and fruit?' (Choosing the meat was far too important for anyone but my father-in-law himself.)

Walking along with Antoinette, who would be proudly wearing one of her best hats in my honour, it was difficult to hold a conversation because she insisted upon remaining three paces behind me, paying for and carrying our purchases. There was, I soon learnt, an art in choosing fruit – like pears and melons, for example. You had to weigh them in your hand to check that they were heavy with juice, and sniff the stalk end for a few seconds. If I chose badly, M. Baumier would be very critical.

It was also now my duty to serve the evening soup when Antoinette placed the steaming tureen in the centre of the table on its silver stand. I learnt how to dip the bowl of the ladle into the soup a second time before carrying it to each plate to stop it dripping on the immaculate tablecloth.

I learnt what is meant by a *pet de nonne* (nun's fart) and a *crottin de chèvre* (goat's turd) – not what you might think but rather a delicious pastrycake and a small round goat's cheese. It amused me to see elegant behatted ladies in the *pâtisseries* asking for three *pets de nonne*.

Monsieur Baumier was a wine expert, a gourmet and a gourmand and frequently, as we were finishing lunch, he would ask: 'What have you planned for dinner tonight?'

He had a collection of medieval recipes that had taken him years to put together. He and Antoinette had sampled many of them. Some of the dishes took a week to prepare. Sometimes the ingredients had to be marinated for days; in other recipes you had to stir every four hours or add some vital element every eight hours or even every two days.

For M. Baumier it seemed that life consisted of filling in time between the all-important meals. When he sat down at the table, the first thing he always did was to tuck his table napkin into the neck of his shirt collar, to show that he meant business. He could be embarrassing in restaurants. A few times when we took him out to restaurants in Geneva he made us rise to our feet and march out after one taste of the *sole meunière* or steak because 'this has not been cooked in butter!' Sometimes he demanded that the chef be brought to our table, then berated him because the food had not been prepared correctly.

Once in a restaurant in France I received a severe scolding for unthinkingly putting salt on my food before tasting it: 'Why add salt? That is an insult to the cook! Why, in some restaurants I could take you to, the chef would come out in person and throw you out of the restaurant for doing that. You must understand that cooking is an art in France and when the chef has finished his work with your food, it should be perfect and not need anything added. You wouldn't pick up a paintbrush and touch up a Renoir or a Gauguin, would you? Ah, these English!'

How would he have felt about the bottled tomato ketchup my young brother used to put all over his food, or the Tizer he drank with it?

Papa believed that only the French truly knew how to cook, and he remained very suspicious of Switzerland's offerings.

Once he and Antoinette came for a week's visit while Pouche was away at boarding school. When they started unloading the car, I was intrigued by the number of newspaper parcels that soon covered the kitchen table and floor and even started piling up in the garage. They had brought their own bread with them because even stale it was preferable to Swiss bread. There were enough loaves for their usual quota of two per day. Antoinette had a trick of wetting the baguettes and reheating them in the oven to make them seem almost fresh again. They had also brought their own meat and wine.

'Swiss butchers use different cuts,' explained M. Baumier, deprecatingly.

In came parcels of leeks, onions, mushrooms and a set of sharp knives, a large chopping board and even Antoinette's favourite saucepans. The more I saw, the happier I was that I had insisted upon Antoinette coming too.

M. Baumier sat down and announced that he was tired from driving and not very hungry.

'I shall need very little dinner tonight,' he said. 'Almost nothing. Just a little freshly-made vegetable soup to start with. I presume you have fresh vegetables? And some salad. You do have salad? Perhaps a little cold *rosbif* to go with it or some other sort of meat. Just something light. As for dessert, very little – say, a baked custard or rice pudding, and some fresh fruit of course. Oh, I forgot the cheese. What sort of cheeses do you have in Switzerland? Do you have goat's cheese? Are they good? You'll find the wine in the garage by the car, you'd better bring it in to get it to room temperature. I've brought a bottle of Pernod, too, for the apéritif.'

Sunday mornings with Gérard's family in St Etienne were interesting. Monsieur Baumier occupied the only bathroom from 7 o'clock until the last minute panic when they all left, generally five minutes late, for Mass. I could hear water noises as he took his dominical bath, then trimmed his moustache, splashed himself with eau de Cologne, cleared his nose and throat, cut his toenails, put on his best clothes, polished his shoes and spent considerable time choosing his tie, to be worthy of the Lord. Gérard and I had no choice but to stay in bed late that day. One thing we would not miss, however, was to see them leave for church. Since Mémée's death, Antoinette accompanied 'Monsieur' to Mass and her selection of hats had to be seen to be believed. Feathers and ribbons, velvets and veils were never too good or too elaborate and while she spent weekdays in black, topped with a dingy apron, on Sundays she gave free vent to her imagination and her Sunday best.

When I asked Gérard why he never went to church and his family raised no objection, he said that they all knew about the pact he had made with Virgin Mary when his mother was dying from meningitis. 'One night the doctor told us it was the crisis: either my mother would die or she would live through the night and be saved. We all prayed for her throughout the night and I made my pact: if the Virgin Mary saved her, I would go to Mass every Sunday but if she died, I would never go to Mass again. She died.'

We were having breakfast on our own. I sipped my tea. Now that we were married I had been able to insist that I should always make the tea. They thought I was very wasteful using a whole teaspoonful when a pinch would do, but I sometimes left a packet in the kitchen to compensate. I buttered a long crisp stick of bread and was just about to bite into it when Gérard grabbed it out of my hand and ate it. '*Quia nominor leo*', he said. ('I am the lion and I must have the lion's share'.)

I looked at him in surprise.

'You'll have to get used to that,' he retorted. 'Always remember that I am the lion and that the lion is the king of all animals.'

I shrugged. What did it matter if he wanted to be the lion?

'Tell me more about your pact with Virgin Mary.'

'Well, first, she wasn't a virgin. The Hebrew word used means "young woman" not "virgin". It's a translator's mistake. The Bible's full of them. Don't they teach you anything in England?

'I shall have a lot of things to teach our children. But they won't have the crutch of religion to lean on,' he continued.

'Don't you want them to be Catholics? I had to promise –'

'That's your affair. Do what you like. But I won't encourage them to be Catholics or anything else. And I shall teach them not to believe history, either. "Our ancestors, the Gauls . . ." is what we're taught in France. And even the little brown-skinned children in Tahiti have to repeat the same ridiculous nonsense. I shall teach our children that there is no true history. Only subjective stories. The same as for the Bible.'

M. Baumier and Antoinette slammed the door as they came in, putting an end to our conversation. They both carried white cardboard boxes tied with ribbons from the *pâtisserie*. Each week an important decision had to be made: whether to choose a *Saint Honoré*, a *Japonais*, *un Forêt Noir*, *des méringues Chantilly*, *un vacherin glacé cassis*, *une tarte tatin*, *une bombe glacée à la vanille* or *une tarte aux myrtilles*.

After lunch, we would leave the table and retire to the drawing room where we sat on uncomfortable gilded Louis XV chairs and waited for Antoinette to bring the coffee. Finally the door would open and she would place the silver tray on the table in front of me, saying: 'Coffee is served, Madame.'

I then had the delicate task of pouring the coffee to each person's liking. I had to remember the taste of visiting aunts and uncles – some liked a 'white collar' at the top of the small cup while others preferred their cup brim-full. Some liked one lump, for others I had to master the knack of breaking the rectangular lump exactly in half, or in a third, and putting it in the cup before the coffee. Some had to have a dainty silver spoon correctly placed in the saucer, under the cup handle. (No milk was served with the coffee, of course.) It all had to be done deftly – and quickly, I soon learnt, because the greatest crime of all was for it not to be drunk piping hot 'in order to facilitate digestion'. It also had to be taken immediately after the meal 'before digestion had started'.

I always waited for M. Baumier to taste his coffee before relaxing. He had a way of clicking his tongue to test coffee, wine or brandy. It was not for nothing that he was a member of the famous French *Taste-Vin* society.

On one particular occasion, I thought I had accomplished my task correctly but, after one sip, M. Baumier frowned. His features froze.

'Send for Antoinette,' he said. I got up and rang the bell.

The moment Antoinette appeared in the doorway, I knew she had done something wrong. I sampled my coffee but could taste nothing different. It was the usual strong bitter French coffee. But Antoinette was twisting the corner of her apron between her fingers and moving from one heavy foot to the other.

'You have added water afterwards to this coffee,' said M. Baumier in an accusing tone. 'It is undrinkable! It tastes of water!'

Mumbling something about it having been too strong, she blushed and rushed out of the room, bearing away the tray. Soon she was back with fresh coffee and cups and my father-in-law grunted as he swallowed his first sip, to acknowledge begrudgingly that this time it met his standards.

As I have already explained, my father-in-law had only one eye. As a result, he had difficulty judging distances. Sometimes when serving the wine he would carefully pour it just beside the glass instead of into it. I always tried to help him avoid this by moving the glass.

I still feel guilty about what happened at lunch one day. Antoinette had placed a large bowl of salad in front of me and after helping myself I passed it across to Papa, sitting opposite me. He took some crisp curly lettuce on to his plate, and as he raised the first forkful to his mouth I looked – and looked again: there in the middle of a curved lettuce leaf was a bright green grasshopper, at least three centimetres long, with long antennae. In the two seconds it took me to realise what was happening and wonder how to say it politely in French, he had put the lettuce in his mouth, chewed and swallowed. I decided it was better in the circumstances to say nothing. Even now, after all these years, I still feel guilty that I wasn't quick enough to stop him.

We spent our first Christmas as a married couple with Gérard's aunt and uncle in a little mountain village behind Nice. Midnight Mass was a chilly affair in a draughty village church, grey and dismal at one o'clock in the morning, in spite of the ornate gilt statues in alcoves of Virgin Mary and various saints. There were three masses one after the other and they seemed to last for hours.

'This is the last one, it will soon be over,' Gérard whispered encouragingly. He was proud of my elegance there among the humble peasants dressed in black and grey. I was proud that he was pleased with me.

After the aunts, uncles and cousins had queued up to receive holy communion and returned to their seats I put my arm in Gérard's and smiled at him. 'Thank heavens, we can go now.'

But people weren't leaving. They were once again queuing up and this time the queue included the entire congregation. It wound all round the inside of the church. Facing us stood the priest holding out a doll about the size of a baby, chipped and worn. Each person in turn curtseyed, crossed himself and kissed the feet of the doll. This was more than I could take. I fled outside into the night.

Back in the warmth of the house no-one, fortunately, seemed to have noticed my hurried departure. The *Reveillon* had begun. There was champagne and *pâté de foie gras*, walnuts, marzipan-stuffed dates, special Christmas biscuits and an enormous Christmas tree aglow with candles.

Next morning the fun continued with more champagne and presents for all. An old lady of ninety-six who was someone's great grandmother told me about the Christmasses of her childhood, carefully holding her champagne glass in both shaky white hands.

Pouche, Gérard's sister, looked very grown-up with her hair up, knee-length white socks and shiny black patent leather shoes with a small heel. She was turning into a very pretty young lady. She adored her big brother and listened, eyes shining, whenever he expounded his theories.

New Year's Eve, too, was a happy time, back in St Etienne in the Baumier apartment. The streets were full of revellers, in spite of the cold – all laughing, shouting, singing and even dancing. The cafés stayed open all night and were so packed the pavement in front wasn't wide enough and the crowd spilled onto the road. Gérard and I went from one café to another, meeting friends of his. The talking got louder and louder as the hours went by. When the church clock chimed midnight the bells began to ring and we kissed everyone in sight on both cheeks, starting with one another. I was being carried along on a giant wave of euphoria. I was discovering a wonderful new world and was almost breathless with the thrill of it and anticipation of the joys to come.

Next day everyone continued kissing all their acquaintances as they met them for the first time in the new year and I felt shy as men I hardly knew came up enthusiastically to put a hand on each of my shoulders and deposit a resounding kiss on each cheek while I went through the motions of kissing them in return.

We weren't expected to kiss Antoinette but we did all shake hands with her and the men gave her little visiting-card envelopes containing money. She curtseyed and thanked everyone, getting redder and redder in the face with all the attention.

After a wonderful New Year's Day dinner with Antoinette's speciality, guinea fowl on toast soaked in cognac, and many full-bodied wines, followed by a spectacular *Bombe glacée*, M. Baumier sat in his deep leather armchair, a glass of Armagnac in one hand, and beckoned me over to sit next to him. Leaning towards me confidentially he asked: 'And how do you like being married?'

There was a twinkle in his eye.

'We are very happy,' I replied defensively.

'Yes, yes, yes,' he answered. His double chin rested on his chest for a while and I wondered if he had fallen asleep.

Then he leant towards me again and said: 'You know, you married the wrong man. I'm the one you should have married. The father, not the son! I would have known how to take care of you.'

At a loss how to answer that one, I remained silent. It was the second time he had told me this – the first time was at our wedding.

'Gérard was a terrible child, you know,' he went on. 'He always had the most terrible tantrums. A violent temper. Once he bit Danielle on the thigh when they were quite small. It bled a lot and we had to take her to the doctor. She still has the scar, I believe.'

The strange thing was that he said this quite proudly.

'Even when he was a tiny baby he had terrible fits of temper. He used to scream and rage and kick and go so red in the face it was quite frightening, the little veins stood out so on his forehead.'

Why was he telling me this? He spoke as though it were a joke, yet there seemed to be a seriousness underlying what he said. Perhaps it was a warning. I'd heard tales of Gérard's childhood tantrums before, but paid little attention, although I knew he had a temper. When I started furnishing our house in Versoix the first thing I bought was a set of five leather pouffes which I placed strategically in a zigzag path down the length of the living room. If Gérard got angry he could kick them to give vent to his feelings without hurting anybody. They proved extremely useful.

It was many years later that I received a telephone call from Danielle. Papa had been taken ill and was in hospital in St Etienne. He was dying of cancer. He was asking for me – he wanted to see me as soon as possible.

Next morning early I set off and eventually found my way to the hospital. When I went into his room, I found a crowd of relatives gathered round his bed.

He looked very pale. 'I want to see Val,' he whispered.

'She's here,' they said gently, and stepped back to allow me through.

'That's the first time he's spoken for days,' someone murmured. 'He had a brain haemorrhage last week and hasn't spoken since.'

I bent over to kiss him on the cheek and he whispered in my ear, 'Come back again soon *on your own*. I have something to tell you.'

'I will,' I said reassuringly.

I resolved to come back the next weekend.

But two days later I received a telephone call to say he had died during the night.

Papa's funeral was memorable. He had planned everything: booked the table at Chez Léon (giving the time but not the date), chosen the menu, specified the wines, written the guest list and paid the bill in advance.

I have often wondered what it was Papa wanted to tell me.

Chapter 6

In the summer of 1953, I was sitting on the garden swing reading Montherlant's *The Dead Queen*: 'A little boy with long eyelashes, partly handsome, partly rough, who sighs with pleasure and daydreams in wonder at the beauty of the world around him.'

I put one hand down to rest on my bulge, and sure enough there was a faint movement as if my own little boy were turning over or stretching out in his sleep.

'It is such a wonderful feeling,' I tried to explain to Gérard. 'It's like a special secret you carry around with you wherever you go.'

'You look like a penguin and you walk like one,' he replied flatly.

I was three months' pregnant and my world seemed perfect.

I had bought a tray of African marigold seedlings to plant out. They would make a pretty border for the path leading up to the front door. As I put on my gardening shoes and walked down the path, Gérard followed.

'There's a film on at the cinema that I want to see tonight,' he announced.

I looked up expectantly.

'You're in no condition to be seen, you'd better stay here and rest.'

A moment of disappointment. But after all I would be perfectly happy at home, sewing and nursing my bulge. I had a very powerful Mother Earth feeling. And I did enjoy preparing for the baby. I was making small sheets with a lace border and pillowcases to match. I had recently bought some delicate flowery material to re-cover the wicker basket that Gérard's father had given us. It had been used for Gérard's first months. It had handles and a round hood that could be raised and attached with ribbons on either side and I was looking forward to starting work on it.

Gérard went back into the house and I knelt carefully and started planting my African marigolds.

I had planted two or three of them when he came out again and stood behind me admiring my work.

'They will look nice. How many more do you have to plant?'

Melted by his interest in my gardening, my heart softened. It was so rare for him to notice what I was doing. I sat back on my heels and smiled up at him.

'All these left to do!'

I indicated the tray still three-quarters full of plants. Perhaps he was going to offer to help.

I heard him go back into the house and kick the front door closed.

Some minutes later I stood up and stretched. Now that I was pregnant I certainly needed to go to the toilet more often. I opened the front door to find Gérard on the telephone in the hall. I heard him say: 'I'll pick you up around eight-fifteen then. It starts at eight-thirty. Make yourself beautiful! I'll take you out to dinner afterwards.'

He turned round as he heard me come in. The kind, interested expression I had seen a few minutes before was now an angry scowl of accusation.

'I can't talk any more now. 'Bye!' he said crossly into the telephone and hung up.

Then he turned on me, furious.

'Why are you listening to my telephone calls? Can't you stay out in the garden when I'm on the phone? So you're spying on me now are you? Spying on me in my own home! I can't even make a phone call in peace! God, what has it come to?'

'I'm sorry, I didn't realise. I'm only going to the bathroom,' I stammered, hurt and bewildered, hardly able to make sense of what I'd overheard.

He raised himself to his full height and continued to shout at me, self-righteously as he climbed the stairs to our bedroom. Some minutes later he rushed downstairs wearing his new pale-blue suit. He stormed out to the garage, leaving the scent of his aftershave in the air behind him, and I heard his new sports car drive off furiously. To show his indignation, he had left all the doors and the garden gate wide open.

As I closed them, I felt that the bottom had fallen out of my perfect world.

But later, as I sat sewing in the big armchair (it was a typically Swiss high-backed armchair with earpieces on the sides, where I felt safe), I decided that whatever Gérard was doing was his own affair. It was better not to know. I would be much happier at home alone, sewing, than I would have been in a crowded cinema full of cigarette smoke. Anyway, I was not alone. I would never be alone again. I would have a baby to nurse and love, to stroke and sing to.

After that, Gérard stopped coming straight home from work.

'Don't wait for me for dinner,' he said. 'I generally go and have a drink with my colleagues and we end up eating as well. Don't worry about me.'

He often got home after I had gone to bed. But I didn't let myself brood about it. I was too busy preparing for the baby.

I read all the books I could find on pregnancy and childbirth. Birth expert Grantley Dick Read's 'painless childbirth' methods were much talked about in England and reported in the *Observer* which I received each week from London, though no-one in Switzerland seemed to have heard about them yet. I asked my gynaecologist what he thought when I went for my monthly visit. I also told him my cousin in England had given birth recently without any pain by delivering her baby under hypnosis.

'The only way for you not to suffer is for us to administer gas and air,' Dr Muhletaler said, leaning back in his chair. He was very sure of himself and seemed to think I was a little crazy. After all, it was my first experience of childbirth whereas he had attended many. 'If you do as you're told, when the time comes you will suffer a minimum,' he added with a professional smile, rather similar to Gérard's when he was explaining how superior men are compared to women.

I saw that if I wanted my baby to have as pleasant a birth as possible, I was going to have to take charge myself. It seemed to me that childbirth was a natural event and if I was healthy, relaxed and confident there should be no need for gas or anything else.

Gérard made fun of the little case I had packed which stood ready in the hall but when the first contractions started he panicked.

'Quick! Quick! We must get you to the hospital!'

'I'm not sure it's time,' I hesitated. 'I think I just had too much apple juice last night. I've had a stomach-ache ever since.'

But I was bundled into the car with my little black case and for once Gérard had a good excuse for squealing tyres, though

I was afraid that being thrown from side to side as we went round bends and jolting when we suddenly stopped at red lights (there were no seat-belts then) might frighten the baby.

The nurse was kind in spite of the fact that it was 1 a.m. I was put to bed, shaved and given an enema. Gérard came in to say he had to go home and pack – he was leaving for Paris on the 8 a.m. plane.

'I'll come back to be with you, I haven't forgotten my promise. But you'd better lay your egg before my plane leaves,' he said benevolently, 'so that I know whether it's a boy or a girl. And it had better be a boy!'

I told the midwife I wanted no gas, no pills, no injections.

'But –'

'I will raise my arm if I want the mask,' I said firmly. 'I am the one who must decide.'

'But the pain –'

'If the pain is unbearable I will raise my arm.'

She smiled the smile of one who knows best.

'You'll see,' was all she said.

When things started in earnest the sister prepared an injection.

'What is that?'

'We must slow it down until your obstetrician gets here. Don't worry, we always do that. It'll be all right.'

'But I've told you I don't want any injections!'

'Now you must be good and lie still. I know best. The doctor will be very cross if you don't do as you're told.'

'If my baby is ready to come, now is the time I want it, whether the doctor is here or not!'

I was getting desperate. The contractions were strong now and nature told me to start expelling the warm little body.

Gérard came into the room, out of breath, donning a white overall and mask.

'We'll pay him even if he isn't here in time!' he said sarcastically but conclusively.

His presence was one of authority and I was grateful for his arrival. The nurse looked questioningly at the midwife and I started to push. Just as the baby's dark wet head appeared, the obstetrician burst into the room. He was in the nick of time after all. In the large square mirror above me I could see the baby's head and the joy of it was so great I felt my heart would burst.

'It's a healthy, beautiful boy!' the doctor announced and I felt a wonderful wet warmth against the inside of my thighs.

The umbilical cord was cut and I was shown the wrinkle-faced little creature.

'You have done well,' said Gérard magnanimously. 'You have given me a son. It is the king's choice to start with a boy.' Then, as he rushed out of the door, he added: 'I shall telephone my father from Paris.'

A relaxed feeling crept over me. I had accomplished my mission. I had produced my baby without any medication or stitches in spite of them all! Even Gérard was happy and in time for his plane. Now everything would be all right. He would love his son and we would be a happy family.

Against the fashion of the time I passionately believed that the best way to bring up a healthy baby was on its mother's milk. I breastfed my babies religiously, for as long as I could. I managed to put myself in the right frame of mind to produce plenty of milk by imagining I was a black and white cow with nothing to do but stand in the warm sun in a meadow, watching the trains go by.

With a husband who couldn't bear to be kissed or touched I was hungry to love, to stroke and to hold. I caressed the baby's silky head as he suckled, and sang to him. When we got home

I played all my favourite records for him to hear while he lay in his cot. I tried to eat the healthiest foods possible to produce good sweet-tasting milk for him and I watched him grow with pride.

I had decided to work right up to a week before the expected date of Marc's birth in mid-September in order to keep most of the three months' maternity leave to which I was entitled to spend with him. By adding to that my six weeks' annual leave, I wouldn't have to go back to work until he was just over four months old.

Marc was a healthy baby. We planted a cherry tree in the garden to mark his birth, imagining our schoolboy son a few years later climbing the tree to plunder the cherries – although as yet the tree was hardly tall enough to cast shade over his pram.

We gave a garden party for his christening. He wore the handmade-lace Baumier christening gown and bonnet which our maid had washed, starched and ironed; his grandfather was very proud of his first grandson. Danielle and Bruno, now married, came too and we asked Dany to be Marc's godmother.

'It's thanks to you that Marc was ever born!' I told her.

We all drank champagne and Pouche grew pink-cheeked and shiny-eyed as she led me away from the crowd to tell me she was in love and hoped to get engaged soon.

After a month or two, Marc was thriving and I went back to my flamenco dancing which I had missed so much during my pregnancy. I practised while he slept in the afternoons and my figure improved rapidly. Soon I was ready to dance in public again and could fit into my flamenco dresses once more, although I had to let the bodice out a few centimetres because of my milk-heavy breasts.

Now I had a wardrobe of flamenco dresses in every colour and bright-coloured fringed shawls to go with them, as well as mantillas and tall combs to keep my long hair up. Before going on stage, I would pin red carnations on top, making sure not to fix them too securely so that when I got into the passion of the dance and shook my head suddenly, the flowers would fall out round me and gradually my hair would come loose and fall over my shoulders. Oh, how I enjoyed that moment!

My favourite dress, a *bata de cola*, I had made in Seville for dancing the Soleares. It was deep red; the bodice was well fitted and tight at the waist. Then at the hips, the frills started, layer upon layer of them, down to my ankles — except at the back where the skirt formed a pointed train that dragged behind me so that, when I danced, I had to jerk my hips to one side suddenly to make the train swing round. I felt like an insect about to attack its victim when I did that.

I didn't want to leave Marc, so I took him with me to the theatre in his carry-cot. A few months old, he would be there in the wings, tucked up in his cosy little bed and in between dances I would go and talk to him and make sure he was all right.

One evening I was performing in the Grand Theatre in Geneva. Marc was in a corner of my dressing-room in his carry-cot while I put the combs in my hair, the red carnation on the top of my head and stiff soap-curls in front of each ear. Finally the big ear-rings, the sturdy-heeled shoes and the dress. Then we both headed for the stage and I put his carry-cot in the wings.

While the audience applauded the end of the programme I rushed off to see if my baby son was all right and found him crying. He was hungry. And he was right. It was time for his feed. So I sat on a chair next to his carry-cot and breastfed him during the applause. Someone came to get me.

'They want an encore,' she said.

'Tell the guitarists to play something and then I'll come back on stage,' I whispered.

The baby was replete and gurgled happily as I put him back in his cot. So — back into my bodice, on with my castanets, and back onto the stage where the guitars were playing another 'Soleares'. Soon I was a red-tailed insect once more, about to sting my victim. Head held high, I stepped forward in rhythm, both arms behind my back, my castanets clicking like a death rattle behind me. Looking down, I saw that I was not symmetrical. Breastfeeding mothers will know what I mean.

One morning while I was having breakfast, someone knocked at the door. A slender woman, her grey hair in a bun, was standing hesitatingly in the driveway, stamping her small booted feet to keep them warm and rubbing her hands together in their knitted mittens. Her eyes were a sharp shining blue.

'Would Madame like –?' She gestured towards an old wooden cart standing outside, laden with crates of vegetables, apples, pears and a basket of farm eggs. The long handles of the cart must at one time have had a horse between them but now the Vegetable Lady pulled it herself. It was downhill to the village; the problem must have been to hold it back. She didn't look strong enough.

That was the first time I met her. After that she called every Wednesday and Saturday morning, her face sometimes pinched with cold, a hand-knitted bonnet on her head. Her face was sensitive and deeply lined but it is the sharpness of her blue eyes that I remember most clearly.

Behind her in the distance the Swiss Jura Mountains were crisp and sparkling white with snow against the deep blue of the sky.

'Mary-Ann!' I called. 'Come and meet the Vegetable Lady!'

Mary-Ann had just arrived from England in response to my advertisement in *The Lady* for a live-in nanny. She had brought with her one sensible suitcase with a tennis racquet tucked inside the leather strap. She was in her early twenties, her hair was short, her face reliable and shiny as if from scrubbing. She wore a pale blue uniform with white elasticated cuffs and practical lace-up navy-blue shoes. We made friends immediately. She was kind and gentle with the baby and right from the start I felt confident about leaving Marc in her care when I went back to work. She was also a reassuring presence when Gérard behaved irrationally. He had a tendency to throw things and I particularly remember Mary-Ann patiently and methodically picking congealed spaghetti bolognaise off an oil painting on the wall of the dining room after he had flung his dinner at it, slammed the door and driven off in a fit of temper one evening.

Mary-Ann came out to join us, crossing her arms over her pale blue twin-set and uniform to keep the cold out.

'Do you grow all these yourself?' I asked the Vegetable Lady, for I knew Mary-Ann would not dare to try her schoolgirl French out on a stranger.

'Yes, my husband and I live just up the hill on the left. That's where we grow our vegetables. All this was the Domaine de St Loup in the old days and where you have your garden was the vineyards. At the top of the hill was the castle belonging to the Duke of Burgundy. You must come and see us some time when you go for a walk in the woods.'

That same afternoon we decided to investigate. Mary-Ann strapped the snugly-dressed baby into the little chair fixed to the sledge, for it had been snowing again, and as she pulled it along, I bent down to hold Marc's gloved hand in mine. In the other hand I had the dog's lead, for we had recently purchased a green-eyed puppy we called Ulla (after a Swedish friend of mine with green eyes). A cross between a german shepherd and a boxer, Ulla was large, adorable and full of mischief.

Soon we came to an old two-storey building, brick at each end with elaborate carved doors and window frames. In the central part were glass panes up to the grey slate roof, which I thought must have been the Duke of Burgundy's conservatory that I had read about. He kept two hundred potted orange trees and palms in it during the winter. The Head Gardener's pink cottage was still there, a little way down the road. There were over one hundred gardeners working there and in the vineyards in the Duke of Burgundy's time.

On our left were rows and rows of silver beet, spinach, cabbage, carrots, potatoes, leeks and brussels sprouts all sprinkled with snow but obviously well taken care of. The Vegetable Lady's husband was stamping about in his heavy waterproof boots and thick apron, string dangling from the front pocket. He picked off a dead leaf here, tied a plant to a stake there.

'*Bonjour, Mesdames,*' he called out gruffly at our approach. 'You will keep that dog on a lead, won't you?'

'Of course I will.'

'Well, at least until you get to the end of the cultivated part. Doesn't matter so much when you get to Cemetery Field at the bottom there by the fountain.'

'Why is it called "Cemetery Field"?'

'The story goes that when they ploughed it up some years ago they found rows of human skeletons. All lined up in rows, they were, and all buried in a crouching position, which is how they used to bury smugglers. You see, the border is there some-where in the woods – it's not clearly marked. But the other side of the field is France so it must have been a good place for smuggling.'

'What did they smuggle?'

'I suppose that changed with the times. Whatever was worth while at the time, one might say . . .'

The sledge slid along easily in the fresh snow and the dog pulled at the lead, sniffing rabbits. I was glad to release her when we got to the end of the track and found an old drystone bridge with clear, clean water rushing beneath it. Fish could be seen in the water in spite of the cold. A few years later we'd play 'Pooh sticks' there with Marc, throwing sticks in on one side of the bridge and rushing to the other side to see whose stick came out first.

I let the dog off the lead and she rushed away, tail wagging, barking with joy at her freedom. Looking after her, I saw it. I suppose you would call it a mountain spring. Clear, sparkling water spurted out of a hollow formed deep in the intermingled roots of three enormous trees. Looking up, I marvelled at how tall the trees were and how old they must be. Bending down to look more closely, I saw that many years earlier someone's deft fingers had fitted together pieces of rock and pebbles like a jigsaw puzzle to form a wall about one foot high, arched like a church window. From its centre the water gushed, gurgling and splashing, catching the golden sunshine before disappearing into the ferns.

We stood for some minutes, entranced.

'It must have been here for at least a hundred years,' Mary-Ann said at last.

The tall trees seemed to lead one's spirits straight up out of the shadows into the clear blue sky.

We tasted the water and it was fresh and pure. Mary-Ann carried some in her cupped hands for Marc to try. I bent down and drank some and the dog came running back and drank greedily too. There was something special about that water. As you drank it, it seemed to give you zest for life, pure joy to be alive. Standing beneath those trees was like standing in a cathedral. Instead of stained glass windows filtering the light, the dappled sunlight shone through a roof of green leaves.

Now that I had discovered them, I often went for walks in the woods behind our house when I needed to think through a problem. Along by the stream, deep in the autumn leaves, I would walk fast at first in my anger for something Gérard had said or done – he was often rude to the tradespeople or to the maid – but gradually I would slow down and feel calmer, stopping to look at a reflection in the water, a patch of mauve autumn crocuses or, in March, primroses growing down by the water's edge. By the time I reached the spring, I would be at peace with the world. It was my thinking place, my green cathedral.

Seeing one another most Wednesday and Saturday mornings when she made her rounds, the Vegetable Lady and I became good friends. During the worst of winter, she ceased her rounds but with the spring I would hear her familiar knock on the door and we'd be able to comment on the forsythia buds by the front gate and the cherry trees' buds gradually turning into blossom as the weeks went by.

It was the Vegetable Lady's husband who told me about Fanny. I came upon them working among the rows of carrots and onions one afternoon as I took Ulla for a walk after work.

'My husband has brought a book down from the attic to show you,' she said, and bustled off to fetch it.

'We knew you would like to see it,' she continued, returning with an old volume in her hand. 'It has a picture of the castle that was here in the old days – the Duke of Burgundy's castle. It's only about ten years since they took away all the ruins and used them to build a beautiful home for a rich American in another village not far from here. See? There used to be a pond here for boating.'

We pored over the book for a few minutes and she urged me to borrow it for a closer look.

I had a question I'd been wanting to ask: 'Who was this Fanny you mentioned?'

'Oh, she wasn't up here on the hill. Fanny lived down in the village, many years ago. She was quite a character.'

The Vegetable Lady hesitated and her husband took over.

'She was unmarried, you see, but she had so many children the Mayor started to get worried because the municipal authorities had to provide for them. She had no money. When her twelfth child was born the Mayor decided he should speak to her. So he asked: "Do you know who the fathers are of your children? If you can tell me, I will try to get some contribution from them towards the children's upkeep."

'Fanny shook her head.

' "Please try to remember," the Mayor insisted. "Sit down quietly and see if you can think back."

'Fanny thought for a moment.

' "Look, Sir," she said. "If you sat on an ants' nest and one of them bit you, how would you be able to tell which one it was?" '

Marc grew into a tall, slim little boy with golden brown eyes and curly hair so fair it was almost white. He and Mary-Ann were good friends and I admired her patience and common sense. I felt she looked after him better than I did – Mary-Ann respected all the rules, like meal–times, table manners and bed-time, and never ever raised her voice. She seemed happy in her new life and had soon made friends, especially from her weekly French class. (I let her use my bubblecar to go into Geneva for French lessons and at weekends.) She chose the fabric for new curtains, bedspread and cushions for her room. Walking along by the lake in the afternoons with Marc in his pram, she had made the acquaintance of two other nannies, one of whom looked after the five princesses of the exiled Royal family of Romania, who lived by the lake. The three nannies would go on picnics with their charges, taking it in turn to bake cakes and make sandwiches and thermos flasks of tea. They would walk to Creux de Genthod, the next village along the lake, and, as the children grew bigger, took them to paddle in the water there and sail toy sailing boats.

Gérard adored Marc: he played with him, danced round the room with him, exhibited him to family and friends and boasted about him until people were tired. To Gérard, Marc was perfect. I was happy to be on the fringe of Gérard's happiness – even though he never said so, I knew I had played a part in producing such a wonderful little boy.

Gérard seemed to be doing well in his career and was gradually rising in the company hierarchy. He started going overseas on business trips and always brought me back a piece of expensive jewellery. I was honoured to be able to help when he asked me to translate articles he had written for publication in foreign journals. Sometimes I would be preparing for bed when he called out: 'You can't go to bed yet! I've got a twenty-three-page article here that's got to be translated tonight. It has to be posted to the magazine publishers in America first thing in the morning.'

So I would put on my dressing-gown and go downstairs again.

To me, Gérard was like a force of nature, a storm that could not be averted. In a way, I respected him for being so forthright. My upbringing had made me over-polite and considerate of people, I felt. Perhaps Gérard was right and the English way was hypocritical. Gérard, on the contrary, gloried in being uninhibited and unrestrained, much closer to nature and what he felt to be the truth. His anger was quite unpredictable and sometimes violent. I often longed for someone to confide in, but I could not betray him by discussing my problems with any of my friends or colleagues. We had a tumultuous relationship, but when Gérard was in a good mood, everything seemed wonderful.

Then, two years after Marc's birth, something happened to make me suppress any doubts I might have had. I discovered I was pregnant again. Fortunately unpredictable Gérard reacted well to the news and even helped me re-organise the bedrooms to make a 'baby corner'. Mary-Ann was excited too and started knitting baby clothes in her spare time.

As with my first pregnancy, it was a serene, complete feeling and I revelled in it. Once again I felt that special quiver inside me. Once again I had a secret joy to carry around with me that no-one could take away. Gérard could joke unkindly about my increasing girth and go off to spend his evenings with his friends as much as he liked. I was impervious to any bitterness – even if he was having an occasional fling – for I had my own special secret inside me, filling me with happiness and illuminating my world with a special glow.

Stephanie was born in 1956 with the first snow. She was the most perfect, dainty little girl. Her birth was easier than Marc's, maybe because I knew what to expect and what to do but also because the obstetrician and nurses, having now heard of Grantley Dick Read, didn't treat me like a madwoman as they had the first time.

The previous day had been grey and dull but as we walked to the car early that morning our snowboots left footprints in the deep white carpet of fresh snow and we were part of a hushed, white world. The fir trees in the garden were heavy with snow. I climbed into the car and Gérard put my little black case on the back seat.

Later that morning I felt overwhelmed with joy as I lay back on my pillows, the delicate little baby girl in her cot beside me. I dreamily imagined the pretty feminine dresses I would buy for her, the dainty shoes, the hair ribbons, while Gérard sat on the side of my bed, thumping it with enthusiasm as he described his new research project. As usual, he couldn't stay – he had a meeting in Poland – but would be back in time to take me home at the end of the week.

Perhaps I enjoyed Stephanie so much because I was more

relaxed with her now that I had some experience of babies. Mary-Ann was thrilled to have a new charge. Gérard, too, was smitten and I knew she would soon twist him round her little finger.

She developed into a smiling, contented baby who gurgled with happiness in her pram in the shade of Marc's cherry tree, watching the bees buzzing in the lilac bushes and the birds chirping and darting in and out of the cherry blossom.

We planted another cherry tree a few yards from the first.

Stephanie's christening took place one sunny spring morning. She looked like a beautiful doll in the Baumier christening gown and bonnet. My friend Pierrette was her godmother.

'I'm not experienced in holding babies,' she warned, as I put the lacy bundle in her arms outside the church. Gingerly she held Stephanie out to the priest for him to put salt on her tongue and holy water on her forehead. Steffi seemed to enjoy the experience and smiled angelically.

Later we arranged her under the cherry trees in the garden, her lace frills arrayed around her artistically, for the photographs to be taken. She had smiles for all those who came to admire her and even seemed to enjoy the drop of champagne Gérard put on her tongue from a silver spoon.

At three, Marc felt very grown up and manly compared to the useless little bundle in the pram. He studied people thoughtfully before speaking to them to gauge which language they spoke and once he had decided, it was forever. It was no good trying to change and say something to him in the other language. Once he had labelled you English-speaking you got English from him, whichever language you used. His English was very polite, for he had heard no English swear-words from Mary-Ann or myself. Not so with French! He was very impressed with his father's vocabulary, as well as that of the milkman and even the quiet little butcher, thanks to whom he learnt many new French words. He thought French was a much more expressive, manly language than English.

Stephanie's chubby little arms were dimpled at the elbows and soon turned a delightful golden colour in the sun. I loved playing with her as I bathed her, Mary-Ann hovering in the doorway in case she might be allowed to help. I could see that Mary-Ann longed for the day when I would go back to work and she would be allowed to bathe and feed her and take her for walks in the afternoons in her pram.

Chapter 7

The Secretary General had fallen ill soon after I had gone on maternity leave with Steffi. He had returned to the United States for surgery and would be spending two more months there. As it happened, his absence was much longer because while in hospital he contracted typhoid. Back at the office, I tried to pretend I was busy to justify my presence, but that became very boring after a while. All I had to do every day was deal with the correspondence – which sometimes took less than an hour.

One morning at the coffee bar I shared a table with Isobel, one of the permanent translators in the Linguistic Service. She looked pale and tired and told me how busy they were, preparing documents for a forthcoming international conference on television colour standards, but the texts were so specialised and highly technical that they did not have time to train new translators, unfamiliar with the terminology. I offered to help out, since I knew the vocabulary and was available during the Secretary General's absence. I could prepare a draft translation which Isobel or one of the others could then revise. At least we could try it out and see if I was good enough. And that is how

I was transferred to the Translation Department. In the end, the Secretary General had to resign for health reasons so I never returned to work in his office. I officially became a professional translator.

Translating the information on the television colour standards used by the various countries interested me because there were so many non-technical aspects; differences in terminology could often be explained by different cultural backgrounds. This applied particularly to the USSR documents; translating them into English was a great challenge because their television vocabulary had developed in isolation from the rest of the world over the years and often the word used bore no relation at all to the word used in French, English or Spanish, their approach being from quite a different angle.

Some months later the television standards conference took place in Geneva.

It had been hoped the member countries would agree to recommend one of the standards which they would all adopt but the conference ended with a decision not to decide. In other words, countries would continue using different standards, some PAL, some NTSC, some SECAM and the USSR would continue to use their version of SECAM. Changing from one system to another would have involved considerable expenditure for the countries concerned, which is no doubt why no decision could be reached.

I should explain at this point that a translation is written. In other words, translation involves taking a written text in one language and translating it into a written text in another language. During a conference, most of the translation work is urgent. Sometimes the whole conference of over 1000 delegates would be waiting while I translated a Resolution, or a proposed amendment to a text. The typist would be hovering over my shoulder, waiting to grab the sheets of paper as they came out of the typewriter so that she could rush off and type them on a Gestetner stencil, and they could then be mass-produced with a conference document number and agenda reference for the delegates. Sometimes reaching agreement would just be a question of changing all the 'should's or 'shall's in all languages to 'may', or amending all 'admissible's to read 'permissible'. The same word could have different meanings for people of different cultures; sometimes a phrase that seemed absolutely innocuous in English, French and Spanish would be offensive to the countries of the Mahgreb. When an amendment to a text had been put forward in one language, the speakers of the other three generally refused to consider it until they had it in writing in their own language in front of them, so the whole conference had to wait while the translators performed their task.

The USSR specialised in footnotes. They often expressed agreement with the text, provided they could have a footnote added. This appeared to be a very reasonable request. The footnote might simply say 'except for the USSR'.

The translation department comprised four sections: English, French, Spanish and Russian. Each section had four offices, with two translators in each, all working into their mother tongue from a variety of languages. I translated from French and Spanish and, after a few years, also from Russian into English. The chief of each section had an office to himself, and was also the reviser. No translation could leave the department without the signature of the reviser. Each section had a secretary who kept track of all the incoming and outgoing work.

My fellow translators were a fascinating group. Working together on conferences, often under stress, we got to know one another well. In the French translation section were Brodsky and Vladimir, who was also a playwright; I occasionally heard his plays broadcast over Swiss radio. He was tall and spoke in a deep theatrical voice – in fact, he was rather a theatrical figure altogether. There was an intriguing little grocery shop right on the Quai facing the lake, tucked into the wall of a majestic building. It was small, badly lit, and rather like Aladdin's cave full of treasures; it was run by a gnomelike, almost-bald Russian émigré. One could spend hours browsing among his overloaded shelves full of specialities from many countries, especially Russia. Vladimir married the grocer's daughter. He liked good food and enjoyed Vodka ('little water'), so for him it was the perfect union.

The head of the French section, Monsieur Revoy, had a brilliant mind. He was extremely well read and had an excellent turn of phrase. He delighted in puns and *contrepetteries* (spoonerisms). There used to be a programme on French radio on Sunday mornings called *Les Chansonniers* which was full of ascerbic French wit and wordplay and gave us food for many a discussion at Monday morning coffee breaks. We often went on conferences together but M. Revoy never participated in sightseeing tours or excursions, preferring to stay in the comfort of his air-conditioned hotel room and read the guide-books.

Steffi's godmother, Pierrette, was also a French translator. Her husband was rotund and suffered from gallstones but in 1960 the medical means available for their treatment and evacuation were not as scientific as those of today. After an unsuccessful attempt to remove a stone in hospital, he ended up at home, immobilised on a steeply sloping bed, the head end of which was built up with bricks. She told me he had a piece of fine string hanging from his posterior to which she had to attach a weight, such as her bunch of keys, watching day by day as they got closer to the floor. The advantage, of course, was that she always knew where to find her keys.

In the Spanish section Cardeña, a tall curly-haired Basque, played the guitar and introduced me to his artistic and musical friends. One of them, Jimmy Bowen, had a guitar on the wall of every Spanish restaurant and café in town so, if inspired, he always had a guitar to hand. We had wonderful musical evenings. The head of the Spanish section, Señor Moreno, was even more theatrical than Vladimir. He had black wavy hair and could sometimes be seen striding through the streets of Geneva wearing a black cloak, its scarlet silk lining flashing as it billowed in the wind.

In the English section we were all good friends and often went out to lunch together. There was quiet, intellectual Isobel, Bill with his endless stock of jokes and Norman who typed his translations with the red half of the typewriter ribbon and with the page sideways in his machine, just to be different. But whatever he did was always forgiven because he was the only one with so many passive languages. (A passive language is a language you work *from*; an active language is the language you work *into*.) It seemed to me that his erudition knew no bounds, he translated from Sanskrit and Arabic as well as Russian, Spanish, Italian, German and French; he was learning Chinese in his spare time. He also spoke fluent Swahili.

Norman taught me a Turkish idiom which I rather liked: *cami yîkîlmîs ama mihrap yerinde* (the mosque is in ruins but the pulpit's still in place) – applied to a woman no longer young but still attractive.

Hedley was the head of our section and he had an enormous repertoire of tales. He was also artistic and greatly enjoyed good food and wine, which meant that he often had very late nights. As a result, he specialised in being late for work in the morning but always had the most amazing excuses. I remember on one occasion the Secretary General was expecting him to take part in a meeting convened for the organisation of an important forthcoming conference. Hedley arrived just as the meeting was closing and explained that he would have been on time, but just before leaving home he had opened the medicine chest on the wall above the bath to look for something. A bottle of ether had falled into the bath and broken and he had been overcome by the fumes. He had lost consciousness and only just recovered. I must admit this was the most original excuse for being late that I had ever heard.

Pinned on the message board of the Linguistic Service was a quotation from G.K. Chesterton: 'A translation is like a woman: if she is beautiful she is not faithful, and if she is faithful she is not beautiful.'

Another apt quotation is from *The Rubáiyát of Omar Kháyyam*:

The Moving Finger writes; and having writ,

Moves on: nor all thy Piety nor Wit

Shall lure it back to cancel half a Line,

Nor all thy Tears wash out a Word of it.

Omar knew what he was talking about. Once written, a translation takes on an existence of its own and can be criticised years later. You cannot hand in a translation unless you are perfectly satisfied with it. The finished product has to read as naturally as possible so that the reader would not necessarily know it was a translation.

Sometimes to get the same end message in another language, you have to use quite different words because of cultural and historical differences. For example, when I first went to visit Dany's family, her father and brother had taken great delight in teaching me to recite:

Après la soupe, un verre de vin

Remplace une visite chez le médecin.

It rhymes in French and trips off the tongue rather pleasantly but in English ('After the soup, a glass of wine replaces a visit to the doctor') there is nothing very special about it. I used to have to recite it to all their friends amid much mirth and applause because of my English accent. It was only many years later that I realised that in fact, this was the French equivalent of the English proverb 'An apple a day keeps the doctor away'.

Occasionally, instead of going to the coffee bar for our sacred fifteen-minute coffee breaks, we would make our own coffee in the office, especially if we needed to get together to discuss a word or phrase we were trying to find an equivalent for in another language. These discussions would haunt us for days until we found a satisfactory translation. I remember us all trying to find an acceptable translation for 'dead reckoning' in the other languages. One English expression I have never been able to find a good French translation for is 'the rat race'. I have found many terms that represented something similar but nothing that covered all the implications of the English expression.

Sometimes English is so concise that in the other languages a whole sentence is needed to translate just two or three English words. This also means that English is an imprecise language, particularly when compared to French, Spanish and Russian where every adjective has to be masculine, feminine or plural and the reader knows to which noun or verb each adjective or adverb refers. Often a text in English is quite ambiguous and presents many problems for the translator who has to decide himself to which noun or verb the adjectives and adverbs refer. I sometimes wonder if this is why English became the language of diplomacy. Each delegate could understand a text differently and find it to his liking. In the United Nations and all its Specialized Agencies, it has always been the French text of any document which was the official reference text (*qui fait foi*). However, there is no doubt in the minds of non-English speakers today that English is a flippant language because of the use of phrases like traffic 'bottleneck', satellite 'footprints' and computer 'mouse'.

When I was once given a telephony document to translate, my imagination ran away with me when it referred to an 'artificial mouth' – I pictured a pair of big rubbery lips. I thought I had better go down to the laboratory and ask to see an artificial mouth before going any further. It turned out to be a metal stand, holding vertically a piece of wire about as thick as a human hair, with a switch on the base so you could adjust the sound to cover all the frequencies uttered by a human voice, but in the right order, making the measurements easier. No big rubbery lips – what a pity.

I learnt to use words like 'implementation', 'communication', 'indication', 'hereunder', 'above-mentioned' and 'heretofore' instead of simple one syllable words.

There is no glamour in being a translator. You are rarely seen or heard, truly a 'backroom boy'. The best you can hope for in the United Nations is to become a reviser, after translating a certain number of pages satisfactorily over a period of some five years. Then you are entitled to an office of your own, however small, with a window, a Persian carpet and a picture on the wall. There used to be a dictaphone – now there is a computer, a telephone on your desk and a bookcase full of dictionaries. And you can take your coffee break whenever you choose. Your only ambition as a reviser is to one day become the head of the Linguistic Service.

In my day we each typed our own translations and though slow, this worked very well. Some years later, however, to make us more efficient and speed up our work, we were provided with shorthand typists to whom we dictated our translations. Then we were 'modernised' even further and had to use dictaphones – that was when I began to find translating boring. In between conferences I missed the social contact, especially when I was promoted to reviser and had an office of my own, where I sat all day with the sole company of a dictaphone. The final straw was having to translate a document the length of a book about the working conditions of nurses in Peru. I spent day after day without seeing another human being, except for coffee breaks. I felt isolated, completely cut off from the rest of the world and envied the glamorous life of the simultaneous interpreters, who were always at the forefront of whatever was happening. But I had little hope of becoming a simultaneous interpreter without a university degree.

My morale improved when I worked on the Plenipotentiary Conference, held in the Bâtiment Electoral in Geneva in 1959. It was much more exciting to be working in a conference environment amid so many people from more than 140 countries. Passing through the Assembly Hall, I noticed a place had been prepared for the delegation of Afghanistan. There was the name card right in the first row as you entered the Assembly Hall. I was curious – there had never been a delegate from Afghanistan before – so kept an eye out to see what he looked like. At the opening ceremony I was astonished to see that the delegate of Afghanistan was the tall, slim, dark young man who had been working at document distribution during the previous conference. How was it possible that a document distribution clerk could become a delegate? After the Plenipotentiary Conference was over, instead of returning to his country like most delegates, he reappeared in the Secretariat as a high-ranking technical engineer on the permanent staff. This was how I learnt about the sacred rule of geographical distribution. In the early days of the United Nations the most suitably qualified candidate obtained each post, regardless of where they came from. But before long, the quota for recruitment of nationals from Switzerland, France, America, the United Kingdom, Canada and Australia was full. From then on, because of the geographical distribution rule, vacant posts went to nationals from other countries, such as India, Africa and Asia. However well qualified you were, you could not hope to get a job unless you were from a country with few nationals on the staff. If you came from Afghanistan or Zimbabwe, you could be pretty confident. ('*Les Nations Unies se noircissent*' 'The UN is getting darker', said the interpreters.)

At the coffee bar during breaks the main subject of conversation was the six-week Los Angeles telecommunications conference planned to take place in six months' time. Typists, secretaries, accountants, engineers, technicians, translators and interpreters would be needed, but the big question was: who would be chosen? Those who had been asked if they would like to go found it difficult to keep it a secret and tongues were wagging. I was approached by the Head of the Linguistic Service and asked whether I would like to go as one of the English translators. A voice in my mind said that it was out of the question for me to go away and leave my children. But the voice of my spirit of adventure was stronger and hinted that it would be good to get away from Gérard for a break, and that the children would be fine with Mary-Ann. Gérard made no objection to my accepting the offer. Besides, we needed a new washing machine, and I had told him that when working overseas I would get a special allowance in addition to my normal salary.

It was the custom in those days in Switzerland for nannies and maids to work on Saturdays but I wanted to have my children all to myself when I was at home. It was only during conferences that I had to work on Saturdays, so I suggested to Mary-Ann: 'Let's say that you're free every weekend unless I have to go away and then you will work Sundays as well to compensate. How about that?' Mary-Ann was delighted and so was I. She was a very keen tennis player and skier and had made many friends at her French class. Besides, our arrangement meant she would not normally be there at weekends when Gérard was most likely to make scenes.

I explained to Marc that I would be away for six weeks but that I would telephone him twice a week and bring him back a big present from America. 'A cowboy outfit?' he asked.

To give him an idea of when I would be coming home we put a calendar up in the kitchen so that he could cross each day off with Mary-Ann's help. He had now started going to nursery school two mornings a week in Geneva and was very proud of his independence. Mary-Ann would drive him there in the new turquoise Fiat 600 that had replaced the Isetta. So I was off to my first international conference.

Chapter 8

About fifty staff members flew from Geneva to Los Angeles. In those days, air travel was a luxury most people couldn't afford. There were always porters to help you with your luggage and guide you in exchange for a few coins and there were never long queues. Children on planes and in airports were a rarity: in those days I never experienced the torture of children sitting behind me on a plane and kicking me in the back during the entire trip.

This particular flight was in five stages. I remember this because we had five breakfasts in a row due to different time zones and refuelling stops. One of these was in Baffinland in the Arctic Circle, where we waited in a freezing corrugated iron shed for over an hour without any refreshments. No-one dared go outside into the ice and snow to see if there were any toilet facilities. One of the flights was in the brand new Boeing 707 which made some of the staff nervous for it had only just started flying.

The conference was held in the enormous Biltmore Hotel. We were anticipating something bright, modern and larger than life, as that was how we pictured America from Europe but in fact it was a gloomy, old-fashioned hotel with bad lighting. The air conditioning didn't work in my room. The lifts were old and creaky; they trembled and seemed to hesitate before stopping at each floor. And you couldn't just grab a lift and zip up to the floor you needed as in the Palais des Nations in Geneva. You had to wait for the liftman, who was old, slow and often difficult to find because he would be tucked away out of sight, sitting in a comfortable chair to save his feet. The liftman was the only one with the key to work the lift. He was tall, thin, grey and almost bald and wore a black top hat and a dark uniform with gold braid on the shoulders and round the sleeves. Once persuaded into the lift, his aim seemed to be to make the most of your company and keep you talking as long as he could.

There were about 2000 delegates from some 165 countries; the meetings were held in enormous window-less ballrooms in the basement of the hotel.

I had a small office with a big desk with an 'in' and 'out' tray. Every hour a messenger would come and collect the contents of my 'out' tray and fill my 'in' tray with pieces of paper and brown envelopes. It seemed never-ending. The messenger was a tall gangly language student with dark skin and black frizzy hair. He was studying French at university but when I tried him out in French it was too embarrassing so I reverted to English. I asked him if he liked classical music. 'Oh yes!' he replied eagerly. 'What in particular?' I asked. 'Anything,' he said, 'so long as it's played by Mantovani.' (Mantovani's orchestra popularised the classics by playing them in his smooth 'easy listening' style.)

After a day or two I could take no more of the gloom and moved out of the hotel into a small furnished apartment about half-an-hour's walk away, which I had found through my friend the Mantovani messenger. I felt I would get to know the city and its people better by having my own apartment, buying my own food and talking to people. Also, I needed fresh air and exercise so intended to walk to and from work each day. I took a taxi with my suitcase to the address my friend had given me and was welcomed by a plump landlady in a voluminous flowery nylon overall, hair in curlers, who was sweeping the entrance. Her chubby feet overflowed from her slippers. For the remaining five and a half weeks I never saw her with her hair out of curlers. I wondered about it and tried to imagine when she would take them out. But even in the evening if I knocked on her door for something, she was still wearing the flowery overall and her hair was still in curlers.

'I'm on a very good diet,' she confided, leaning against my open door.

I looked up sympathetically from my unpacking for she was indeed generously proportioned.

'I've tried the grapefruit diet – have you? And the grape and milk diet. And the carrot diet – nothing but carrot juice. And I've tried all those packaged ones you can buy,' she continued, leaning on her broom.

'But this new one is best. You just have smaller meals. I have small, light meals like salads, vegetables, steak, but only a small amount.'

She paused to take a nutty biscuit out of her pocket and have a nibble. Whenever I saw her she was munching biscuits or eating chocolate. 'Snacks are OK,' she said with satisfaction, 'because they reduce your appetite at meals.'

When I went to the drugstore on the corner later to buy some washing powder and soap I found her there, perched on a high stool at the counter, enthusiastically tackling a boysenberry sundae.

I unpacked, investigated the bathroom and it suddenly occurred to me that there was no bed. I looked everywhere again, unsuccessfully. In the end I had to give up and go and ask. My landlady obviously thought I was really strange not to know that the large wooden panel on one wall had to be pulled down to produce the bed. The first night I had nightmares about someone coming into my room at night and closing it up with me inside, but after that I got used to it . . . Oh to be a burglar and know which knob to push! Would anyone hear the cries for help?

I was very proud of myself the first two evenings when all the others went back to their miserable grey hotel rooms and I could step out and walk back to my apartment. I enjoyed the walk, looking around curiously and stopping occasionally to consult my map, go into a shop or talk to someone. The only difficulty was crossing the road. It was often impossible because of the traffic and the fact that there were no pedestrian crossings even at traffic lights, and I had to make a complicated detour instead. I was fascinated by the huge automobiles (as the Americans called them) all in pastel shades: mauve, pale pink, lemon and pale green. I saw few other pedestrians, which seemed strange.

On the third evening as I stepped out of the Biltmore and set off I realised there was a car driving slowing along the kerb beside me. I tried to ignore it but after a while it stopped and a policeman got out and asked me for my papers.

'What are you doing? Why are you walking? Don't you have a car?' he asked.

'I am walking because I want to walk,' I replied. 'I enjoy walking.'

'Where is your car?'

'I don't have a car. I don't live here. I want to walk.'

He sighed and gave his colleague a significant look. Obviously another crank.

'OK. We can't stop you. But we can't allow you to walk alone. If you insist upon walking we shall have to accompany you, all the time, all the way. We shall drive alongside the sidewalk at your speed.'

'Please don't,' I pleaded. 'I shall be quite all right. I can look after myself.'

'Either you take the bus or we accompany you.'

After that, I took the bus home at night. The only unpleasant thing about that was waiting at the bus-stop. I felt vulnerable, standing there so visibly, with no escape until the bus finally arrived. People would come up to me with all sorts of requests, often to ask if my soul had been saved and whether I had heard the call of Jesus; it was not easy to answer without offending them – or opening myself up to further soul-saving activities.

One middle-aged lady noticed my diamond engagement ring and stopped to say: 'I hope that's a paste copy and the original is in the bank.'

I tried to explain that I enjoyed wearing my ring because of the way it reflected the sunlight.

'But darl,' she persisted. 'You don't realise what you're doing. Someone will come along and cut off your finger with the ring on it. Now you just take my advice and put that ring in the bank. Are you married, then? What salary bracket is your husband in?'

This was a question I was often asked in LA. Fortunately, this time I was saved by the arrival of the bus. But I heeded her words and after that kept my left hand in my pocket.

I was still musing over this when a truly wonderful thing happened.

Bus drivers in LA were always black and so were the passengers; they often hummed to themselves as they drove along. It wasn't long before I joined in too and we all had an enjoyable time. But on this particular trip, a tall, slim woman jumped on at the first stop. Lithe and agile she walked to the back, swaying slightly with the movement of the bus. She was the most beautiful woman I had ever seen, and the most elegant I'd come across in LA. When she got to the back seat she sat down, arranged herself and started to sing.

She had a rich contralto voice which filled the bus with melody and warmth. It was a moment of pure magic. I dared not look round for fear of embarrassing her and causing her to stop. I wanted to join in and sing with her but most of all I wanted just to listen. I could have listened to her forever.

Suddenly I could forgive the hair-curlers, the salary-bracket lady, even the police car that prevented me from walking home. I felt at peace. I was sorry when she got off the bus and I smiled at her with gratitude as she passed me. She had shown me an America I could be happy with.

An American girl I had met in Geneva had given me the telephone number of Barbara, a friend of hers who lived in Los Angeles. I rang her and she came to pick me up after work one evening to show me around. Barbara's car was the most enormous I had ever seen with chromium points at all four corners. Driving along the eight-lane highways with her was an anxious experience as Barbara paid no attention to the road but talked all the time and gesticulated wildly with one beringed, blood-red-nailed hand. She took me home to admire her refrigerator and kitchen stove which were truly huge – they covered a whole wall – but it seemed to me that the cooking she did mainly consisted of brightly iced and decorated cakes. However, Barbara boasted about her cooking skills while we had soup and cake so I asked her for the recipe for her home-made vegetable soup.

'You put a can of tomatoes in a large saucepan. Then a can of beans and a can of peas. Add some water and a can of mushrooms, a can of . . .'

Barbara took me to a Farmers' Market one Saturday morning. It was a hive of activity. The strawberries were the largest and reddest I'd ever seen, the oranges giant-sized and vivid, the bananas very yellow and shiny, but none of these larger-than-life fruits had much taste. In a window a white-hatted chef was icing cakes at top speed before an admiring crowd. That afternoon we went to Blum's for afternoon tea: delicious cakes which were as good to look at as they were to eat were piled up in glass cases. As I glanced around I was puzzled to find that many of the faces at the tables seemed familiar.

'They're all film-stars,' Barbara explained. 'You must know them, even in Europe.'

The whole time I was in LA I pined for my children. I hadn't realised how hard it would be. Almost every day I sent postcards home to them, as well as to Gérard and Mary-Ann. I kept buying presents until I had to buy an extra suitcase to put them all in. Now I was the one who was counting the days. Marc and Stephanie were my life and yet here I was voluntarily thousands of miles away, entrusting them to the care of a nanny. I went about my work automatically, wondering what they were doing at that instant. One morning I could bear it no more. I telephoned home and Mary-Ann answered.

'Everything is fine. Mr Baumier calls in sometimes to see we are all right. Stephanie has another tooth. Marc is doing very well at nursery school and he's being a good boy. There's nothing to worry about. Would you like to speak to him?'

Then an anxious childish voice: 'Mummy, I need some special pencils for school tomorrow. It's good you phoned because I must have them for tomorrow morning. They're special soft pencils for drawing and teacher said –' His voice trailed off.

'Let me speak to Mary-Ann.'

Mary-Ann took over. 'It's too late tonight,' she said. 'The shops are shut.'

The ridiculousness of the situation should have been funny but it was not. Here I was, so far away, how could I get him his pencils? I was failing him, my precious boy, because I couldn't get him his pencils for school. I rushed blindly out of the telephone booth straight into the arms of a surprised stranger.

'Sorry,' I murmured, my face awash with tears.

'Here, what's this? Tears?'

He kept a fatherly arm around me. His soft yellow-green eyes seemed to have the sun shining in them. They looked kind.

'Let me get you a coffee,' he said.

'No, no, I'll be all right.'

'Come, come. Just let me look after you.'

His comforting arm was warm and protective.

He dragged a pink velvet armchair from a corner and sat me in it gently.

'Wait there a moment. I'll be right back.'

I was in no mood to argue.

The coffee was scalding hot and revitalising. But the kinder he was to me, the more I sobbed.

Producing another chair from somewhere he sat down opposite me and his frank, clear eyes looked into mine, conveying calm and sympathy.

'Let me tell you where I come from,' the quiet voice said, trying to keep my mind off my own troubles.

'In Poland in my village it is still very cold now. I was on my way to the telephone booths to ring my parents to see if they are all right. They are old and my father is ill. He is not expected to live much longer.'

The softness of his voice and his accent seemed to give extra meaning to his words.

'I am called Janek. It is written with a "J" but pronounced like a "Y" – "Yanek".' He told me that he had emigrated to America as a refugee and now worked as an engineer. He was at the conference as an observer.

I relaxed in the gentleness of his voice. I let it wash over me like warm water, soothing my hurt.

After a while, I was calm again.

'I must get back,' I said at last, getting to my feet.

'Let me take you to lunch,' he replied, standing up also. 'I'll wait for you here at twelve-thirty.'

And that was the beginning of our friendship. We had lunch together several times during the rest of the conference, each time finding more to say to each other and discovering a mutual passion for music.

The last occasion was at Easter. It was difficult to find a restaurant open. Finally we found an all-you-can-eat with plastic palm trees and neon lights, and as we went in, the backs of our hands were stamped so that we could help ourselves as often as we liked to the food on the counter. Our knives and forks were in a plastic bag marked 'Sterilised' in red letters and on our table, in the centre of a small bunch of plastic roses, was a 'Thought for Today' in the form of a quotation from the Bible.

We sat by the window and talked. I noticed that Janek had the long-fingered hands of a musician.

'I live with relatives here,' he said. 'Sometimes I go to Geneva for my work. I hope I may see you then?'

The softness of his voice prevented me from saying: 'No, no!' Instead I pulled myself together and said primly: 'I must warn you that I am married and have two young children.' Then I added: 'I love my husband and I am faithful to him.'

The words sounded hollow and trite, but Janek accepted them.

'Then let me be your friend,' he said simply.

I knew something was missing from my life. Something I longed for and yet could not define; an emptiness lurked in the shadows that even my children could not fill. I knew Janek was right when he said: 'Human beings are animals. We are not just cerebral beings. We tend to forget our animal side, that also demands satisfaction.'

A chattering group of middle-aged ladies went past outside, all wearing extraordinary hats for Easter. There were plastic flowers, plastic birds, feathers, and veils of all colours.

'It must be a convention or a club outing' we agreed. Afterwards, walking in the park, we came across several more groups of women wearing similar hats and shiny jewellery. Gradually I stopped feeling a need to criticise. I was more relaxed than I had been for years. I had no need to defend or justify myself. I wasn't in love with Janek and he wasn't in love with me, I had no need to live up to his expectations so it didn't matter if my hair was untidy and I didn't look perfect or if I said something he didn't like. We had indeed become friends.

When we finally reached my front door, Janek bowed and thanked me for my company. I thanked him for his and we both stood awkwardly trying to find something else to say.

'When do you go back?' he asked.

'In two days' time. But these last two days will be very busy. I'm afraid I won't have any free time, we'll be working night and day. It's always panic at the end of a conference and on the last night there'll be the official closing dinner.'

'So it's goodbye now, is it?'

'I'm afraid so.'

We shook hands and Janek walked briskly away, his back very straight.

When I stepped off the plane in Geneva, Gérard was waiting. He bent and gave my cheek a hasty peck. I was bursting to tell him all about Los Angeles and my first overseas conference, hoping that he would be proud of me.

'I'm very busy at work,' he grumbled. 'I've had nothing but late nights all the time you've been away. And there's a pile of bills to be paid, I don't know how we're going to manage for money. It's difficult to make ends meet. I hope they gave you your cheque before you left. Oh, and you'll find an article on your dressing table to be translated. I've promised to post it off before the end of the week. I'm so tired . . .'

He didn't ask me anything about my trip. He deposited my suitcases inside the front door and hurried off, calling as he went: 'I shan't be home till late tonight. Don't wait up for me. I have to go to a lecture a friend of mine is giving.'

Mary-Ann was smiling with Stephanie in her arms and Marc and Ulla were bouncing about with excitement.

'Did you bring my cowboy outfit, Mummy?'

'Yes, I did. And there are lots of other surprises as well for you all when I unpack.'

Marc was trying to drag me into the dining room.

'Come, Mummy, come and see what we've prepared . . .'

The table was laid for afternoon tea and in the centre was a special 'Welcome Home' cake, the words written on top in pink icing.

'I helped Mary-Ann with the icing, Mummy. And at school, we did drawing today and the teacher said . . .'

Marc had so much to tell me I was afraid he would never go to sleep that night. Stephanie gurgled contentedly as I tucked her up in her cot and I was glad to be home.

It concerned me that I had had lunch several times with a man other than my husband and that he had had such an effect on me. I felt a confession was due. Accordingly, the following evening, Sunday, I put Marc and Stephanie to bed early and lit a log fire in the lounge.

'Come and have a drink by the fire. I have something I feel I should tell you,' I told Gérard.

He turned on his charming smile.

'In that case, I too have something to tell.'

Sitting by the fire, I took a sip from my glass to give me

courage. Gérard pulled his pouffe closer to the hearth and prodded the logs, turning his back to me.

'In LA I met a man from Poland. He was very kind and we had lunch together a few times. There's really nothing more to tell . . .' I petered out, not sure how to continue.

'Just a minute!' As usual, Gérard barely seemed to hear me. He jumped to his feet and went to get his wallet out of his coat pocket. Passing me some photographs of a tall, slim blonde, he said: 'What do you think of her? Just look at that figure! And she's intelligent too. Yes, this is my mistress. For about six months now. You can be proud – you couldn't be ashamed for me to be seen with her, could you? She dresses well, too. She works with me, as a matter of fact, and I am trying to help her get on. She even helps me with some translations, the easier ones – so less work for you! Monique is the ideal age for a woman, just twenty-seven. Younger than I am, I know, but that's how it should be. I can give her guidance, help her career through my contacts. She's a real beauty. Almost as tall as I am and so well made. Wait, I think I've got a picture of her in a bikini some-where –' and he handed me another photograph.

She was indeed very attractive.

I was at a loss. I had no idea what to say. Gérard seemed to expect my approval.

I knew I must not cry. My eyes filled and my voice trembled but I knew that tears would only make Gérard angry. He couldn't stand women who cried, he had told me many times.

'I had no idea . . .' I started to say.

'Oh, for heaven's sake, you must have guessed. Surely you're not as stupid as that! I suppose it's because you come from that backward island of yours. In France it's the accepted thing. All my friends have mistresses, there's nothing wrong with that. I'm not taking anything away from you and the children. I'm probably a better husband as a result. You should be pleased my mistress is attractive and you can be proud. I want you to meet her and then you will see.'

He prodded the burning logs with the poker.

'For heaven's sake don't cry – you know I hate tears! After all, *you* are my wife. You have the privileged role. I have chosen you to bear my children. Just think how miserable it is for her when I go away on holiday with you and the children and leave her all alone. Just think how she feels when I leave her to come home to you, knowing you are the legal wife with all the rights and she has no claims on me at all.'

I could find no words. There was no room in my heart at that moment to pity her.

'It's not as though I ask *you* to be faithful,' he continued. 'You are free too. I'm glad you went off to America. Travel as much as you like, it's good for you and enriches your life as well as Marc and Stephanie's.'

What he said sounded so reasonable, I felt I must be wrong to feel so hurt. I must be old-fashioned.

'All I ask is that you let me know ahead of time when you plan to go abroad so that one of us is always here to keep an eye on the children and Mary-Ann. I shall be travelling more and more now. I may even take Monique with me sometimes. But so long as there is always one of us here, there should be no problem.'

I looked at him in silence, miserable and confused, as he continued excitedly.

'Traditional marriage is out of date anyway! It was all right in the old days when people died younger, but nowadays couples live longer and outlive their marriages. It should be renewable on a five-yearly basis right from the start and only if both parties want it. Haven't you read your Bertrand Russell?'

He fetched the bottle of wine and refilled our glasses.

'Let's drink to modern marriage and to our freedom! You are

free to do what you like so long as you are discreet and people don't gossip. The same applies to me.'

He raised his glass.

That night as I cried myself to sleep, I heard Gérard's sports-car start up and with a roar set off in the direction of town. I was glad it was the weekend and Mary-Ann was staying with her friend, Hilda.

It was Alexandre Dumas who wrote that 'The bonds of wedlock are so heavy that it takes two to carry them – sometimes three.'

Some months later I accepted the offer of a six-week conference in India with relief. I needed another break from Gérard, who now talked openly to me about his mistress and their plans. Gérard and Mary-Ann raised no problems, the children were healthy and happy and came to the airport to see me off.

Chapter 9

I left the Swiss winter behind me and arrived in New Delhi in brilliant sunshine. After unpacking my bags, I walked along Janpath to the Vigyan Bhavan building where the conference was to be held, to see how preparations for the grand opening the following day were progressing.

There were workmen everywhere, ladders, buckets of paint, electricians putting in cables, rolled up carpets and squatting flower-arrangers making pictures with flower heads and petals on the floor along each side of all the main corridors. Out of the windows I could see sunshine and flowers. Next door to the conference building was a museum with a statue garden where gods and goddesses stood on pedestals surrounded by a profusion of flowers that were all new to me. There was nothing useful I could do until the workmen had finished and the translators' offices were ready, so I went out into the sunshine and wandered along the paths, admiring the statues. There were many of Ganesh, the god with the elephant's head and also curvaceous goddesses with tiny waists and high round breasts. After a while I grew bolder and gave some of the statues a little pat – there seemed to be no-one around. I felt as if the garden were

143

there just for me. Not another human being in sight. And no FORBIDDEN signs anywhere that I could see. It was all so different from Switzerland.

'In Switzerland,' said Coluche, a famous French comedian, 'everything that is not forbidden is compulsory.'

If you have ever been to Switzerland, you will have noticed that you are never allowed to walk on the grass. Whenever you visit a public park, or the Quai by the lake, you see signs saying it is FORBIDDEN TO WALK ON THE GRASS and DO NOT TOUCH THE FLOWERS. If you live in Switzerland you accept this as the norm and it is quite shocking to go to London, say, and see people actually sitting or lying on the grass in Hyde Park, right in the centre of London. But of course the English climate with its plentiful rain means that grass is green, healthy and not easily damaged. In Switzerland it is much hotter in summer, colder in winter and it rains much less, so green lawns are difficult to come by and need a lot of nurturing. Along the Quai in Geneva, you must be careful to just *look* at the dazzling display of blooms in the rose garden and not touch them. Sometimes I was tempted, after a precautionary glance left and right, to actually bend down and *smell* a rose, never quite sure if this was allowed or not.

Now the unfamiliar Indian flowers attracted me like a magnet. One bush drew my particular attention. It was covered with tiny bright orange flowers with a wonderful scent. Brightly-coloured birds darted in and out of the branches. I bent to sniff the perfume and, since there was no-one to see, I furtively broke off a small stem. I would put it in my dismal room at the Janpath Hotel – that would brighten it up.

I walked a few more steps and there before me was a delicate mauve flower with bees buzzing round it and again the most delicious scent. Just a small piece, I thought, my fingers itching, no-one will notice. After that I grew bolder. A little pink would look nice with the mauve. A few tiny white flowers . . . Just as I stopped in the shade of a tree to admire my posy, out of nowhere a gardener suddenly appeared. He was dressed in a ragged dhoti, with a shabby turban on his thin boney head; I noticed his arms and legs were thin as matchsticks. But his eyes were the colour of honey. As he approached, I knew he had seen my flowers and there was nowhere I could hide them. I had been caught in the act. I started to apologise but he smiled.

'Memsahib, I am happy you like them,' he said in halting English. 'This one is called . . .' and, in a friendly voice, he told me the names of all the flowers I held, and whether they liked the shade or the sun. As we spoke, gardeners appeared from all around. They had all kept out of sight as I wandered down the paths and alleys, not wanting to spoil it for me, but now they came out of hiding, each in turn breaking off flowers to show me and tell me about, and to add to my bunch. I was over-whelmed by their gentleness, the softness of their voices, their smiles. Soon my hands were full of flowers, I could carry no more. 'Thank you, thank you,' I murmured, but as I left a young gardener shuffled after me as fast as he could, leaning on his stick. 'I don't think you have one of these,' he said shyly, holding out a magnificent red bloom.

My posy of Indian flowers welcomed me back each evening after work and turned my gloomy room into a sweet-scented friendly place, especially when I remembered the gentle gardeners. Sometimes during my six-week stay I went back to wander in the museum garden and they greeted me with a humble 'Namasté'; I felt we were old friends.

When I arrived at the Vigyan Bhavan the next morning there had been a transformation. Carpets and furniture had appeared during the night, as well as flower arrangements, draperies and elegant chairs, banners and flags. All along the main corridor and on either side of the entrance were elaborate floor designs made from flower petals of all colours. The workers I had seen the day before must have continued throughout the night.

To my surprise, Janek was attending the conference. I had seen him at the airport with a strange mix of joy and misgiving. He hadn't seen me.

For the inaugural ceremony the first night, I wore my favourite mauve dress (refusing to acknowledge to myself why I wanted to look my best). As I came down the stairs into the main hall I noticed with a quickening of my heartbeat a familiar figure standing at the bottom of the stairs, looking up at me and beaming with delight. We greeted one another then, my face burning, I hurried off to join my colleagues, resolving to avoid him as much as possible to prevent any embarrassment. I knew I had to be careful not to betray my feelings or let him guess how much he had been in my thoughts.

The inaugural ceremony took place in a vast packed amphitheatre. The opening speech was by Pandit Nehru, the then prime minister. I took an instant liking to this gentle, humble and homely man who spoke straight from the heart, in contrast to the other speakers who read carefully polished speeches from printed texts. He gave the impression of an honest man who saw a straight path ahead of him and knew what was right and what was wrong. He referred to politicians as 'quarrelers'. He didn't try for effects, used no impressive long words. He began simply with: 'When I was a boy . . .' and concluded: 'We tend to overlook the wonder of it all.' Nehru was speaking from a platform and there were several thousand listeners yet I felt, and I think everyone else felt too, that he was talking to me alone.

A few days after I arrived I called home and Mary-Ann answered.

'Oh, Mr Baumier has been very kind to us,' she said. 'After you left he took us all out to lunch at the Creux de Genthod, by the lake. Marc thought it was fantastic because he had wine to drink – just a taste! We all got a bit light-headed. Steffi enjoyed herself too. Then he drove us home and said he was taking a holiday down on the Riviera but I have his phone number in case of emergency and he telephones us every two or three days to make sure everything is all right.'

There wasn't much I could do, and Mary-Ann assured me she could cope. In any event, walking through the dusty streets of Delhi, I saw such poverty and hardship that my personal diffi-culties seemed trivial indeed. Emaciated beggars settled down on the footpath for the night, rolling themselves in their rags, one arm extended with open palm in case some passing benefactor with a guilty conscience felt moved to give them a few annas.

One evening, I happened to look out of my hotel room window at nightfall and saw the back of the hotel next door. Through the brightly lit window I could see into the kitchen where people were clearing up after the day. As I stood there, looking at the sky and wondering whether the stars were different from the ones I saw at home, the back door opened and someone put some dishes of leftover food on the ground outside. For the cats, I thought – there were so many mangy, skeletal cats around, especially at night. But before the cats could get to the food, beggars appeared from the surrounding bushes, on hands and knees. The food was gone in a flash. I might have thought I had dreamt the scene if it weren't for the clean, empty dishes that remained.

As well as beggars, there were an enormous number of cripples (you were allowed to call them that, in those days): handsome young men with legs folded uselessly underneath them, scooting about on wheeled pieces of wood, darting in and out of the cars stopped at traffic lights, holding up a begging hand to car drivers. Lepers holding out a hand with no fingers. Teenage boys on crutches selling cigarettes one at a time and small boxes of matches or lottery tickets.

The streets bustled with so many people trying to eke out a living. I saw snakecharmers wherever I went, mongoose fights on street corners and fakirs performing yoga feats in all the busy public places. I had never seen such incredible muscle mastery, the ability to control one half of the body and make it behave differently from the other half, as if a line had been drawn down the middle. They were able to perform the most twisted contortions with legs and arms in all directions, and often the fakir would balance on one hand, upside-down and motionless, for five or six hours at a stretch.

Transistor radios were new then, rare and precious. In India they were unheard of, with one exception. If you saw a man with a transistor radio you knew he had had a vasectomy – that was the government-supplied prize.

Often in the evenings, as I walked along Janpath back to my hotel, I'd find a blind storyteller sitting at a street corner, surrounded by a spellbound crowd. Young and old had gathered round, with wide-eyed children, sitting cross-legged in the dust, concentrating on every word. I couldn't speak more than a few words of Hindi, but after a while I too was following the story. The eloquence of the storyteller, his dramatic gestures and the reactions of the crowd brought it all to life. It was a story of love when his voice grew soft and tender; hatred when he seemed to brandish a sword and his voice changed. When he mimed the cutting of a throat I could see the blood spurt forth into a red pool in the dust.

Even in those days there were tourists. Once outside a temple I saw a crowd of angry tourists gesticulating in the direction of the domed roof where a monkey could be seen holding on to the spire with one hand, a ladies' white handbag in the other.

'It's got my passport in it and my air ticket and all my money!' bemoaned a mauve-haired American. She looked like so many American widows I had met on planes and in airports, whose husbands had died recently, and who were spending some of their new inheritance on a world tour.

The guide shouted angrily at the monkey and menaced him with clenched fist, but the monkey merely opened its mouth in pink mockery.

It was difficult to come to terms with the contrasts of India: the anguish and ugliness of the poverty and the dirt; the bright acid colours of the saris draped over bushes to dry. The richness of the temples and the carvings of gods and goddesses. The silver bangles and earrings the women wore, their grace and elegance as they walked barefoot draped in their vivid saris, designed to follow the line of their bodies.

'We do not try to force our bodies to adapt to our clothes, like European women do,' an elegant Indian lady explained to me in a fitting room in the Emporium, one evening. 'It horrifies me to think of strapping myself into a brassière!' She had come up to talk to me, having recognised me from a few days earlier. 'You are the lady who ran!' she exclaimed. 'I was there! I saw you!' It was true: a few evenings before I had nearly missed the hotel bus come to pick us up in town. I had had to run to catch it. As she spoke, I realised I had never seen an Indian woman in a sari run. Running was unladylike. Very unfeminine. Not a graceful thing to do. Indian ladies do not run.

I was struck, one day, by the grace of a slim young woman walking in front of me down the street, silver bangles round each ankle and wrist sounding like little bells as she walked. She had jewelled rings on her toes. On her head she bore a large circular basket; her back was as straight as a rod. She walked unhurriedly down the road, barefoot, and her gait was so elegant that unconsciously I began to follow her – until we came to a group of women digging a trench, many of them with babies strapped to their backs. She suddenly stopped, bent forward and emptied the basket. It contained bricks. She was a human wheelbarrow, working on a building site. The serenity and resignation in her gentle face was a lesson for me. In the whole of my six-week stay in Delhi I never once saw a wheelbarrow. Only the female kind.

I often took a taxi to visit the Red Fort after work and stood as the sun was setting, fascinated, watching thin bearded crafts-men replacing inlaid semi-precious stones in the marble panels of the inner courtyard. Sometimes one of them spoke a little English: 'My father did this before me and when I die my son will take over.'

For me, those were the days of the 'real' India: with all its poverty there was yet a sense of continuity, timelessness, of con-nection with days of old – before the impact of Western culture.

One weekend the whole conference was taken on an excursion by night train. I had a comfortable sleeping compartment all to myself. Early in the morning I was awoken with a cup of milky sweet pinkish buffalo-milk tea – 'bed tea' – and a bowl and pitcher of warm water to wash with.

The train had stopped at Agra where we were to visit the Taj Mahal and Fatehpur Sikri.

With a flutter I had caught a glimpse of Janek boarding the train in Delhi. So far I had been fairly successful in keeping him at arm's length. Whenever we came face to face at the coffee bar or at conference receptions I either pretended not to see him or smiled briefly and fled to join my colleagues because of the voice in my head which kept repeating: 'You are not free. You are a married woman.'

We had heard so much about the Taj Mahal, seen so many pictures, we were ready to be *blasé* but it took our breath away.

It was not only what you saw, but also what you felt as you looked. I could hardly tell which was more beautiful, the misty white Taj in the crisp early morning air or its shimmering reflection in the still water before it.

Janek was standing just behind me and I was very aware of his nearness. The frail old man who was our guide murmured in his cracked voice, 'It was built in 1629 by Emperor Shah Jahan to house the tomb of his wife Mumtaz Mahal who died giving birth to their fourteenth child. It symbolises love, which is the secret of happiness for all men and women.'

Janek and I didn't speak. We didn't even look at one another.

That afternoon, despite all my manoeuvring, Janek and I entered the abandoned city of Fatehpur Sikri together – the others were dawdling and chatting far behind us. I found myself walking beside him and couldn't avoid saying '*bonjour*', though few words were spoken after that. Together we passed lavender water fountains of marble inlaid with precious stones where elegant ladies had once cooled their wrists. We visited the Royal Astrologer's abode where the stars were consulted each day and the Emperor's horoscope drawn up. The guide told us that the colour of the Emperor's jacket and trousers was determined every morning by his astrologer.

We said nothing as we walked through the palace Akbar had built for his beloved and stood admiring her white marble bathroom. Around the sunken bath, the mosaic walls were set with curved pieces of mirror so that when she bathed her beauty was reflected a thousand times. Jasmine-scented water flowed from one side and rose-scented from another. It was like a fairytale but it had really happened. I imagined the background music – the sounds of the *veena* played by delicate fingers – and felt like a beautiful Mogol princess.

We wandered over carved marble bridges crossing the waterways that had cooled the palace, rose petals floating on the water, scenting the air. In the sumptuous bed chamber, the lacework of the carved marble screens let the sunshine through so gently that it cast intricate patterns on the white marble floor. We stood very close together, bound by the magic of the place, in a world that had existed hundreds of years before.

An old, bent man with a wrinkled face and wispy white beard must have thought we were lovers – he came up and whispered confidentially: 'They used to burn the skin of their fingertips deliberately, to increase their sensitivity to touch when making love.'

My first visit to India finally came to an end. My flight to Geneva left half an hour later than Janek's flight to Washington. Surreptitiously watching him queue to check in, I felt envious of the others catching his flight and wondered who would be sitting next to him in the plane.

After he had disappeared, I went into the airport bookshop and spent my last rupees on a copy of the *Kama Sutra* to read during the flight. It was a bad translation; parts of it were incomprehensible. But it appealed to my imagination and set me thinking: why was it that in India, making love was a way of reaching God, whereas where I came from, making love had sinful undertones and chastity was the quickest path heavenwards?

Chapter 10

I had been back from India for some time and life had returned to normal. One sunny spring morning after Marc had left for school with Mary-Ann and Stephanie, I was wondering what to do with my free day when the telephone rang.

'This is Janek. I'm in Geneva and I've got a free day. It is so beautiful, the trees are all in blossom and the birds are singing. How about a walk in the country?'

'As a matter of fact, I am free today too. Until about three thirty.'

We met. He was solid and square, not so tall as Gérard but there was something reassuring and reliable about him that made me feel safe and protected. His feet seemed to be firmly planted on the ground. He gave an impression of warmth and kindness and his skin looked soft to the touch. We walked some way in silence, rather shy of one another after so long. As he stopped to hold some branches back for me to pass, he looked at me and said:

'I have been waiting for this moment all the time we have been apart.'

'Janek!' I said in a warning tone.

'I just wanted to see you, to be with you. I ask for nothing.'

The sun disappeared and after a while it started to rain. We had no umbrella but the rain didn't seem to matter. I started to sing out of sheer happiness. We were walking in single file down a narrow path, Janek walking ahead to hold back the branches for me. I sang all the songs I could think of. Then I sang a love song. I had an irrepressible urge to sing something tender to express how I felt. Without a word he put his strong hands on either side of my head and looked into my eyes. We stood for a few moments without moving, the rain pouring down on us. Then gently he led me back to his car, one arm round my shoulders.

'I'm taking you back to my place to dry your clothes,' he said.

He had rented a small studio in Geneva, and soon I was enveloped in his dressing-gown while he spread my clothes over the radiators to dry. He gave me a mug of steaming tea with rum and lemon in it, put some cushions on the floor so that I could sit with my back to the warm radiator, and said:

'I have brought my violin with me. It has some things to tell you.'

Tenderly, softly, he played. There was a sweet sadness in the music and without a word being spoken I realised they were Polish love songs.

When he put the violin back in its case carefully, lovingly, and came towards me I knew we would make love. It was the natural consequence of the music, our walk in the rain, my singing.

He kissed me hungrily. I felt he was eating me, drinking me. I had never known such feelings existed. We made love and I discovered tenderness. We seemed to melt into each other, our skins seemed to fuse. My armour had gone. I gave myself up to the waves of voluptuousness washing over me.

We lay still afterwards, stroking one another's bodies. When I touched his back ever so lightly it seemed that his flesh rose to meet my fingers.

I lay back luxuriating in a feeling of wellbeing I had never known before. Life would never be the same again. I had discovered the secret. I was a real woman after all.

Janek spent three weeks in Geneva and there were many more visits to his studio, many more violin recitals. He prepared Polish dishes for me and promised to bring special Polish delicacies with him next time as well as books and records. He played the violin and I sang. He taught me haunting melodies from his country.

When I looked at myself in a mirror I was amazed at the change. I looked softer, my features looked blurred and velvety. After making love at lunchtime I went on foot along the country lanes to meet the children from school, moving as if a gentle breeze was blowing me along and I was walking a few inches above the ground.

'Love is the best beauty treatment,' I had heard people say.

I wondered whether my friends would notice the difference, or Gérard. But Gérard noticed nothing. I doubted whether he ever really looked at me. Janek's love and uncomplicated down-to-earthness gave me a new feeling of self-confidence. I was able to view Gérard in a new, more detached way.

I seemed to have more time for Marc and Steffi, more time for special goodnight stories, more time for cooking their favourite dishes – more time for everything. When the children were asleep, I left Mary-Ann in charge and slipped out to meet Janek. Gérard was rarely at home and even when he was, he would be working in his study and didn't seem to notice. When the three weeks were over, it was hard to say goodbye. Yet we were so full of new hope and happiness that we could not feel sad. He promised to phone and to return to Geneva as soon as he could.

Even after Janek had gone, my newfound happiness remained. And anyway, it would be hard to be sad in the full glory of a Swiss spring. The two cherry trees that we'd planted for Marc and Steffi burst into bloom and the forbidden municipal roses flourished.

Gérard, the children and I joined in all the traditions of a Swiss spring with great enthusiasm.

In the woods around Geneva in spring you are allowed to pick wild primroses and on the first day of May you must respect the tradition of going out into the woods to pick wild lily of the valley to the sounds of the first cuckoo calls, because you are expected to give a sprig to each of your friends. (At the end of the day, those who have accumulated a big bunch feel much loved.) Also, around mid-May on a Sunday the Genevese go up to the mountains surrounding the lake to pick wild narcissus. The scent is heady and wonderful (except for those suffering from hayfever). We used to take the children and the dog – which delighted in bounding about over the mountainside as we picked all we could, filling a basket or two with the strongly-scented flowers. Unfortunately, these days, the farmers who own the land have realised that they had been neglecting a way of making easy money. They have put fences round the fields and charge anyone who wants to pick narcissus an entry fee.

One afternoon Marc and Stephanie were invited to the birthday party of one of the Romanian princesses.

We dressed them in their best and off they went, accompanied by Mary-Ann in her St Christopher's uniform. I can still see Marc, aged five, in his grown-up-looking white shirt with bow tie and grey trousers, holding a posy of flowers that we made with rosebuds from the garden and a paper doily. We could think of nothing else for a birthday present – the princesses had everything. Mary-Ann had told me that their huge day nursery was full of toys, games, stuffed animals, music boxes, dolls' houses, books and paintboxes. The toys were mostly official gifts from famous people or from magazines which had been granted interviews.

The first thing the children had to do upon arrival, they told me later, was to bow and click heels (Marc) and curtsey (Stephanie) to the ex-king and queen. (Fortunately we had practised this at home beforehand.)

Apparently they were the only guests and after a few words of polite conversation, they were allowed into the day nursery to play with the princesses. Tea, hot milk, sandwiches and the birthday cake were brought in on trolleys by two maids dressed in black with frilly white aprons and headbands. The ex-king and queen joined them for the blowing out of the candles and cake-cutting and the king screened some Charlie Chaplin and Laurel and Hardy films for them. He also showed them a film of the small planes he piloted. Before leaving, they once again had to curtsey to the queen and bow to the king.

Strict protocol was maintained at all times because the family expected to regain the throne eventually. The princesses came to play once or twice under the supervision of their nanny and boasted that even at four years old they could stand absolutely still for an hour. As they got older they would be able to do it for longer.

There were more birthday parties but after some years the protocol must have relaxed a bit because once I saw the queen shopping in the supermarket incognito and occasionally I saw her driving her own car. As they grew up, one by one the princesses left home to go to boarding school and we saw no more of them or their nanny.

During this time I was sent abroad for several more conferences and found that life was becoming too hectic.

I wanted to be able to spend more time with the children.

When one of them caught chickenpox or measles, I hated having to go off and leave them even though I trusted Mary-Ann completely. I decided to go freelance, which would make me more independent and I would be able to say 'No, thank you' during school holidays and the week before Christmas. I hoped that I would have no difficulty finding freelance work with the other Specialized Agencies of the United Nations, and the idea of working for different conferences on different topics, and with different colleagues, was very appealing.

My colleagues thought I was mad to give up the security of a permanent contract, so coveted by those who did not have one, but they gave me a big farewell party after work in the staff lounge, with speeches and champagne, canapés and petits fours. Miranda was there and Mickey, a former WREN officer who had taken over my old office and was now Administrative Assistant to the new Secretary General, a tall, distinguished, greatly respected Tunisian.

Luckily, from then on I was offered short-term translator contracts from most of the international organisations in Geneva, as well as elsewhere in Europe, with the result that in fact I was working almost full-time as before, but it was much more stimulating and interesting. I now worked frequently at the European UN headquarters (the Palais des Nations), as well as for the World Health Organization, GATT (which later became the World Trade Organization), the International Labour Organization, in Geneva and Turin, the Food and Agriculture Organization's offices in Rome (with their 'breads of the world' display in a glass cabinet in the entrance), and many others.

Each international organisation had regular series of different types of conference (Plenipotentiary, Plenary Assembly, Administrative Council) which would meet at regular intervals, sometimes in Geneva but mostly overseas. For example, a Plenipotentiary Conference would meet every five years. The pace of the preparations would gradually build up for the staff until the climax of the Opening Ceremony or Inaugural Session. When the conference was over, they would be able to recover, relax and settle down again before beginning the build-up for the next one. But the freelance translators had no such quiet period in between. We enjoyed the excitement of going from one conference to another, from one state of panic and crisis to another.

Over the years I collected many examples of mistranslations, mostly during my travels: 'Don't look at me in that tone of voice!' is one of my favourites. I once heard '*Voilà l'anglais avec son sang-froid habituel!*' translated as: 'Here comes the Englishman with his usual bloody cold.' And recall being told solemnly that: 'Lincoln wrote the Gettysburg Address while travelling from Washington on the back of an envelope.'

Signage is always a rich source of mistranslations. In Malaysia: 'Take one of our horse-drawn city tours: we guarantee no mis-carriages.' In Rome, outside a laundry: 'Ladies, leave your clothes here and spend the afternoon having a good time.' In a hotel in Tokyo: 'Room service: you are invited to take advantage of the chambermaid.' From a helpful Japanese road sign: 'When a passenger on foot heave in sight, tootle the horn. Trumpet him melodiously at first, but if he still obstacles your passage then tootle him with vigour.' In a Prague hotel room a sign on the television set advised: 'If set breaks, inform manager, do not interfere with yourself.' In an East Berlin cloakroom: 'Please hang yourself here.' In Romania a sign by a museum lift: 'The lift is being fixed for the next few days. During that time we regret that you will be unbearable.' A sign over a Bombay bakery: 'We are No.1 loafers, best in whole town', and an Ankara hotel brochure suggested: 'Visit our restaurant where you can eat the Middle East foods in an European ambulance.' In a Tokyo hotel:

'Is forbidden to steal hotel towels please. If you are not a person to do such thing is please not to read notis.' A dentist in Hong Kong advertised: 'Teeth extracted by the latest Methodists.' And finally, the ring of truth from a Copenhagen airline ticket office: 'We take your bags and send them in all directions.'

Someone told me that at a conference in London General de Gaulle had refused an interpreter, declaring that his English was excellent. He then proceeded to upset the English by 'demanding' this and that because he did not realise that 'demand' in English is not the same as *demander* in French (to ask).

At a conference on aircraft landing procedures, a novice interpreter called the joystick a *bâton de jouissance*.

Tant pis and *tant mieux* are French expressions meaning 'too bad; what a pity' and 'so much the better'. Together they mean 'It might be worse!' but I once heard them translated as: 'Auntie went to the toilet and Auntie felt better'.

A chairman once spoke of 'anglophones' (English-speakers) and 'francophones' (French-speakers); one of the delegates announced he was an Anglo Saxophone. And I've always wondered why English say 'shallow water' when the French say *haut-fonds* (the sea bed is high).

We were once asked to test one of the new translating machines that had just appeared on the market in the 1960s. We entered: 'Out of sight, out of mind' and 'The spirit is willing but the flesh is weak', requesting a Russian translation. Then we put the Russian translations back into the machine and asked for them to be translated back into English. The result was: 'Invisible idiot' and 'The vodka is good but the meat is off'. I am still not convinced that computers will fully replace human translators and interpreters any time soon.

In 1961 I was working as a translator in the English section of the first international Space Conference in the Bâtiment Electoral in Geneva when something happened that changed my life forever.

Lunchtime was almost over and I was at my desk when I heard a commotion in the corridor outside. In the office opposite mine, Señor Moreno, the Chief of the Linguistic Service, was shouting into the telephone, watched by a group of stunned-looking colleagues.

An important meeting was about to start at two o'clock. The simultaneous interpreters were always there ten minutes before the meeting started, sorting out their documents and checking the agenda. The English-speaking Rapporteur on the podium could see two faces in each of the French, Spanish and Russian booths, but none in the English, the most listened to. It was he who had telephoned Sr Moreno in a panic: where were they?

Panic spread. The French chairman was anxious to begin the meeting. He was well known for his impatience, his bad temper and his tendency to criticise the interpretation; he must not find out the English interpreters were not even in the building!

Finally, Sr Moreno received a telephone call from the hospital. The two interpreters were most apologetic: they'd lunched together in town. It was pouring with rain and on the way back the tyres of their car had got stuck in the tram lines and they had ended up crashing into an oncoming tram. The pair had been taken to hospital for a check up. They were shaken but not seriously hurt. But all this was going to take time – in fact, most of the afternoon.

How to replace them? Sr Moreno could certainly try telephoning all over Geneva to see if any English booth interpreters were free and available at such short notice. But that would take a while. It would take time, too, for whoever he found to get to the Bâtiment Electoral. How could the impatient French chairman be told he would have to wait an hour or two when all the delegates and members of the Secretariat were in their seats, documents in front of them, agendas in hand and ear-phones on, waiting to begin the meeting?

I volunteered to give it a try. I had never been inside an inter-pretation booth, I had no idea how the equipment worked, how you switched your microphone on and off or where the volume control was. But if someone would explain that to me, I was willing to see if I could do it. Ecstatic, Sr Moreno ushered me to the booth.

The meeting began. For a few seconds – looking down at the rows of delegates in the hall, pushing their earphones closer to their head with one hand to be sure of hearing what I was saying – I panicked. I strained to catch the words delivered machine-gun style by the French chairman but I was too nervous to make sense of them. I think at first I uttered sounds, not words. Fortunately after a few seconds I was able to pull myself together and focus my attention not on the audience but on the speaker, the chairman himself, and it happened. Apogee. Perigee. Attitude. Precision tracking systems, yaw, pitch and roll; polar, geostationary and elliptical orbits, geostationary synchro-nous orbits, payload, trajectory, thrust vector control – the jargon went on and on, but it all made sense: I could do it.

Fortunately, I didn't realise the most nerve-racking part of it until afterwards, when an out-of-breath colleague came in to relieve me after forty minutes or so and I could sit back and take stock. The chairman was of the variety most dreaded by inter-preters: a Frenchman who thought he knew English. He was actually wearing two headsets across the top of his shiny bald head. I could see them quite clearly now. Apparently one was switched to the French channel and the other to English; he was checking every word I said as I said it, and pausing in the middle of sentences, to see how I would translate this or that. The inter-preters' worst nightmare.

It was a triumph. As I drove home afterwards, I couldn't wait to tell Gérard my terrific news. But Mary-Ann reported he had phoned to say he wouldn't be home that night. So after the children went to bed, she and I had a glass of sherry to celebrate my new career.

Chapter 11

My days as a faceless 'backroom boy' were over. For the remaining ten days of the conference, I went to my office in the translators' section every morning but found I was usually assigned to meetings as an interpreter. After that, all the conference offers I received were for interpreting. When the next series of interpretation examinations were held at United Nations' headquarters in Geneva I asked to sit for them, as I was already working as a simultaneous interpreter. I passed and soon started receiving offers from UN headquarters as well as from the Specialized Agencies.

For me it was an easy transition, especially as I knew so many interpreters already. It helped that they were grateful to me for helping out and preventing a disaster. I was lucky: most beginners found the experienced interpreters, who felt there were enough interpreters already, quite hostile. I will always remember, however, my first WHO meeting which happened to be the Finance and Budget Committee – in other words, there were a lot of figures. (For example: 'Replace 6,788.09 in column 10 on page 30 of Document FCBC219 with 7,688.09 and remove the decimal point in the last column on page 40 of the same document', delivered at high speed.) My elderly booth-mate announced she was going out for coffee as I switched my microphone on at the beginning of my half-hour. She then left the booth, picking up all my pencils, pens and writing pad as she went and taking them with her. Somehow, miraculously, I survived in spite of her.

At first, interpreting at large meetings in the main Assembly Halls was intimidating, especially when I realised the power the interpreter could have: the effect of intonation, a hint of sarcasm or even a strategically placed moment of silence. But after a while, as with all things, interpreting became routine.

Sometimes there were more than one hundred interpreters on a conference. The first thing you did upon arrival at the Palais des Nations was to go to the Interpreters' Room to look at the giant blackboard on the wall and check your assignments. On one occasion, my contract had specified I would be working on Anthrax so I had spent ten days or so studying it. (Sometimes you spent more days studying the subject beforehand than actually working at the conference.) When I arrived on the first day, however, I discovered I had been reassigned to 'Coal'.

I found I was working with a colleague I had never shared a booth with before. His name was John. We introduced ourselves and he explained he had been with Atomic Radiation in Vienna. His first ever conference for the United Nations in Geneva had been Coal Mining.

'In fact,' he joked, 'I cut my teeth on coal.'

With simultaneous interpretation, two interpreters sit in each glass booth (one booth per language), wearing headphones and with a microphone, volume control, channel switch, etc., in front of them. Each time a delegate takes the floor, the interpreters immediately interpret their words into English, French, Russian and Spanish, each one of which is broadcast through a separate audio channel – the other delegates can then tune in to the channel of their preference. For example, if I am working in the English booth in a trilingual meeting, say English, French and Spanish, I have to interpret into English what the French or Spanish speakers are saying, as they say it. It is a task requiring intense concentration – you cannot afford to miss a single word. You also need to ensure that the volume in your earphones is adjusted correctly so that you can hear the speaker but also hear yourself, otherwise you run the risk of omitting to finish your sentences. Interpreters generally work half an hour on, then half an hour off, alternating with their booth-mate, but they mostly remain in the booth to listen even when they are not on the air, in case an unusual word is used that may come up again, or in case their colleague needs help in locating a document, or a word to be amended in a document. If the French delegate asks to 'Amend "might" to read "may" on page 7, third paragraph', you can be sure that in the English text it is not on page 7 nor is it the third paragraph.

In the early days documents were produced with 'parallel pagination', which meant that if you wished to refer to something on page 22 of the English text, it would also be on page 22 of the Spanish, French and Russian texts, making amendments much easier. Then some bright bureaucrat decided that this was an uneconomical use of paper as the English was always shorter than the French, which in turn was always shorter than the Spanish, so while the Spanish page would be filled completely; there would be blank space at the bottom of most English and French pages. As a result, parallel pagination was dropped, resulting in even more uneconomic hours of confusion and discussion.

For smaller meetings and for negotiations, consecutive interpretation is occasionally used. These days there is little consecutive work but in the 1960s and '70s, simultaneous interpretation was used only for Plenary meetings; the main work of the conference was done in smaller groups with consecutive interpretation. In consecutive, the interpreters sit with the delegates round the table, take notes during a speech and then at the end interpret the speech.

Before our professional association took a hand in regulating such practices, we often had to interpret consecutively into two languages. In the old days in the Maison des Congrès, I found the most difficult subject was Radioastronomy. After the scientific expert had spoken for thirty minutes, say in French, pointing to diagrams on the blackboard, I would have to give an interpretation first in English and then in Spanish, a truly daunting task. Every specialised subject has its own particular jargon, and outer space is no exception: line-of-sight, electromagnetic waves, celestial bodies, white noise, radio noise, random hiss, static, ionospheric refraction, directional antenna, cosmic radio emissions, VHF and UHF, interstellar space, magnetic field, microwaves. (Did you know there are no microwaves on the other side of the moon?)

Monsieur Boithias, a brilliant French radioastronomer, was so enthusiastic about his canting raindrops and their effect on radio propagation that he would get carried away, and after forty minutes or so I would have to interrupt him. There was also a rather voluble Italian scientist who, because Italian is not an official United Nations' language, had to speak in French. Because of his strong Italian accent, he pronounced *en-dessus* (above) exactly the same as *en-dessous* (below). This made things very difficult for the interpreters as it was vital for the other delegates to know whether he was referring to frequencies above or below 27.5 Mhz – this was the crux of the debate.

Yet the other interpreters and I somehow managed to enjoy working in consecutive on these arid subjects. We were always laughing; my memories of those days in the old Maison des

Congrès are all happy ones. I particularly used to enjoy working with one interpreter, André, as when the discussion got too esoteric and impenetrable, we would pass ridiculous notes to one another to relieve the tension ('The delegate from Romania has concave dentures!').

Today there are about 2500 professional conference inter-preters throughout the world, mostly freelance. Yet postgraduate interpreting schools have sprung up like mushrooms all over the world, turning out many would-be interpreters each year, who find it difficult to find an opening in what is now a crowded profession. The prerequisite for a conference interpretation course is four working languages – preferably also with a uni-versity degree.

In the post-war heyday of conference interpreting however, it was a very different story.

In the 1950s and '60s, when interpreters were the élite jetset; the distinguished, elegant, witty actors on the world stage, interpreters and translators were self-taught, few in number and they all knew each other. When the total number worldwide reached five hundred, interpreters were afraid of becoming commonplace.

Their manners were impeccable, their command of five or six languages perfect and their dazzling wit in all languages as sophisticated as their knowledge of wines. They were well-educated and much-travelled aristocrats: white Russian princes and princesses, barons and baronesses, counts and countesses, sons and daughters of diplomats who had lived in different countries and learnt not only the languages but also the culture, religion, history, customs and literature of the countries where these languages were spoken, as well as the mentality of the people, their body language and gestures.

They were following the traditions of an age-old and very noble profession.

The word *interpreter* goes back to ancient Roman times. There are records of the official status of interpreters in Carthage (that is, between the fifth and first centuries BC) and Caius Julius Caesar mentioned Roman military interpreters in his *De Bello Gallico*.

An interpreter was described by Saladin in 1192 in a letter to Richard the Lionheart, and when the Americas were discovered, interpreters made possible the first contacts between Europeans and American tribes.

In the eighteenth and nineteenth centuries, international business and particularly diplomacy was most often conducted in French, the language of the cultured at the time. In the twentieth century, between the two world wars, the League of Nations held its meetings in French and English with consecutive interpretation.

At the Geneva Peace Conference in 1919, conference-room seating was arranged in a semicircle, with aisles running from the back to a central point, dividing the audience up like pieces of a semicircular cake. The interpreters stood at the central point, side by side, each responsible for a different language: the language of his slice of cake. You can imagine how difficult it was to be heard – each interpreter had to shout louder than his colleagues so that his slice of audience could hear him.

On 4 June 1927 the first meeting with simultaneous interpretation opened at the International Labour Conference in Geneva with a system developed by one A. G. Finlay, for which he won a prize of $200.

At the end of World War II there was an urgent need for interpretation in English, French, Russian and German at the Nuremberg trials of Nazi war criminals and this is where simultaneous interpretation came into its own, its great advantage being that it takes up no extra time. With the creation of the United Nations and the new mobility of air travel, more and more international conferences were held using simultaneous interpretation, developing into today's flourishing worldwide conference industry.

Interpreters lead a privileged life, brushing shoulders with top scientists, architects, musicians, philosophers and writers, able to talk to them freely on social occasions. They are up to date with the latest research on cancer, SARS or AIDS, and are often privy to information that is kept from the general public.

Even today, in top level meetings between world leaders, interpreters are there. They are among the first to know when something of importance happens. Ambassadors have to wait outside during meetings between heads of state, but even the most secret negotiations cannot take place without interpreters.

It is a satisfying feeling, too, to think that you have contributed to the eradication of smallpox, to peace in Cambodia or to an understanding of the latest scientific developments. You cannot help a flash of pride when you recognise your own wording in an international treaty or a document.

When I started my interpreting career, we usually travelled first class and there were always porters to carry our luggage – which was just as well because on some conferences we needed a second suitcase for evening dresses, evening shoes and handbags, a fur cape or stole and jewellery for the many social functions. We stayed only in the best hotels, we were all *fins gourmets* and ate only in the best restaurants, drinking only the best wines. We were invited to receptions in palaces, we were on familiar terms with world leaders like Marshal Tito, Fidel Castro, Indira Gandhi, Pandit Nehru, Giscard d'Estaing, Ferdinand and Imelda Marcos, Prince Sihanouk and Hun Sen. Many famous statesmen were dependent on us – they relied upon us to get their message across, to 'be their voice', and so we were taken good care of.

Sometimes I needed to take yet another suitcase, to bring

back my purchases because the per diem (in local currency) had to be spent in the country of the conference. If I had money over at the end of my stay, I would have to spend it. I bought furs in Canada, Burberries and tennis racquets in London, amber in Senegal, turquoises in Persia, citrines and topazes in Brazil, amethysts and rubies in India and perfume and designer clothes in France. There were practically no customs formalities with a United Nations *laissez passer*. We would swan around airports, scattering witticisms and wisdom like pearls. We had fads and idiosyncracies. For example, an interpreter I knew refused to work in the afternoon unless her pencils had been sharpened during the lunchbreak. My friend Pierre Lambert told me that, in the early days, he used to have a message sent over the pilot's radio as his plane approached Java, Rangoon or Suribaya: 'Have a couple of girls put on ice for me . . .'

One of the first and most brilliant of the post-war interpreters was Jean Herbert, who maintained that our profession was like a vast itinerant international university: working as freelance interpreters, he said, 'we were in contact with the front line of new ideas and new knowledge in many diverse fields. In the course of our work, as well as statesmen, diplomats and politicians we also met famous philosophers, writers, artists and research scientists. Many brilliant interpreters also used their travel air tickets to pursue their *real* interests such as archaeology, oriental art or obscure languages'.

There were many glamorous figures amongst the interpreters: gentle Prince Galitzin and the heel-clicking, hand-kissing Prince Sviatopolk Mirsky with their dazzling humour. Although they spoke Polish or Russian to their servants and in their families before becoming refugees during World War I, on formal occasions they had spoken French, the elegant language then as well as the language of diplomacy for some two hundred years until World War II, when economic power and the technological prowess of the English-speaking world imposed the English language.

The quick wit common to interpreters often enlivened our time in the booth.

Working with Pierre Lambert, the most entertaining of colleagues, was something to look forward to. Once, during a meeting about African diseases carried by animals such as warthogs and groundhogs, he kept me amused with impersonations of each while I was interpreting and he was 'off'. He knew what each one looked like and would put up his hands for ears or horns, or stroke his chin if the animal had a beard. It was not easy to keep a regular tone of voice when you were so close to mirth.

Pierre was working the following week for the Pope's visit to Geneva. There was to be a vast open-air ceremony at which various dignitaries, including the Pope, would be speaking. A passing colleague put her head round the booth door to say hello. She would be working there too and she asked, 'What does one call the Pope? His worship? His . . . what?' Quick as lightning, Pierre replied, 'His Holiness, the Pope. Not His Popiness the Hole. Nor his Poliness the Hope. Avoid at all costs His Hopelessness the Pole . . . Thank you, Mr Chairman. I wish to comment on the proposed text on page four . . .' He had switched his microphone on because it was time for his half-hour to begin and someone had asked for the floor.

Emperor Charles V, who dominated much of Europe in the sixteenth century, could have been an interpreter. He is said to have boasted: 'I speak Spanish to God, Italian to women, French to men and German to my horse.'

There were also some eccentrics: Hélène, a brilliant French-booth interpreter, always said she worked much better in really difficult conferences if she could knit at the same time; knitting helped calm her nerves. The delegates would sometimes complain of a clicking sound in their earphones and ask if the technician would please do something about it.

Over coffee one morning, a colleague was telling us about her financial difficulties. Another interpreter, Charlie, said without any hesitation that he would buy her house in Malta to help her out. He had trained as a pilot and owned a small plane. After a while he moved to Malta and flew himself to conferences. Rumour had it that when offered conferences in out of the way places, before accepting he would ask, 'Is the conference venue near a landing strip, a flat field or a sandy beach?' I often worked with Charlie in those days and he would talk of the joy of flying yourself around and not being bound by commercial flight schedules. He also thought it unfair that men had to shave every day and tried as a rule to do it in his employer's time. He brought one of the first electric shavers on the market into the booth, unplugged the table lamp and plugged in his shaver, smiling at the thought of actually being paid for the time he spent shaving. Once again there were complaints from the delegates, this time of a 'buzzing sound in the earphones'.

One older colleague in Geneva, Olga, later went to live in Addis Ababa where she became the second wife of a young man and 'put him through university'. They all lived happily together as an extended family, Ethiopian-style. Olga took with her all her Russian icons and shawls and brass ornaments and helped raise the first wife's four children as though she were their grandmother. When any of us went on a conference in her part of the world we would write to ask what she needed us to bring – mostly household items, chocolate for the children, clothes for a four-year-old boy, or pyjamas for an eight year old.

Georges de Modzelewski was a brilliant interpreter from Russian, Polish, German and French into English which he did in an inimitable rich, deep, fruity voice. Sometimes in the middle of the morning he would send for our secretary. Handing her a bunch of keys, he would ask if she minded driving over to his flat – he wasn't sure whether he had turned off the electric kettle after breakfast and wanted her to check.

Rather plump, kind American Ruthalma was a motherly figure who also knitted, but in her case it was during her half-hours off the air. She knitted the most enormous garments in bright shades of red which were often draped over the arm-chairs or table in the Interpreters' Room. Ruthalma must have had a large collection of spectacles because whichever bright colour she wore, the extravagant frames of her glasses always matched. She also wore glamorous wigs and sometimes in the afternoons delegates stared up at her booth, fascinated by the sight of her wet bathing costume hanging on the coat hook on the inside of the booth-door with her wig hanging above it, also drying out after her lunch-time swimming session. Ruthalma had a heart of gold and was always giving money away. I believe she had forty-eight cats at home in America and remembered all their names.

Tita was from Peru. In those days she spent six months of the year in Peru with her family and six months interpreting in Geneva. One day the meeting finished early. It was unusual for us to have a free afternoon. Tita was delighted and rushed off to buy ten metres of telephone wire. 'Where do I go to buy that?' she asked. Her wires at home in Peru were mouldy because of the damp walls. 'You can't buy telephone wire in Switzerland,' another colleague explained. 'It's not allowed. You'll have to buy it in France and get it through the customs somehow. Be sure to check French wire is the same as the one you have in Peru.'

The other item on her shopping list was a blue glass eye. Her great-uncle in Peru was blind in one eye. Once when he left his eye in a glass of water overnight, the maid emptied the glass of water down the toilet the next morning and the glass eye was gone. He managed to get a message to Tita just as she was leaving

Lima for Geneva: 'Please buy me one blue glass eye (right side) in Switzerland.' He was convinced that glass eyes *must* be better in clean, modern Switzerland.

We helped Tita find a telephone directory and enquire about the best eye-makers.

Next morning she told us about her visit to the glass-eye factory. She had been shown drawer upon drawer full of rows and rows of blue glass eyes, all different. Some were wider, some narrower. 'You needed to know the exact measurements, the eye pressure, and so on. It all seemed too complicated, so I said: "Forget it!"'

When Tita returned to Lima, her great-uncle was furious.

'You see how serious this is to you. You don't care about me. You forgot all about your poor old half-blind great-uncle.'

So, six months later when Tita returned to Geneva, the first thing she did was go back to the glass eye factory and look at the drawers of blue glass eyes. She picked out one at random and took it back to her great-uncle in Lima.

It turned out to be the very best glass eye her great-uncle had ever had. It fitted perfectly and he proudly told everyone it had come all the way from Switzerland.

Simultaneous conference interpreting is a very stressful occupation at the best of times. But it's particularly nerve-wracking when you may be televised or recorded for radio and when certain universally-dreaded, hard-to-understand speakers are scheduled to make unpredictable headline statements. For such occasions some feel they can only do their best if wearing a certain colour, a certain dress, or a particular pair of shoes or have been to the hairdresser the previous day. Others feel they cannot do their best unless they have had two cups of strong black coffee before starting work. And there are still others who cannot perform unless they slip outside the building every now and again to have a surreptitious cigarette. With Bernadette, it was a cup of blood before breakfast.

We often worked together in the English booth. Bernadette was short and dumpy and lacked the sophistication of other interpreters. Her main interest in life was food. She had been living with Antoine now for twenty years and seemed to think no-one knew. Marriage with Antoine was unlikely because he was already married. His wife had been in a mental hospital for twenty-five years and was therefore, according to Swiss law, unfit to provide a legal signature. So there could be no divorce. Rumour also had it that Antoine was a very wealthy man.

When Antoine fell ill, Bernadette devoted herself to him. She was up at the crack of dawn to get him washed and dressed before she left for work and arranged for a nurse to call in every day while she was at work.

Then one morning Bernadette arrived at work with a sparkle in her eye and a grin on her round pink face. Antoine's wife had died. She bought a round of drinks at the conference bar before we all went home that night.

Next day she started planning the wedding. Antoine was now permanently in hospital, but she arranged for him to be allowed out for his wedding day in a wheelchair accompanied by a nurse.

It was a grand wedding. Bernadette was resplendant in shiny purple. Antoine, frail, pale and shaky, looked as if he might not last another five minutes. The food and wines were the best that money could buy. The catering was by the most exclusive restaurant in town, the hall was furnished and decorated by the top hotel. We were seated on gilt and plush Louis XVth chairs, except for Antoine in his wheelchair. There was no doubt that this was Bernadette's day. She was now a rich woman, owning four cars including a Daimler, as well as two apartments, stocks, shares and properties all over the country.

There could be no honeymoon because Antoine died the

next day. The doctors said the excitement of the wedding had been too much for him. He died in her arms.

Bernadette worked at only one more conference before retiring to enjoy her wealth – she had signed the contract a few months earlier and was legally bound. At the coffee bar on her last morning she confided the secret of her health and vigour: every morning she drank a cup of blood before breakfast.

She told me she was the illegitimate child of a famous man whose name she could not divulge. She had never known her mother and had been brought up by peasants on an isolated farm in the Swiss Alps. From her earliest childhood, every morning first thing they had given her a cup of blood to make her strong.

In Geneva Bernadette always walked to work through the covered market. The butchers, setting out their steaks and chops on the marble slabs in their refrigerated glass display cabinets, knew her well. Her regular supplier would have the cup of cooled blood ready for her, knowing she would call by on Saturday morning to collect her week's supply of meat and settle the bill.

Pink Pills for Pale People may have done the trick in the old days, but from what I have seen, there's nothing like a cup of blood before breakfast.

Marcela de Juan, half Belgian, half Chinese, was still interpreting in her eighties, as tall and straight as ever. After work, she would rush off to her rumba and cha-cha dancing lessons. She was a Chinese princess whose father, a real pig-tailed mandarin (magnificent in his silk robes in the photographs she showed me) and Chinese poet, had later become a diplomat. To become a mandarin, he'd had to pass a very difficult poetry examination, she explained. For centuries, civil servants in China had to write poetry as part of their qualifying examinations. They were shut in a cell and not released until the poetry was written. Marcela was also a writer and poet as well as a simultaneous interpreter. She wrote in Spanish and worked in the Spanish or French booth. She was a member of the fifth branch of the line of Emperor Wang-Li, thirteenth emperor of the Ming dynasty. This is the Emperor who was famous for inviting the Italian jesuit Mateo Ricci to the Imperial Court of China and giving him a pension in exchange for teaching all he knew to the Emperor's son.

Incredibly, Marcela's sister had served in the Chinese army, disguised as a man – and a very handsome man too, judging by the photographs Marcela showed me.

In addition to working as a conference interpreter, Marcela de Juan (Juan was the Spanish version of her Chinese name, Huan) was an eminent translator of classical and modern Chinese poetry into Spanish, as well as a diplomat. When I visited her in Hong Kong, where she was Cultural Attaché to the Spanish Embassy, I was impressed by her regal posture as we sat on the ferry boat, her white rice-powdered face protected from the sun by her parasol for fear of suntan. A real princess's skin was white. Over a Chinese dinner of fish cooked in its scales; golden, crisp and delicious, she told me unforgettable tales of her childhood when her amah bound her feet every day so that she would have the required hoof-shaped 'lily feet' – a sign of high breeding, while her Belgian mother crept into her nursery every night to unbind them in secret. Marcela's long slender fingers were white and soft and her long pointed fingernails immaculately mani-cured and lacquered bright red. As she talked, her expressive hands reminded me of butterflies.

Then there was the extraordinary red-headed Génia Rosoff, who had been deported to Germany for her work in the French Résistance and who, when I worked with her, was dying of cancer. Black-haired Gedda Preisman, so kind and encouraging at the beginning of my career. Bright-blue-eyed Paul Tolstoy (grandson of *the* Tolstoy), Chrysanthème Liou and her tinkling laugh, Sonia Drake (who went to school with Margot Fonteyn), – all famous names in our profession.

But even with all that wit and wisdom, interpreting was not always plain sailing.

The stress of simultaneous interpreting has been compared to that of air traffic controllers. We do not know beforehand what the speaker is going to say. Sometimes we do not know whether he is in favour or against until he gets to the end of the sentence. You are constantly on tenterhooks, waiting to hear what you are going to say next. While you are working, the adrenalin is flowing and you surpass yourself – you are in a state of heightened awareness. I once heard tapes of a conference twenty years earlier – I was amazed that it was my voice I could hear, because I was using words I do not know, talking about subjects I know nothing about. A strange experience.

There are many pitfalls. Proverbs, for example, are always a headache.

Often a proverb doesn't work if translated into another language. One colleague had his personal passe-partout proverb to save the situation in case of emergency: '*Il ne faut pas essayer de tondre un oeuf* ('It's no good trying to shave an egg') if working into French, and 'You can't boil an egg twice' if working into English. Pierre's favourite proverb was '*La plus belle fille du monde . . .*' – a French saying about the most beautiful girl in the world not being able to give any more than she has, however beautiful she may be.

Figures of speech can be tricky, too. On one occasion, an American delegate took the floor to say: 'The delegate of the UK is pussyfooting with a red herring.' We had been talking together during the coffee break about the difficulties of interpretation – he must have spent some time working out something clever to say, thinking it would amuse me. It did not!

It was no easy matter to put that into French and Spanish at the drop of a hat.

Jokes can be awkward to interpret because however funny they may be in one language, they are rarely funny when translated into another. If a delegate tells a joke and you don't 'get it', it is impossible to translate it and make people laugh. If the joke-teller's listeners do not laugh, he has lost face. Some colleagues admit defeat without even trying and simply say into the microphone: 'The speaker is cracking a joke. Would you please laugh.' But I find that solution lacks imagination. The best thing to do, of course, is to understand the joke and interpret it brilliantly so that everyone laughs at the right moment and no-one loses face, not even the interpreter. But, just in case, I always have a little joke of my own up my sleeve, that I can shorten or expand, to ensure that everyone laughs at the right moment.

At a meteorology conference the World Weather Watch was being discussed and we were going round the room so that each country could announce how many vessels they would place at the disposal of the World Weather Watch the following year, to monitor weather conditions over a given period of time in their part of the world. The UK offered three, France offered three, the USSR meant to say four to five but what came out of the interpretation booth sounded like 'forty-five'. There was great excitement and the press gallery emptied in a few seconds while phone calls were made to ensure the incredible news of the USSR's generosity hit the headlines promptly.

At a telecommunications conference, the agenda item was 'New Technologies'. It was my colleague's half-hour on air, so I was reading the newspaper. Suddenly she switched her microphone off and asked urgently: 'What's "*guidon*"?'

Without lifting my eyes from my paper, I answered 'handlebars'.

I vaguely heard her say into the microphone: 'I am referring to the new handlebar technique.'

Then it was my turn to take over. The chairman was asking the French delegate to explain the new handlebar technique in greater detail.

When the Frenchman referred to '*guide d'ondes*' I realised what I had done. Carefully I had to guide them back to 'wave guides'.

'The new handlebar technique, more commonly known as wave guides, consists of . . .'

After another handlebar or two, I weaned them back to wave guides, which is what it should have been in the first place.

The following week I was working with Ina, who was reading the paper beside me. In a desperate whisper I asked: 'Did he really say "elephants everywhere"?'

'I think he said "of relevance everywhere",' she replied coolly.

I was in Manila for a Forestry conference and happy to be back in a warm tropical climate, far from the Swiss winter. Upon arrival we were met at the airport by government officials: there had been a spate of hotel fires in Manila. We were handed an official letter of warning, telling us to be watchful, to carry our passports, travel documents and travellers' cheques with us at all times, how to crawl on all fours to avoid smoke inhalation, where fire exits were situated and where to pick up flashlights.

At the meeting we talked of swamps and fish breeding and the vital role mangroves play in the ecosystem. Of nitrogen-fixing trees, soil and water conservation, forests, woodlands and shrubland, watershed management, man and the biosphere, felling and firebreaks, shifting cultivation, catchment protection. A tall, dignified white-bearded Italian professor kept referring to fruit-bearing mammals.

Now when you have been doing simultaneous interpretation

for as long as I have, while one part of your brain is interpreting, in another you are trying to think about more pleasant things to prevent complete stultification of the poetic side of your brain. Sometimes something one of the delegates says starts me off on a fantasy trip in the unconfined realms of my imagination. This particular fruit-bearing mammal created wonderful, exotic pictures in my mind.

I could see a beautiful furry creature rather like a large fox, with a long, bushy tail and a well-groomed coat, gliding through the forest with its head held high. It advanced on its paws as if on tiptoe. On its head was a basket of fruit, Carmen Miranda-style: pineapples, peaches, mangoes, bananas, oranges, lemons, perhaps even a watermelon sliced to show the beautiful colours. There was something regal and graceful about it as it glided among the tropical ferns and palms of my mind.

Every now and then I came back to reality and tried to work out how one would say 'fruit-bearing mammal' in French or Spanish. I tried switching to the other channels to catch what my colleagues were saying, but was never quick enough.

The conference lasted five days and the graceful fruit-bearing mammal glided elegantly through all of them. It wasn't until the last afternoon coffee-break that I found myself at last face to face with the tall, dignified Italian delegate who had referred to it in the first place.

'Could you tell me more about the fruit-bearing mammal?' I asked him over coffee.

'Many mammals are fruit-bearing,' he replied. 'You see, they eat the fruit they find on the ground in one place; then they may travel miles and miles before they excrete the fruit seeds, and the fruit grows in the new location.'

I had the answer at last; but I preferred my own picturesque fruit-bearing mammal.

A most embarrassing thing happened to me when I was

working in consecutive in my early days. In consecutive, there is no booth; the interpreter sits up on the platform next to the chairman. In the front row of the hall sat a Frenchman called Monsieur Bès. He was an easy-going, rather portly father figure from the south of France, with a strong *accent du midi*. Fortunately, he was also a very understanding man, because I had never encountered his name before and wasn't sure how to pronounce it. When talking to him, I just called him 'Monsieur' which was fine, but when interpreting I had to say 'Monsieur Bès says . . .', or 'Monsieur Bès suggests . . .' I pronounced his name as if it were written 'Bez' in English.

During the coffee-break, M. Bès came up and asked if he could tell me something that had happened to him during the early days of his marriage, many years earlier.

'You'll understand why when I get to the end,' he said kindly.

'When I was first married, someone telephoned us in the middle of the night. I was half asleep but I answered the telephone. A voice asked: "Monsieur Bez?" Being half asleep I didn't think twice, I just said, "Oui?"

'Then the voice asked: "*Madame est contente?*" ("Is Madame happy?")'

He walked away, leaving his words to sink in. After a minute or two they did and I blushed and never called him 'Monsieur Bez' again, but rather Monsieur 'Bess'. *Baise* (pronounced 'bez') is French for 'makes love'.

Not long afterwards I was again presented with the challenges of pronunciation, but this time it was Japanese.

We were working in consecutive for a technical working group. The only two languages being used were French and English, so whichever of those languages was used, it was my job to take notes and repeat what had been said in the other language. Unfortunately we had a problem with the Japanese expert who spoke both English and French – equally incomprehensibly. The problem was that we never knew before he started which language he was going to speak. Sometimes it was difficult to tell the difference even after he had begun.

On this occasion the Japanese delegate took the floor and I sat forward, concentrating, pencil in hand, ready to take notes. After he had been talking for a few minutes I still had not understood one word. I couldn't even tell what language he was speaking. No-one in the room seemed to understand a word. The delegates had resigned expressions on their faces as they sat back, waiting for him to finish, so that the interpreter (me) would make it all clear.

He spoke for twenty minutes. Obviously what he had to say was important because he was reading from a paper in front of him, but I had not understood a single word. When he finished, I rose to my feet, taking my courage in both hands, and walked round the green-baize table, behind the seated delegates, to where the Japanese delegate sat. Bowing politely I said:

'Sir, in order to be sure I have the figures right, I wonder if you would be so kind as to lend me your notes?'

He bowed politely and handed me a wad of paper. I returned to my seat, drew a deep breath, turned on my microphone and prepared to start. The notes were in Japanese. I did not speak Japanese.

My expression must have given the game away. The tactful chairman said, 'Ladies and gentlemen, it is almost lunchtime. Since the Japanese statement is obviously of great importance, I propose we hear it after lunch. Perhaps the Japanese delegate would be so kind as to hand it to the Chair in writing, in French or English, at the beginning of this afternoon's session.'

I could have given him a big hug.

I think the greatest interpreting challenge I ever had was at the hands of an Australian who in the 1980s was elected to the post of Secretary General of one of the Specialized Agencies of the United Nations. He gave a celebratory cocktail party that evening with live music and I was invited.

When I arrived at the party I shook his hand and congratulated him. He said, 'I might say a few words, later. Would you mind interpreting them for me into French and Spanish?'

'Of course,' I agreed politely.

So when he climbed the steps up to the podium, beckoning me, I followed like a lamb.

He took the microphone and, after a few words of thanks, announced, 'The interpreter will now sing "Waltzing Matilda" in French and Spanish.'

The band struck up . . .

Chapter 12

Conferences are wonderful occasions for lonely people to meet under the most auspicious circumstances: away from home for long periods in exotic, luxury hotels with palm trees swaying in the wind and parties almost every night. At one such conference cocktail party I stood, glass in hand, talking to a bright young secretary. It was getting late and gradually people were starting to leave, often in couples. The delegates had been away from home for two weeks now.

'You can always tell if a man is married, whatever he says.' She was matter-of-fact. 'They usually say their wives don't understand them and that they are separated and live alone. But when it comes to the big moment, they always have *their* side of the bed. You can always tell . . .'

A certain number of secretaries were needed for all overseas conferences so for the months leading up to it they were all on their best behaviour, buttering up the right people. Those chosen were the envy of all the others. Even the plainest could be assured of a good time with cocktail parties almost every evening, official conference dinners and weekend excursions at the invitation of the host government. Even the dullest could be sure of a romance or at least invitations to dinner and a night-club or the theatre from lonely delegates far from home.

Many conferences in those days lasted six weeks. Some had only seven hundred delegates, some had two thousand or even five thousand, nearly all men. They were away from their wives and families and must have felt lonely. After a week or two, couples formed, delegates paired off with secretaries, translators or interpreters. Since many of the conferences met regularly every six months, every year, every two or three years, couples that had formed at a previous conference would meet up again and carry on where they had left off. Between conferences there would be no contact – they were usually happily married, after all. After a while, though, some of the conference couples became like old married couples. You could hear them nagging one another at corner tables in the coffee bar.

One couple who caused a scandal in the early days of the United Nations were a certain Secretary General and his secretary. The Secretary General was an aristocratic Frenchman, very tall and rather heavy, with straight white hair and a pink face. He was married to a drab French lady who was rarely seen; they had a number of children whose photographs figured prominently on his desk. He was a practising Catholic and always wore a dark suit and tie and highly polished black shoes. The Secretary General was exemplary in every way, extremely polite and always dignified. He addressed everyone as 'Madame', 'Monsieur' or 'Mademoiselle' and generally gave a half-bow as he shook your hand.

The Secretary General's secretary (later she was called his administrative assistant and given a raise) was a widow, about ten years younger than him, with dyed black hair. She was not pretty or attractive – rather overweight in fact, and not very tall. She wore dark, rather dowdy clothes but always shiny black high-heeled shoes. (There was a rumour that she wore white gloves in bed to protect the sheets from her handcream, but there was no proof of this.) She frowned a lot and was not very talkative or friendly to the other members of the staff. In fact she gave the impression that she was much too important to talk to anyone.

Everyone treated them with reverence: 'The Secretary General wants this.' 'The Secretary General's secretary asks that this be done.' Very few knew either of their first names. No-one ever questioned a decision taken by the Secretary General (on the advice of his administrative assistant). The system was not in any way democratic but had the advantage that each member of the staff knew exactly where he stood. There was no need for a staff association because no staff member had any complaint. If you wanted to keep your job, you accepted what came your way.

A select group of high-ranking officials had been sent to Mexico as well as a few secretaries, a typing pool, translators, revisers, interpreters and a few accountants to service the conference. It lasted six weeks, everyone travelled first class; the conference was held in the ballroom of a brand new hotel. The hotel had all the very latest equipment and luxuries and was situated right next to the Catholic cathedral in the centre of town.

It was the custom in those days for all staff on overseas conferences to be given two free three-minute telephone calls home per week. Some sacrificed one of these occasionally to call their colleagues in the office to tell them the latest news. Rumour had it that the Secretary General's administrative assistant had telephoned her assistant at Geneva headquarters asking for a tin of instant coffee to be sent by diplomatic pouch marked 'confidential documents'. (Apparently the new Nescafé had not yet reached Mexico.)

Everyone knew that the Secretary General and his administrative assistant were having an affair. Some members of the staff lived across the street from the Secretary General's administrative assistant and had seen the Secretary General leaving her block of flats in the middle of the night on more than one occasion. The staff smiled to themselves about it, but no-one actually said anything out loud. Amazingly, the couple themselves seemed to have no idea that everyone knew. They carried on day after day decorously behaving as if they were office colleagues and no more, laboriously calling one another '*vous*' formally in the office – never the more personal '*tu*' which would have given them away. (Secretly I wondered whether they even said '*vous*' in bed or whether they took the risk of relapsing into '*tu*' when alone.)

On Sunday mornings in Mexico many of the staff attended mass in the Catholic cathedral next to their hotel. The Secretary General and his administrative assistant were there too, both dressed in black. She wore black gloves and a black felt hat with black feathers on one side. As usual, they arrived separately. When the time came for communion, they both rose and joined the row of kneeling communicants in the front.

(At this point I must explain that in those days the bell-boy in the big hotels had a task that he no longer has today. He had to polish all the guests' shoes early each morning. At night when you got undressed for bed, you placed your shoes outside the door of your room and in the morning you found them freshly polished and a-shine.)

On the soles of the shoes of those kneeling for communion a number could clearly be seen, written in white chalk. The room number, written by the bell-boy. And there for all to see: the number written on the soles of the Secretary General's shoes was the same as that on those of his administrative assistant.

Many interpreters married diplomats and conference delegates: Australian Anne Robson married the then Governor General, Sir John Kerr, in 1975, after interpreting for him at diplomatic conferences.

Some independent, free-thinking interpreters wanted a baby but not a husband. This was quite shocking in the 1960s.

Sometimes a group of us, waiting for a delayed meeting to begin, would survey the rows of delegates below to see if we fancied any of them.

'I think Poles are the best lovers. What do you think?'

'Italians make marvellous fathers but are not so good as husbands. I would say they're good lovers. If only they wouldn't keep checking when they're walking down the street to make sure their genitals are still there.'

'They amuse me on the beach, strutting about in their bathing trunks with their bulges to the fore, when everyone knows they've stuck a handkerchief or two in as well to make it look bigger!'

'The Greeks show off their virility by spitting, have you noticed? They seem to think the farther they can spit, the more virile they are.'

'Some men think their car represents their virility and the faster they drive, the better they are at making love,' I added, thinking wryly of Gérard.

'When I was in Chile, I couldn't help noticing the llamas with their mournful eyes and long eyelashes. Someone told me men aren't allowed to go on long treks across the Andes with llamas because they have sex with them – apparently they're the nearest thing to a woman.'

'Frenchmen are wonderful with words, poetry and flowers, but not so good in action.'

'Have you ever tried a Finn?'

'Yes, but what would you want for the father of your child?'

'Must be handsome and tall, definitely. Intelligent and good sense of humour. Kind. Witty. Sporty and healthy.'

'Fair or dark-haired? Blue or brown eyes?'

'I think I would like a dark Latin-American.'

At coffee break we would talk to the delegates, hoping our conversation would give us an idea of their intelligence, breeding, and whether they had a good sense of humour, so that we could report back to our group.

We looked along the rows of 1500 delegates from some 180 countries trying to pick those who would make the best fathers. Not that they would ever know they were fathers. The idea was to sleep with them a few times and never see them again. In the days before the Pill, all you had to do was forget to put in your diaphragm.

Three or four of my colleagues went through with it and there must have been others. The interpreters' lifestyle made it much easier to be a single mother. Working freelance, it was easy to take time off as needed, and our high salaries made nannies possible when work was resumed. To make up for the lack of a father, we all rallied round on birthdays and at Christmas with parties and presents. Many of the mothers, though, gave in and got married sooner or later.

Affairs were also the perfect way to improve your language skills.

My advice to a beginner interpreter who had problems with, say, a French-Canadian accent or a Cuban or Chilean accent in Spanish, would be to have an affair with a delegate speaking that language. It is amazing how much easier it becomes to understand and interpret the language.

As for me, despite my affair with Janek I was still in love with Gérard and hoping our marriage would work out. Before Janek I had stayed faithful to Gérard, however, if I'd wanted to stray, plenty of opportunities presented themselves. Indeed, on one occasion I received an extraordinary proposal.

I was working in Brazzaville (French Congo, then) for a medical conference on communicable diseases: relapsing fever, trachoma, yaws, plague, measles, cholera, tinia, smallpox and kidney-flukes.

I generally got up early and went for a gentle swim in the outdoor hotel pool, which was surrounded by bougainvillea and flowering trees. My spirits were lifted by the sight of the delicate bougainvillea flowers floating on the surface of the water and the way my hands brushed them aside as I swam. It felt like floating tai chi. Moving gently so as to disturb them as little as possible, I bathed luxuriously in the pink and mauve flowers and cool water.

On the last day of the conference we were invited to a farewell cocktail party at the presidential palace. I wore a slinky blue shot silk dress I'd had made in India the month before.

The president of the Republic of the Congo at that time had been a Catholic priest before becoming president. He continued to wear a cassock but now had them made in Paris by Christian Dior; the colours changed according to the time of the year and the proximity of religious occasions. On this particular day his cassock was of sky-blue silk because it was Ascension Day.

There were a few speeches I had to interpret but after that I was free to enjoy the sumptuous food passed round on silver trays by white-gloved servants, the overwhelming selection of drinks in tall glasses and the music played by the orchestra.

Towards the end of the evening, one of the white-gloved, gold-braided servants approached with a tray bearing a small white card. It read (in French): 'The prime minister requests to speak with you.' I looked up, puzzled, and the servant whispered: 'If Madame would care to come with me . . .'

I followed him into an alcove where the prime minister waited, looking serious and rather pompous. Very formally he bowed. Then he coughed and announced in a solemn voice: 'The president has asked me to convey a message to you. He is waiting in his suite for your answer. He would like to invite you to consider doing him the honour of becoming his fourteenth wife.'

At a loss for words, I paused to let the significance of his message sink in.

'But I'm already married!' I blurted out. 'I have a husband and two children.'

The prime minister bowed once again.

'That is no problem whatsoever, Madame,' he said. 'We can make all the necessary arrangements.'

After our three wonderful weeks in the spring, Janek had been spending more and more time in Geneva and had rented a flat in the city centre. Whenever he was in town we would meet there several times a week for lunch. That is to say, we generally managed a little lunch, but not always, because we spent most of the time making love. Sometimes he had prepared wonderful Polish dishes for us. Other times we would just eat a quick endive salad.

Janek was a passionate but considerate lover. He would close the curtains, put on my favourite music and strew cushions on the floor in front of the fire. He did everything he could to make the mood right and give me pleasure, which was a novel experience for me. Afterwards, the world was a wonderful place and I smiled at everyone I met. I was aglow with happiness. I sang as I drove home, I sang as I tidied up the kitchen, I sang while weeding the garden, I sang as I bathed the children.

Sometimes, if we had an hour or two free, he would play his violin and I would sing. We discovered we both knew many of the same jazz tunes; his playing reminded me of the Hot Club de France with Stephane Grappelli and Django Reinhardt. He often played 'I want to be happy' and it became our theme song. At home, whenever I played the Barbra Streisand recording of 'Stay until it's time for you to go' or 'I was an oak, now I'm a willow – I can bend', I would think of Janek. It was like watching my own private television show. I would recall every detail of the last time we had been together; everything we had said, the expression on his face, his voice, the clothes we had been wearing. I could spend hours daydreaming about him.

I was glad to retreat into my dream world. Ever since our 'Open Marriage' talk, Gérard took no pains to hide the phone calls from his girlfriends – there seemed to be at least three, although Monique was the main one. He often spent nights away from home. Once when I came back from an overseas conference I had found long blonde hairs on my favourite armchair. Another time I came across a love poem in Gérard's handwriting, addressed to his tall fair princess. It was crumpled beneath his pillow when I made the bed one Sunday when the maid was off duty. I read it several times, studied the words that had been crossed out, imagined how he had felt when he wrote it and I was wild with jealousy. It used to be *me* he wrote poetry to. How I hated the 'tall, fair princess'. Finally I screwed the poem into a tight ball and threw it down the lavatory. But as I flushed it away I realised that it had not gone – it was still in my mind. I knew it by heart. It would torment me for weeks.

Gérard could still send me into a whirlwind of emotions – despite myself, I still loved him. I had discovered that it's possible to love different people in different ways. My feelings for Gérard and for Janek were very different yet equally important. Janek filled my life with romance, tenderness and intimacy. Waiting for the day when we would see one another again, I would plan what I would wear and note down things I wanted to tell him. I dreamt of our last time together and imagined the next. But Gérard was quite different. He was part of a 'package deal' that included the children, our home and lifestyle. He was the price I had to pay for all that.

In December Gérard told me there was to be an office Christmas party and that he wanted me to go with him. I was to wear my long dark-green empire dress and the amethyst jewellery he had brought me back from his last trip to Poland. This gave me hope: perhaps the Christmas party would be the turning point I had been hoping for. If he wanted to 'show me off' to his work colleagues, surely that could only be a good sign.

By seven o'clock he was already there to pick me up. He had changed into his smart pale blue suit. He looked very elegant and smelt of expensive aftershave.

He came into the bathroom where I was putting the finishing touches to my make-up.

'Women, women!' he taunted. 'Why is it that women take so long to get ready? I can be ready in five minutes, that's all the time it takes me.'

He seemed in an unusually good mood, which also raised my spirits. He sat on the side of the bath. It was full of soaking sheets and pyjamas for Stephanie had had a bilious attack and I had told Mary-Ann she could leave the washing to soak there until the morning, since Gérard was not coming home that night. She was in a hurry to prepare supper for herself and a friend who was coming to keep her company that evening while she was babysitting for me.

Sometimes in his rare good moods, Gérard liked to act the clown. Once, some years before, we had seen a horror film about a man who pretended to drown in the bath and then rose with the whites of his eyes showing to haunt his wife, who had a weak heart and promptly collapsed, dead.

Out of the corner of my eye I saw Gérard pretending to slip and fall in the bath. With exaggerated gestures he floundered and flapped his arms, then turned his eyes upward so that the whites showed, trying to look like a drowned man. I laughed and continued dabbing on mascara.

Suddenly there was a sinister splash. Gérard had miscalculated. The bathmat had slipped and he had fallen into the bath with its unpleasant-smelling contents.

I can't say I rushed to his rescue. I watched him struggle for a moment, his bottom in the noxious yellow water, his arms outstretched trying to regain his balance and hold on to something. With a sudden determined effort he heaved himself out of the bath, his beautiful suit dripping wet and his face distorted with fury.

I was ready and waiting for him by the front door while he changed his clothes. I refrained from pointing out that sometimes men take longer than women to get ready.

We were not talkative as we drove into town but as he got out of the car he switched on his charming smile.

We sailed into the reception, he smiled at everyone and took my coat with a bow. Then he handed it to the cloakroom girl with another dazzling smile. Taking my elbow, he led me into the hall and I felt all eyes on me.

He guided me to a group of people and after the usual introductions, fetched me a drink and, with a bow and an 'excuse me', disappeared.

'Monsieur Baumier has been telling us about your travels,' my husband's colleague was saying. 'He is very proud of you, you know.'

Gérard was gone about twenty minutes. Then he reappeared in the entrance, walking towards me, leading by the elbow a tall attractive girl with long fair hair. I knew it must be his mistress, Monique.

'May I introduce . . .?'

He was behaving like a film star, certain that all eyes were upon him. He was 'living dangerously' again – in fact, he was in his element, watching to see how we'd react to each other.

We were the centre of attention and I could tell everyone was aware of what was going on. I stood very upright while Gérard continued: 'This is "our Monique" I've told you about. She speaks several languages, she's on the organising committee and has worked very hard to make the arrangements for this evening.'

Monique was smiling as if she were a débutante being presented to the queen.

If only I had surprised Gérard by making friends with her, whisking her off to tell her that the real Gérard snored, shouted and had a bad temper – that there were at least two other girl-friends I knew of: he wasn't even faithful to her! Instead, I just looked at her, searching wildly for something to say and finding nothing. After a few moments I mumbled an 'Excuse me' and fled to the ladies' room.

But I still didn't want to give up on the marriage. Life continued and we both travelled more and more.

Chapter 13

In the 1960s WHO was engaged in an energetic campaign for the eradication of smallpox and yaws in Africa and India and I spent much time working in various African countries, both French- and English-speaking. The sun was always hot, there was always a profusion of flowers. There were conflicts, too, but I was fortunate enough never to get caught up in them, even when they were taking place in the very country I was in. It wasn't until I got home from Lagos, for example, that I heard about the barbaric events that were taking place there during the civil war although I do remember, as we were driven from the airport to the hotel, we passed a crowd of shouting people surrounding a line of men chained to a metal fence, with car tyres round their necks. We went past very quickly and I didn't understand what had been happening until I got home after the conference and read the newspapers.

My memories of Cameroon in the 1960s are of bougainvillea and flame trees against an electric blue sky and of friendly shop-keepers as I wandered among sacks of rice, spices and other produce, talking to other customers in their elegant headdresses and beautiful brightly coloured gowns, homemade baskets over their arms. You could happily spend an hour or two wandering about the shops and chatting, without realising the time had passed.

In those days I always had a car and a driver waiting for me when I arrived at the airport. They were at my disposal for the whole of my stay. In Senegal I remember we worked all week including Saturday but Sunday I was free so I asked my driver to take me somewhere. 'Not a tourist place,' I said. 'Take me where you would choose to spend your Sunday afternoon.'

So we drove to Poto-Poto.

It seems there is often a Poto-Poto outside town: a village of mud huts where women pound cassava with a pestle while children play, splashing one another with the water they are carrying in buckets. On this occasion, a group of men sitting cross-legged on the ground were cutting one another's hair; another group were carving wood to make statuettes to sell in the market. They held a rough piece of wood between the soles of their agile feet, using their prehensile toes to hold it exactly in the right position. I watched, fascinated, as an African face emerged from a lump of wood, its expression, its eyes and lips beautifully carved in great detail, even to the wrinkles at the corners of the eyes.

'I would like to buy the carving he is just starting,' I said to my driver as one man picked up a fresh piece of wood. 'When will it be ready and how much will it cost?'

After a conversation between the two of them, my driver explained that the sculptor did not know about Western ideas of time. He had no watch and there were no clocks in the village. He counted in sunrises and sunsets. The best thing would be for me to leave it to him, he would drive into Poto-Poto in a few days, pick up the carving and tell me how much it cost.

We wandered about the village; I had been careful not to

bring a camera or a handbag because I did not want to look like a tourist. No-one spoke any language I knew so all we could do was smile at one another.

In the centre of the village was a much larger hut with a thatched roof and a packed-earth floor. This was the Sunday afternoon meeting place. It was crowded with people, sitting at tables and standing about. At one end was a bar. 'What would you like to drink?' my driver asked. There was no wine, no beer, just soft drinks like Fanta, Sprite and Coca-Cola. 'I'll have the same as you,' I replied. My driver found us two chairs at a table and as I sat down, I realised that everyone was staring at me – I was the only non-African in the whole crowded room. People were friendly but curious. They looked me up and down, noting my shoes, my clothes, my face. I smiled at them and they smiled back.

I knew that my driver would look after me.

A group of strong, virile-looking young men, naked to the waist, very dark-skinned and very muscular were squatting on the floor opposite us. They had a selection of drums of all shapes and sizes in front of them. The moment the drums started to play the crowd fell silent. They played many different rhythms and seemed to produce sound waves that put my soul in harmony with the universe and the people (perhaps similar to the vibrations produced by the didgeridoo). No other instruments were necessary.

Couples started to dance; some men danced in groups, but there were no unpartnered girls – they were proud and shy. I was overwhelmed by the powerful beat of the music and the grace of the dancers, all barefoot. Some of the women were monumentally tall, others enormously fat, but the moment they started to sway to the beat of the drums they were all graceful. Their black skin was radiant, their teeth so white (they ate no sweets, cakes, biscuits or ice-cream) when they smiled. They all looked healthy, well-fed and happy. I wondered why Europe and America didn't import missionaries from Africa to teach us how to live contented, healthy lives. The contrast with the haggard unhealthy-looking faces of people going to work in the morning in Paris or London, crowding into the Metro or the Tube, was striking. I also thought of couples dancing in night-clubs in Europe and America, tight-lipped and serious, concentrating on getting the steps right or holding serious con-versations while they danced; hardly anyone looked as though they were having a good time. Here everyone was thoroughly relaxed and obviously enjoying themselves.

The women wore close-fitting bodices, their hips swathed in elegantly draped brightly-coloured skirts, some gathered to one side of the waist. On their heads they had arranged brightly coloured kerchiefs, often of the same material, twisted and tied with an upturned point to one side in a most chic manner. I could have watched them for hours.

Suddenly from nowhere a tall, elegant, very dark-skinned woman appeared in front of me. Towering over me where I sat, she said something I did not understand in a guttural, impera-tive voice. It sounded quite menacing. Then she beckoned me to follow her. I looked at my driver questioningly but he just nodded. 'She wants you to go with her,' he explained.

I rose and followed her, wondering where on earth we were going.

She led me to the centre of the dance floor. The drums started and we danced. She was teaching me to dance the African way. No-one joined us, they all sat round on the floor, watching. I took off my shoes and did my best to copy her movements. She encouraged me with a smile from time to time, showing me how to move my arms, how to sway my hips. It was an incredible experience, one I shall never forget. I felt we were engaged in a language-free dialogue. Complicity and understanding gradually grew between us. After a while, the drums changed to European-style music. They started to play a cha-cha-cha. I was at home with that and my companion happily copied my movements. Everyone watched admiringly. Then a waltz. Then a tango. After that some more African dances. A warm feeling of goodwill and harmony engulfed us.

Being married to a Frenchman did have the occasional advantage: having two passports, French and British, was useful because most countries I worked in favoured one or the other and I rarely needed a visa. Except for Egypt, which at that time didn't much like either. While working on a conference there I had a United Nations *laissez passer* but if I wished to stay on an extra week to explore the country, I had to report to an Egyptian police station every morning.

On one such visit to Egypt I stayed with Gaby (my friend from the Secretariat) and her family. She took leave in order to show me around Cairo for a few days before I went on to Alexandria for a WHO conference (WHO has a regional office there). Aristocratic Copts, the family's hospitality was limitless; they took pride in their generosity to guests and took me to dinner at various cousins' houses, where we sat on cushions on the floor at low, latticed tables. Water bowls and elegant pitchers were held out for us by courteous servants so we could wash our hands before helping ourselves to food. I was introduced to *Pain du Palais*, a sort of sweet bread or cake dripping with honey which we had with strong sweet black coffee, sitting on low cushions in coffee-houses. We usually travelled in horse-drawn open 'fiacres' in a most dignified fashion, my friend's mother sitting very upright opposite us. However when the time came to pay the driver, she would argue about the fare in a most undignified way – this seemed to be the expected thing to do – and was always reluctant to give a tip. She explained to me in

French that one should not tip too much or the drivers would come to expect it.

My kind hosts were so anxious to protect me from tourist traps, beggars and thieves, they wouldn't let me out of their sight. If I went into a shop they came with me and often stopped me buying something that had taken my fancy because they protested that it was too expensive. I asked if they would take me to see the pyramids. My hosts were amazed: why would I want to see them? They were just piles of old stones, all in ruins, that's all. There would be a lot of tourists and it would be very hot. On the other hand (it was suggested), there were some wonderful modern hotels in town where we could have a look round and then take afternoon tea. They could take me to Shepherds, for example, which had a waterfall in the middle, going all the way from the top floor to the atrium on ground level, and there was live music in the afternoon and evening.

When we had visited most of the modern hotels and all of the cousins, I raised the subject of the pyramids again and at long last we drove to El Gizeh in an air-conditioned taxi. It was hot and dusty in the desert and my friends were not very keen. They waited for me in the shade while I had a quick look at the pyramids and the sphynx. I was disappointed the sphynx wasn't bigger. I asked my friend to take a picture of me in front of it, with a row of camels behind me. I knew Marc would be thrilled to take a picture of the sphynx and camels to school. As Gaby adjusted the camera, the camel driver grabbed me by the waist and sat me on the nearest camel. I screamed, the camel driver gave orders in Arabic and the camel rose – first one end sending me backwards, then the other sending me forwards – and walked round in a circle. The camel-driver's aim was to charge me for a ride. I paid up like a good tourist but my friends were furious. I should not have paid, they said, as I hadn't asked for the ride. They shouted Arabic abuse at the camel-driver, who shouted

Arabic abuse back at them and I was glad to get in the car and be driven back to the hotel.

I dared not raise the subject of a visit to Cairo Museum with my overprotective hosts. Instead, I hatched a secret plan. After the conference in Alexandria I would come back to Cairo alone to do some real sightseeing. As well as the museum, a shopping spree at the Khan El Khalili copper market was on my list. And the glimpses I'd had from the car window of the Nile, the graceful feluccas gliding swiftly along the peaceful water, their one triangular sail rounded by the wind, made me want to enjoy it unhurriedly.

So a couple of weeks later I was getting off the train from Alexandria at the chaotic Cairo railway station. There were people everywhere, rushing in all directions, shouting to one another in Arabic. I put my heavy case down a moment while I looked for the taxi stand but before I knew what was happening, a fat, ragged porter had picked it up, put it on one shoulder, and was running out of the station with it. 'Stop, porter! Wait for me!' I cried but he didn't stop. Apparently he spoke no English. I spoke no Arabic so all I could do was run after him and hand him some piastres when he held out his hand. He had deposited my case in a run-down looking car on the outskirts of the station area. I would have preferred the more modern looking taxi-cars at the taxi rank. However, what was done was done so I jumped into the car and sat next to my case. I announced the name of the hotel I'd booked at, but the driver seemed to pay little attention to me. He drove off as fast as he could, amid much coughing and spluttering of the engine. The car windows were down but there were no handles to wind them up. Oh, well, the breeze was pleasant in the heat even though it made a mess of my hair. There seemed to be no floor to the car except down the middle. It was rather disconcerting to look down and see the road rushing past underneath me. I made sure my feet were safely on the middle piece and held my handbag tightly to my chest. We passed the giant statue of Ramses II, towering above us.

I tried to establish some sort of contact with the driver but he waved me to leave him alone to concentrate on the driving. It is true that traffic was speeding past in all directions. The engine wheezed and jolted every time we slowed down. I decided the best thing to do was just sit back, relax and hope for the best.

After some time we were out of the city centre and driving as fast as we could along a main road away from the traffic. 'Please, driver,' I said two or three times, but he took no notice of me whatsoever. So I just kept repeating the name of my hotel. 'Hotel Zara. Hotel Zara please.' My brain started ticking over now the panic was past and I realised that we were no longer in the busy part of Cairo. Surely my hotel was in the city centre? I had chosen one near the museum. Where was the driver taking me ? He obviously had some sort of deal with the porter.

The driver looked unwashed and unshaven; he wore a grubby long-sleeved shirt with a stained black waistcoat. There was no taxi meter. I had been crazy to get in this car without checking it was a proper taxi. But if I hadn't I might have lost my suitcase.

By now we were out in the countryside. Nobody in sight, just fields. Gradually I began to understand that I had been kid-napped. Or was it my suitcase that had been stolen, and I just happened to be there too? Where was he taking me? He seemed to know exactly where we were going. I had better prepare a plan of action for when we arrived. I thought desperately. I knew foreign passports were very valuable in Egypt, perhaps the driver would let me go if I gave him one of mine – I would still have the other. He would probably take my money too, so if he let me go, how would I pay for a taxi back to the hotel?

Just then, the car started to make strange noises and suddenly heaved, jolted and stopped at crossroads. From nowhere, children materialised with an unhealthy-looking monkey they put on my lap and forced to dance, with jangling bells and cymbals. From the other side a grubby hand appeared with an array of tattered postcards. I tried in vain to push up the window but there was no escape, so I held my handbag tight on my knees and wondered what on earth to do.

A man appeared and started talking excitedly with my driver, who got out of the car. The two of them opened the bonnet and disappeared under it. This was my Big Chance! Summoning all my energy and courage, I rose, pushed away the monkey, the postcards and the begging hands, grabbed my suitcase and escaped from the car. I set off in the direction we had just come. Looking back, I could see two rather fat trousered behinds under the open bonnet of the car. I had gone quite a way before the driver realised I was no longer there and started shouting. Resolutely, I kept walking. The case was heavy and getting heavier by the minute, the midday sun was beating down on me, I was wet with perspiration. But I kept on walking, ignoring the shouting. I walked and walked. After a while, I stopped for a breather, changing the suitcase to the other hand. In the distance, the driver was still shouting. I hadn't paid my fare. My old Anglo-Saxon self almost made me go back and give him some money. But my tougher European self made me keep on walking.

Eventually a car came along and I was able to get a ride back into town. When finally I reached the Hotel Zara the gold-braided doorman refused to let me in. I can't say I blamed him: my hair was stuck to my head with perspiration, I was covered with dust, my clothes were dirty and exhaustion made it difficult for me to speak. Fortunately I had in my handbag a letter from the hotel, confirming my reservation.

My Egyptian friends were probably right: travelling without them was not such a good idea.

Marc loved the photograph of me on a camel, my mouth wide open, screaming, both legs in the air and a petrified expression on my face. So did his teacher.

I was packing my suitcase one December for a trip to Alexandria, once again for WHO. I had already written all my Christmas cards and bought all my Christmas presents, including a furry musical donkey. When wound up, it played a nursery rhyme and the donkey's head turned round and round, its long, soft, furry ears waving forwards and backwards. I knew my new baby niece would love it and take it to bed with her, and the music would be the signal to close her eyes and go to sleep.

When in Egypt earlier, I had been struck by the poverty and, travelling around in my spare time, had noticed the fact that the children had no toys. They played in the mud by the riverside, or in the dust, with sticks and stones and were delighted if they found something out of the ordinary to play with. I was ashamed to think how spoilt my family was and how many toys, chocolates and sweets I had accumulated for them for Christmas. So I decided as I was packing to take the toy donkey and some of the sweets and lollipops with me to give to the deprived children of Egypt. I would buy another donkey when I got back.

It was a two-week conference, so I had a free Sunday. I booked a seat on a bus trip out into the countryside, visiting some villages on the way. Excitedly I packed a carrier bag with all my treasures, happily thinking of the joy they would bring. I managed to find a window-seat on the coach. When we stopped in a village the driver said we would be there for half an hour; everyone scrambled off the bus into the heat to have a look round. After exploring a bit I found a group of barefoot children in rags, with matted, dirty hair. I called them over and distributed my treasures. They opened wide their beautiful dark brown eyes and thanked me politely in Arabic, running off shyly with their gifts clutched to their chests. I explained in gesture to one of the children that the sweets were to be eaten and she put one reluctantly into her mouth, then ran into a doorway where she thought I couldn't see her and spat it out in disgust. After a few minutes, my mission accomplished and feeling quite faint with the heat, I climbed back into the coach where it was slightly cooler. As I put my head back to relax, happy that I had brought joy to some Egyptian children, I realised that out of the window I could see my group of children playing outside a squalid hut in an alleyway. The girl with the bag of sweets passed them round, they each took one, pulled a face and spat it out in disgust. Then I heard shouting. Further up the alley the little boy with the musical donkey was being beaten mercilessly by his mother, who had taken the toy from him. It was not difficult to imagine the envy and trouble that toy donkey would cause until the mother managed to sell it, probably as an Egyptian souvenir to a gullible visiting tourist.

Next time I wanted to give something to the children, I went to the local market and purchased some of the fruit the local people were buying.

It was in the mid-1960s that I took another trip to India, once again for for the Smallpox Eradication Campaign.

I had to keep up to date with my vaccinations and inoculations for smallpox, yellow fever, cholera and poliomyelitis, because sometimes I had only a few days' notice of a conference in countries where these diseases were endemic, especially if there was a sudden emergency or disaster. I had a yellow WHO

health booklet to keep an account of vaccinations and inoculations. Unfortunately this time I had been away and had left my
smallpox vaccination to the last minute. The reaction was at its
worst when I arrived in Delhi, so I spent the whole time
travelling around on buses, sitting next to peasants accompanied
by hens and pigs, with a big red open pus-oozing sore on my
upper arm. This sore was the joy and delight of the WHO
doctors in India when I arrived – they said I had one of the best
reactions they had ever seen. I was not to cover it up, they said,
it needed air to dry. They took photographs of my arm to put
in their brochures advertising the anti-smallpox campaign.
Apparently my virulent reaction showed that I really needed the
vaccination; without it I would undoubtedly have caught the
disease.

Working time passed like a dream. I was free to spend
mornings sightseeing while the doctors were vaccinating
schoolchildren; the meetings requiring interpretation were held
in the afternoons so that the international team of doctors could
compare notes on what they had found in the villages and rural
areas surrounding New Delhi as well as in the city. Proudly they
reported on the number of schoolchildren they had vaccinated
each day, triumphant about the progress they were making
towards total eradication of the disease.

We had a free weekend so my colleague Gedda and I decided
to take a plane to Benares, the most sacred city of the Hindus,
and take a boat down the Ganges. Friday afternoon after work
we caught a rather small, not very clean, local plane. Looking out
of the window as we descended I saw that there was no airport.
We landed on a stretch of grass. As we came down the steps a
crowd of local people closed in on us: beggars, souvenir-sellers
and curious onlookers. The pilot climbed down and walked
round the aircraft removing whatever he could.

'I'll take these with me. Better be on the safe side!' he said.

Rickshaws were waiting and even some rather decrepit taxis. We hired one of the latter, sharing with two other passengers, and drove to Clarke's Hotel.

It was like stepping back into colonial times. The white-pillared front of the hotel was a mass of purple bougainvillea. Inside, the only form of air conditioning consisted of whirring ceiling fans. My room had an old-fashioned washstand and mosquito nets were draped over a big old four-poster bed. I stopped to glance at the menu posted outside the dining room and saw that supper that evening would consist of steak and kidney pudding or stew with suet dumplings; one of the desserts was suet pudding with jam and custard. The British Raj has a lot to answer for.

We were up at four on Saturday morning for we had to be on board our boat before sunrise. The riverbank was busy with pilgrims washing, shaving and praying. You had to be immaculately clean before you could immerse yourself in the waters of the sacred river. One man performed a form of yogi hygiene through the nose and mouth, standing in the shallow water at the edge of the Ganges. The barbers were busy combing and trimming beards and cripples and blind men were being led towards the water. Among them wandered the usual skeletal cows and hungry eat-anything-that-came-their-way goats.

Our boat had a flat wooden deck and crooked rows of what looked like kitchen chairs. We sat next to a gracious Indian woman who smiled at us as we sat down and later told me her name was Mira. We had brought cameras but felt reticent about taking them out of our bags.

The boat set off. We paid our fares and looked around. Slowly the enormous orange sun rose through the mist and as it did so, the thin ragged people on the ghats (steps) on both sides of the river filled brass vases with the grey Ganges water and poured it solemnly over their heads. Others bent to pick up a passing stick which they dipped in the water and used to clean their teeth. The ghats were crowded as more and more people came down to the water's edge.

'The mantras chanted on the banks of the Ganges today are the same as those chanted five thousand years ago. You see that smoke rising over there?' Mira asked. 'Well, that is a cremation. Hindus believe the soul cannot leave the body except by fire.'

I could see a goat and a cow nuzzling the straw and the shrouded corpse.

'Those people standing by are the family watching the body burn.'

I also saw two children playing with kites, running unconcernedly round the funeral pyres.

'It is the body of a man – the sheet is white,' she said. 'For a woman, the sheet is red.'

As the boat progressed down the Ganges, I stared disbelievingly at the grey bundles floating by, obviously human bodies wrapped in a shroud, tied about with string. My Indian friend followed my gaze thoughtfully and said gently, 'Some bodies are not cremated for it is not always necessary. Pleasure comes from the skin, therefore evil enters the body through the skin. If the skin has been purified by certain diseases such as smallpox or chickenpox, there is no need to burn. We do not cremate Brahmins either or young children. They are given to the Ganges with a big flat stone. Sometimes the stone comes loose and the body rises to the surface.'

'The people bathing themselves in the river and cleaning their teeth in it must be well and truly immunised against smallpox by now. The survival of the fittest,' I whispered to Gedda.

A distinguished-looking gentleman sitting in front of us turned round.

'These people do not understand what's good for them!' he

said in a harsh voice that reminded me of Gérard. 'I am here for a smallpox vaccination campaign and you wouldn't believe the trouble we have getting them to accept vaccination.'

He was one of the delegates from our Delhi conference but he had not recognised us.

I was beginning to understand the Hindu belief that if children who had died of smallpox went straight up to heaven, then smallpox was a short cut and saved them a life of hardship.

That night at Clarke's Hotel, I picked up some magazines in the hotel lobby while waiting for Gedda to come down to dinner and on the front cover of an Indian Medical Association magazine was a cartoon showing an ugly white-overalled doctor brandishing an enormous syringe. His face was diabolical. Beside him was a bottle marked SMALLPOX VACCINE. A mother was holding out her innocent, terrified, wide-eyed baby. The caption was in Hindi but there was no doubt as to its intent.

On the last evening of the conference I set out in a rickshaw to explore Old Delhi. There were crowds everywhere. Religious men daubed with ashes wandered past. Blind beggars, many of whom had the white eyes of trachoma, shuffled by or sat on street corners. Buffalo carts and young men on dilapidated bicycles (but why do they always ride their bicycles with their knees sticking out?) occupied the streets. Cows wandered about freely, helping themselves to vegetables and fruit for sale on the stands. So much poverty. I felt ashamed of my smart handbag and comfortable shoes and glad I hadn't brought my camera.

I left the rickshaw in the central square and wandered on foot down a side street. It was there I came across the smallest shrine I had ever seen. It was the size of a doorway. Over the lintel was a bas-relief of a scowling female face with painted black hair and eyebrows and a scornful scarlet mouth downturned at the corners. On the black hair was a twisted scarlet and gold scarf.

Inside the tiny shrine the walls had been whitewashed. There were a few small shelves with offerings of flowers, brass vessels, garlands of marigolds and smouldering incense sticks. The walls were covered with *ex-voto* red handprints expressing gratitude to the goddess for whisking off a child to a better place. It was a shrine to Sitala, the goddess of smallpox.

The smallpox eradication campaign started in 1967; the last endemic case was reported in Somalia in October, 1977. Exactly two years later WHO announced officially that smallpox had been eradicated. Only two known samples of the virus remained, one in a US laboratory and one in the USSR. We believed that was the end of smallpox.

The plane to Uganda was delayed at London airport and we spent three hours waiting on the tarmac. When finally we reached Uganda we had missed a meal and were ravenously hungry.

During the flight I discovered André from Paris sitting in the seat in front of me. As soon as we had checked into our rooms we hurried down to the dining room.

'It's after midnight,' we were told. 'All the restaurants are shut in the hotel and in town. The only places open where you could get something to eat are the nightclubs.'

So André and I, tired though we were from the long journey, ended up in a nightclub dancing the cha-cha-cha and drinking whisky while waiting for a much needed sandwich.

The next morning I joined a group of five colleagues having breakfast together: my friend Catherine, André and three other men, the oldest of whom was Armand, who always took over and told everyone what to do. Not only was Armand rather bossy, he was also very, very mean. He would spend precious time arguing with shop-owners to get discounts on everything he bought, even postcards. I hated going to a restaurant with him because he always contested the bill. He argued with hotel receptionists when checking out and if he succeeded in getting a few francs taken off, was so triumphant he would boast about it for hours.

We decided we couldn't waste our free Sunday, so we would hire a car and take a refreshing boat trip on Lake Victoria. We wouldn't be given our subsistence allowance in local currency until Monday when the conference opened, but we could hire a car from the hotel using our credit cards and between us we had enough local money to pay for the boat. So the six of us set off in a taxi from Kampala, over the bumpy roads, swerving violently onto the roadside grass every now and then to avoid carts pulled by buffaloes. Finally we reached the boat-hire place. It was a run-down looking hut; a thin man in rags was in charge.

Armand negotiated with the boat-man who, in his limited English, told us that they would hold four people only. They looked pretty dilapidated to me. The boatman insisted that for six people we needed two boats but Armand slapped down the exact amount for one boat, brushed the man aside, and told us all to get in. I put the strap of my shoulderbag round my neck and clutched my camera on my knees as we set off.

Two of the men were rowing and at first we made pretty good speed. When we saw crocodiles we went further away from the shore because, even though they were absolutely still, as if dead (and looked rather like plastic ones I had seen in Disneyland), they were nevertheless very large and rather impressive. I have since been to Kakadu and seen crocodiles there, but never have I seen such enormous ones and so many of them along the bank. We were packed in the boat so tightly that I couldn't even raise my arms to take a photograph of them without running the risk of capsizing the boat so I decided to do without.

Armand was waxing poetic next to me – he told me later it was my hair caressing his face in the breeze (I wore it up in those days but strands always came loose) – and time passed very pleasantly until suddenly a wind blew up and the water started to get rough. It was then we noticed the water in the bottom of the boat.

We were too heavy – we had sunk down quite a way. Gradually the water in the bottom of the boat got deeper until it was up to my knees; I struggled to keep my bag and camera dry. Then there was a sudden gust of wind, the boat tipped sideways and in a few seconds we were all floundering in the water. Fortunately (I am not a good swimmer) it was not deep and we managed to stand, splashing about, trying to keep our balance in the moving water, trying to hold on to our possessions. My bag was still round my neck. I instantly decided not to risk looking for my camera (which must have been at the bottom of the brown, muddy water by then), but to scramble ashore like everyone else before the crocodiles bestirred themselves.

A stroke of luck! I looked up and saw a small sandy beach, miraculously crocodile-free. The only problem was that it appeared to be fenced off and was guarded by a Ugandan soldier. He was dressed in a navy blue serge uniform with boots; on his head he wore a navy blue béret with a badge. A machine-gun was slung over his shoulder. I pulled myself up out of the water and scrambled towards him.

He scowled and unslung his gun.

'You can't land here,' he growled, gesturing me back with the gun. 'Government property.'

His black skin was shiny with perspiration. His eyes were bloodshot. My immediate thought was that perhaps he was drunk or on some sort of drug. One thing was sure: he was not in a good mood and he looked as though he meant business.

The other five stood at the edge of the water clutching their wet things, watching me hopefully. For once Armand seemed content to leave the bartering to me.

In a flash I remembered the emergency cache of American dollars tucked in the inside pocket of my bag. The next moment I was waving them in front of him and his whole attitude changed.

'Can you drive us back to our car down that way?'

He muttered something about six passengers being too much for his car. Catherine came up behind me with a few more dollars. He grunted and ungraciously led us to his jeep. We all piled in. We were saved. Now we just had to appease the boat-owner . . .

Later, the whole conference was taken on safari for the weekend in two military aircraft. After dinner in the evening there was dancing at the lodge to a good dance band. The dance floor was well lit; the tables all round it each had a candle. I was dancing with a colleague. Looking over his shoulder out into the night, I saw shining lights dotted about in the darkness. Staring at them, I realised the small shining lights were in pairs. Then I understood: they were eyes. Leopards' eyes. All day long from early morning humans had been looking at the animals. Now it was their turn. The wild animals had come to see the humans. To watch them dance in the bright light. I was a little unnerved at first but one of the guides explained that we were quite safe – the leopards would stay out in the dark. They would not step forward into the light. No barrier other than the light was needed.

Once upon a time I was the only woman at an official banquet somewhere in Africa, under a thatched roof held up by a few slim timber poles. Behind the long table displaying a magnificent array of food stood the government dignitaries in their colourful robes and elegant headdresses. Smilingly they beckoned me to come forward, as the only woman, to help myself first to the food. Not one dish looked familiar. In fact, there was nothing on display I recognised as ever having eaten before. The centrepiece was a pedestal dish piled high with what looked like fat, white, shelled prawns.

Suddenly I recalled a scene when, having just arrived from the airport in Dakar, I was shown my hotel room and, drawing back the faded curtains, I had stepped out on to the balcony, attracted by the sound of happy children's voices. Outside was a tall spreading tree. Round it children ran and jumped, laughing, jostling one another to catch berries as they fell from the tree into the tin cans they were holding. The bigger boys were climbing the lower branches to shake them; others were throwing sticks into the upper branches to dislodge the fruit. The little ones gobbled up as many as they could, and then ran for more. I smiled as I watched them, wondering if I dared to take a photo, finally deciding not to behave like a tourist. So I waved to them instead. As I watched, a boy nearby held up his tin can towards me, offering me a taste. I looked more closely and realised that what they were eating was not berries. They were live caterpillars.

So, avoiding the fat white prawns – or rather, caterpillars – I delicately served myself to everything else, apologising that I was not very hungry. The prime minister himself came round the table and stood beside me. 'My dear,' he said in a rich Oxford accent as he put one arm round my waist. 'You eat like a bird! I insist: you *must* try this special delicacy.' And with that he heaped a generous helping of the raw caterpillars on to my plate.

There was nothing for it but to swallow them, for the sake of international relations. After all, in France, I enjoyed snails (mainly because of the parsley and garlic sauce) and frogs' legs, and in fact the caterpillars were no worse than eating snake and eel, which I'd been obliged to do on other occasions.

Writing about Africa also reminds me of a Women's Conference in Geneva. After a grim exchange about clitorectomy, the delegate from Ghana announced that legislation had recently changed in her country so that wives were no longer the property of their husbands. Now, when a husband died, his wife could no longer be left to another man in his will. She was very proud and happy; there was a round of applause.

Later a discussion took place about the advantages of breast-feeding. A beautiful African woman wearing a scarf wound round her head and twisted in a most elegant fashion, complained that the experts repeatedly said that each breast should be given in turn. This was not possible in her country, she explained, because the right breast was reserved for one's husband.

Chapter 14

My affair with Janek continued happily. He made life with Gérard bearable and I was gradually able to forget my humiliating confrontation with Monique, Gérard's mistress, at the firm's Christmas party.

One evening, I was hurrying to get the children ready for bed. Gérard was in New York for a week and to my delight Janek had arrived in Geneva the previous day and I had invited him to dinner. I felt so excited. It was the first time I had dared to invite him to my home and I felt very adventurous. I had planned an ambitious meal, bought a bottle of good wine and I was anxious to start cooking. I had given Mary-Ann the evening off and I tried not to appear too anxious for her to leave but it was difficult. 'Take my car,' I offered, 'but don't put the handbrake on when you park or it may freeze to the tyre.'

My excitement must have rubbed off on Steffi; she was particularly cantankerous that night. Fortunately Marc had some sleep to catch up on after a week away – a school excursion in the mountains, skiing – so there was no trouble getting him to bed.

'The bathwater's too hot!' Steffi cried, letting out a wail. I tried it with my hand. It was quite all right.

'When I was a little girl and the bathwater was too hot, do you know what my mummy did? She used to spread the flannel out like this for me to sit on. Here we are. Now, you try sitting on the flannel and the water will be much cooler, you'll see!'

She sat down gingerly, an incredulous expression on her face.

At last the children were in bed, Mary-Ann had left and the dinner was cooking. When the doorbell rang I rushed to open it, flushed with excitement and heat from the oven, my hair falling down my neck in wisps, still wearing my apron.

'Would you like to meet the children?' I asked Janek. He sat on Stephanie's bed and Marc came to join us, chattering about his week's ski camp in St Cergue. He had won his badge for cooking. 'First you half-fill the saucepan with snow, then you put in the potatoes,' he explained very seriously.

I stood in the doorway in my apron, enjoying the scene, feeling strangely moved. Janek told them a Polish story about birds, foxes and a wise old man and they drank in every word.

'Why don't you come to see us often?' Marc asked.

Janek laughed, pleased.

'You'd better ask your mother,' he replied, looking at me significantly.

Once the children were tucked in bed and the lights turned out, we were able to have dinner.

'What do I do if your husband walks in?' he asked, smiling.

'He won't – he's in New York,' I assured him. 'But it would be funny if he came home early, wouldn't it?'

The danger of the situation appealed to us both. It added spice to the evening.

Le 5 à 7 was a French tradition, after all, for many happily married women. Their husbands came home from work at about 7 p.m., so the wives' lovers could safely visit them between 5 and 7 in the evening.

After dinner we sat in front of the log fire in the half-light and I poured Janek a glass of brandy.

Looking at me sideways, playing with his glass of brandy, holding it up to see the reflection of the flames in the amber liquid, Janek asked in a quiet, determined voice, 'Have you ever thought of leaving Gérard?'

'No, no,' I cut him off before he could say any more. 'No, it isn't possible.'

I refused even to consider the matter. It would be admitting defeat: the failure of my marriage. And how could I deprive the children of their home, their stability? Gérard had his faults but he was still their father. It was unthinkable.

Janek stared into the fire for a while before standing up, dignified, and placing his empty brandy glass on the table.

'I want to marry and have children of my own,' he said firmly. 'I would be a good father to Marc and Stephanie, but I also want children of my own.'

Stiffly he put one hand on my shoulder and kissed me on the forehead.

'Think about me sometimes,' he whispered. Then, formally: 'Thank you for a lovely dinner and a pleasant evening,' and he was gone. I was devastated. That was that. I was sure I would never see him again.

Miserably I went to bed and lay in the dark, remembering every word that had been said, every glance, every gesture. The look in his eyes. The way his eyes spoke more than his words. The uncanny way he had of answering my thoughts.

I would just have to pull myself together and soldier on.

Time went by and, as I feared, I heard nothing of Janek. Mechanically I went about my life and gradually a loveless existence became normal again.

One Friday evening Gérard came home earlier than usual.

His neck and shirt collar were marked with bright red lipstick. I was embarrassed for him and asked Mary-Ann to put the children to bed quickly so they wouldn't see the lipstick and ask questions. When Gérard and I were alone, he explained that he had left work early to take Monique to the airport.

'She's gone,' he said sighing dramatically. 'It's all over. It was no good: she wants marriage and children. I told her I could not possibly leave my family. So she has gone back to Holland to start a new life. It was very upsetting at the airport, saying goodbye.'

His hair was beginning to turn grey at the temples. He looked tired and rather pathetic.

He turned away. 'I shall sleep in my study tonight.'

Next morning Gérard announced that we were going to have a grand reconciliation. He had a present for me: a bottle of French perfume. (He was buying one at the airport for Monique as a farewell gift, so thought he might as well get two.) He would take me out to dinner that night, we were going to make a fresh start. How would I like to go on holiday, just the two of us, to Greece or Spain?

The next day he brought me flowers.

Gérard made an effort to be more considerate and spent more time at home. We actually did go on holiday together to Spain. I was proud to be seen with Gérard. Despite everything I still loved him and hadn't given up hope of him loving me again. Perhaps optimism is the mother of stupidity.

Soon I was pregnant again.

In June 1962 my beautiful daughter Cassandre was born two months' premature and weighing less than two kilos. They rushed her into an incubator where she spent several weeks. I went home after a day or two, but every morning drove to the other side of the lake to the Clinique des Grangettes to deliver the milk I'd expressed. I did my best to turn myself into a placid milk-producing cow again. The sister at the hospital had great faith in beer and told me I should drink several bottles a day. I therefore spent much of my time in a very cheery frame of mind as I watched the level in the beer bottle go down and that in the milk bottle go up. No sooner had Cassandre come home than she developed double pneumonia and had to be rushed back into hospital. Cassie continued a delicate baby, small, frail and vulnerable. She caught every illness that was about and I spent night after night walking round the bedroom nursing her and singing 'Summertime' softly to soothe her and stop her disturbing her father in the next room. Gérard seemed to resent our closeness and had little time for either of us.

We planted a third cherry tree and dressed her in the Baumier christening gown for her christening ceremony and garden party.

The reconciliation with Gérard lasted a few months. At first he tried to be more considerate at home but gradually his bad temper got the upper hand and life returned to normal.

Fortunately his trips to Paris, Germany and Poland increased in number and length and were a welcome respite. They enabled me to have a life of my own, see friends, dance flamenco and sing in a choir where I made new friends. And I was very busy with the new baby, too.

I didn't care what Gérard was up to so long as I had my three beautiful children to cherish. Cassandre, with skin the colour of honey, looked so gorgeous in her pink dress and matching hair-ribbons that one weekend I entered her in a baby competition at fashionable Divonne swimming pool in nearby France. Cassie stole the heart of the judges each time she stumbled over, showing off her frilly pink knickers, and won second prize.

When Gérard was away, I was able to have dinner parties

without risk of embarrassment. When he was there he sometimes put his knife and fork down with a clatter if he found the
conversation uninteresting and announced, 'No coffee for me.
I have some work to do in my study.'

At first our guests would wonder what they had done to
offend him and whether they too should leave but after this had
happened a few times they were no longer surprised. There were
times when, having left us at the table, he would return
unexpectedly, throwing the door open dramatically so that we
all looked round, startled. He would stride into the room impor-
tantly and, cutting abruptly into the conversation, ask some
trivial housekeeping question such as: 'Will you take my suit to
the dry-cleaner tomorrow? I've left it on the bed. I shall need it
on Friday.' Or: 'When will my black shoes be back from the
menders?'

The first time this happened I commented on it afterwards
and he expostulated: 'Do you think Einstein, Newton, Descartes
and Pasteur were family men? Good husbands and fathers who
sat around at dinner parties being polite? No great discoveries
would ever have been made!'

Gérard shouted a lot. Shouting has always been difficult for
me to cope with. Especially when driving a car in France or
Italy, where abusing other drivers is mandatory – I do not have
the right vocabulary in any language and I am incapable of
expressive hand gestures, let alone putting my head out of the
window to yell insults about the other drivers' mothers. (Gérard,
of course, excelled at this.) My English upbringing has been
something of a handicap throughout my life. My parents never
raised their voices and I have no recollection of them ever being
anything but courteous – to each other as well as everyone else.
If they were going out to celebrate a birthday or an anniversary, they would each ask the other what they wanted to do.
Then they would each answer what they thought the other

wanted. The result was that they ended up doing something neither of them really wanted to do. But they were always very polite about it.

When Gérard started to shout I felt like the quiet eye of the cyclone. I was so used to having a volume control button in front of me when working, I always thought how convenient it would be if Gérard had one too.

Sometimes when he walked in the door I could see from his face that he was on the brink of an explosion and I would feel as if I were in Pompeii, waiting for the volcano to erupt.

Illness exasperated him. If any of us had a cold, Gérard seemed to think it was due to lack of intelligence – after all, *he* never caught any germs. And coughing drove him mad. He persisted in believing we did it on purpose to annoy him. When Marc broke his leg skiing, Gérard was furious and wouldn't even speak to him at first. How could he be so foolish as to break his leg? He had let his father down.

Perversely, he also resented Marc doing something better than him. He was very angry the first time Marc beat him when they had a swimming race at Divonne pool. And beside himself when Marc got his silver medal for skiing, aged ten.

'I could ski better than he does at the same age!' Gérard declared. 'And I didn't even have skiing lessons. I never went to ski-school, I taught myself.'

He raged about the kitchen where we were having breakfast, then slammed the door as he went out after his last word so that I couldn't reply – one of his favourite tricks. Stephanie sat behind her bowl of sugar puffs, her green eyes wide. She couldn't take them off her roaring Papa. Fascinated, she spooned sugar puffs into her cheek instead of her mouth. At last we heard his car drive off. But he was back two minutes later, opening the kitchen door and putting his head round it to bellow: 'I was way beyond his stage when I was only *five*!'

Gérard had always been hard to live with. He was convinced the maid was purposely ruining his underpants every time she washed them. Once or twice he had woken me with a start, rushing into the bedroom in the middle of the night, turning the lights on and shouting: 'They are full of holes, she is doing this deliberately! I insist you dismiss her tomorrow. Get rid of her!' So when we bought a new washing machine, Gérard maintained that the maid would not know how to use it properly and would surely break it. The honour therefore fell to me. I started by sorting all the clothes and bed linen into piles according to the various programmes. If Gérard had been particularly horrible, unkind to the maid or shouting at the children, I punished him by not doing his washing. Carefully I took out everything that was his: shirts, underwear, socks, handkerchiefs. Holding them at arm's length as if they might poison me, I put them in a corner out of sight.

There they remained for at least a week. Sometimes two. A disgusting pile of dirty pants and smelly socks. It satisfied me to know they were there unwashed. It was the only way I had to get back at him.

And then one evening he would come home from work in a good mood and say something normal. Something not even kind or considerate. Just the normal sort of thing anyone could have said. And with enormous relief, I would feel that all was well again. Gratefully and happily, singing to myself, I would go down to the laundry and do his washing.

He wouldn't even have noticed that it hadn't been done.

Gérard once upset our dentist by accusing him of drilling holes in his teeth one week, so he could fill them during the following appointment. The dentist was not amused.

Once I brought a curved grapefruit knife back from a trip to England. Gérard had never seen one before. He found it in the knife drawer and, brandishing it aloft, triumphantly proclaimed:

'Look what they've done to this knife! Nobody looks after things! And here I am, working to feed you all . . .'

Living with Gérard and keeping everyone around me relatively happy was a challenge. Every minute in his presence required armour; I had to be constantly alert. I doubt if I could have survived, sane, without my career, colleagues, friends and the children.

Looking back now, I have a lot to be grateful to Gérard for. Without his bad temper and lack of warmth, I might never have travelled at all – might never have danced the tango in Argentina or the samba in Rio; never ridden an elephant in Jaipur, a camel in Cairo, a donkey in Spain, a helicopter in Nice, a fiacre in Alexandria or a Vespa in Rarotonga. I would never have had caviar and lemon tea for breakfast in bed in Isfahan or supped on silver in Delhi. Had I been happily married, I would probably have been content to stay at home, bake cakes and knit jumpers for my children. As it was, every overseas conference offered an opportunity for escape.

I had not seen Janek for several years when one day, looking out of a window at the Palais des Nations, I caught a glimpse of him. It was lunchtime and he was leaving the building. The next day at about the same time, I contrived to be looking out of the same window and there he was again. After that, whenever I could I would watch for him. The way he walked sent a tender quiver through my whole body. Sometimes I would stand by the window in a daydream for a while.

Eventually, we bumped into each other. I had been hoping it would happen. Perhaps I jogged Fate's elbow just a little.

He explained that he now had a permanent job in Geneva, in one of the Specialized Agencies.

'Let's go and have coffee together.'

'All right,' I said. 'Just this once.'

As soon as we were seated in a nearby café he clasped my hand and said quietly, 'I still love you, I want you to know. I think about you all the time, whatever I am doing.'

'I think about you too. Perhaps we can see one another every now and then. That would be nice.'

'I want more of you than that.'

'You shouldn't waste too much time on me. You should be enjoying the company of eligible young ladies. Geneva is full of them. There is plenty of choice.'

'It's you I want.'

'You know I won't leave Gérard.'

'Well, just have lunch with me sometimes to cheer me up and I promise to look all the pretty girls over,' he said.

His long pale fingers on the tablecloth made me think of the music they drew from his violin. And the music they drew from me.

'If the music were without and not within, what a beautiful melody it would be,' I remembered reading somewhere.

We arranged to have lunch together the following week.

Inevitably we made love at his flat and I felt transported on a wave of tenderness. After that we found ourselves meeting occasionally at lunchtime just as we used to. It was as though we'd picked up exactly where we'd left off. When I had spent an hour or two with Janek I felt like a ripe pear enjoying the sun. Sometimes after he had gone back to work I would drive home, leave the car, and go for a walk in the woods. I felt so serene, I wanted to walk among the trees and feel part of them, their roots in the earth, their leaves catching the breeze, their branches stretching up into the sky.

About this time, someone asked me how long I had been in Geneva and I answered, 'I came here many years ago with one suitcase and now I have three beautiful, intelligent, healthy children, a house, a garden and a canary.'

'And a husband?'

'Oh yes, and a husband,' I added automatically.

One morning some months after our reunion, the telephone rang at home. It was Janek.

'I need to speak with you urgently. Lunch tomorrow?' I agreed.

We had hardly sat down and ordered our food, when Janek said abruptly, 'I need an answer. Will you divorce and marry me? I will do everything I can to make you and the children happy. I want children of my own – with you if possible. If it isn't possible, I need to know before I get any older. Yes, I have met someone – she is rather like you, actually. She wants to get married. She wants children too. I had to ask you again first, to be sure. If you will not change your mind, then I shall ask her to marry me.'

The words were businesslike and straightforward. But it seemed that all round us everyone had stopped breathing.

That was the last time I saw Janek. I had a phone call from him a few months later. 'Just to tell you we are getting married next Saturday.'

That Saturday I was at a British Legion fête with Cassandre. We walked around lucky dip stands, she rolled pennies, had a pony-ride, fished in a plastic fish-pond and I smiled at the people I knew through tears rolling down my face. I couldn't go home in case Gérard was there. I was too vulnerable to face him just then. I needed time to get my protective armour back. So Cassandre and I stayed out all day. It was late when we finally got home and I put Cassie straight to bed and crept into mine as quietly as possible in case Gérard was in his study.

Right or wrong, I had made my decision to stay with Gerard. But I'd always be grateful to Janek for showing me how to live passionately.

When Cassie was a year old, I had taken her to the paediatrician for her check-up. She seemed to have a slight limp. He sent us to see the orthopaedist who had examined her at birth, who studied her posture and backbone, measured her legs, and then made a shattering announcement. Cassie had been born with cerebral palsy. In fact she suffered from diplegia – in other words, the muscles on both sides of her body were not functioning normally. But those on the left side were considerably more affected than those on the right. Her left ankle was a problem: she would never be able to jump, for example, or walk down stairs one foot at a time; she would always have to put her right foot first. The orthopaedist wasn't sure whether she would ever be able to walk normally. Cassie had to start remedial treatment with a physiotherapist right away. All this had been known from the moment of her birth but her paediatrician had decided to wait until it became obvious before telling me. He handed me a disability certificate that would entitle Cassie to attend a special school for the disabled and go on special disabled holidays in the snow – she would never be able to ski of course. She would have to have a check-up once a year with an orthopaedist and would have to wear special shoes, the left one 'compensated' with a higher heel and thicker sole because of the difference in leg length.

I found all this difficult to absorb out of the blue. I crossed the road to a park, with Cassie in her pushchair, and sat on a bench for a long time, thinking it through.

When I told Gérard, he was furious. His children should be perfect: what had I done to cause this?

From then on Cassie and I visited Lucienne, her physio-therapist, three times a week. Lucienne and I patiently tried to get the thin little legs into a machine which by means of electric shocks, forced the leg and ankle muscles to spasm. It was the only way to make them work because Cassie was too small to understand exercises. She screamed with fear. I dreaded those visits. Lucienne was very patient but whatever we did, Cassie screamed. There was no pause in her screaming from the time we arrived until we left the building.

As she grew older, her knees were permanently grazed because she could not control her left knee and foot. When she tried to walk, they got in the way of the right leg and she fell over. She always needed a steadying hand. Sometimes she forgot and ran ahead but always fell over then cried furiously because she was so cross with herself.

'Marc has gym lessons at school,' I told her. 'You do too, now, with Lucienne.'

'Why do I keep falling over?' she would ask.

'Everyone has to learn to walk without falling over,' I tried to comfort her.

When she was about two, she had to have her tonsils out. I took her home afterwards and she seemed fine. Fortunately I got up in the night to check she was all right. I found her asleep on a blood-soaked pillow. Her sheet was covered with blood too. She was haemorrhaging badly. I wrapped her and her pillow in her blanket, carried her down, propped her up on the back seat of the car (there were no seat-belts then) and took her to the hospital without waking anyone else, leaving a note for Mary-Ann on the kitchen table. After she recovered we spent a few weeks in our chalet in Morzine where the mountain air did her a world of good. We went for walks in the meadows, fed the mountain goats, drank from mountain streams; the air at that altitude was invigorating and we loved to hear the clanging of the cow bells. I had never been in the chalet in the summertime before. Enthusiastically we discovered the mountain wildflowers and put vases of them everywhere we could in the chalet. We discovered the best places to pick wild strawberries and *myrtilles* (bilberries). We ate so many our tongues were dark purple;

I made bilberry jam, bilberry tarts and bilberry crumble. We became good friends with our neighbours and they showed us the good places to go 'mushrooming'. My very favourite mushrooms appeared after some rain: the delicately-flavoured, orange-coloured, unforgettable chanterelles.

The following year the whole family went to the south of France to spend Easter with Gérard's uncle and aunt. After a big Sunday lunch – there were twenty-five of us round the restaurant table – we went for a stroll into the pine groves. Everyone else was far ahead. I held three-year-old Cassie's hand and walked at her tottering pace, doing our best to keep up with the others.

Suddenly, Cassie ran on ahead. A bird? A lizard? Something had attracted her attention. She was a happy, loving child and wanted to stroke and love any creature that crossed her path. She fell. Both knees were bleeding, there were pieces of twig and dead leaves imbedded in the wounds. She sobbed uncontrollably, but not with pain. Rather with anger at herself and frustration.

It was a gentle country road through the woods, dappled with sunshine. There were a thousand shades of green and thyme underfoot scented the air around us.

I called out to Gérard and the others to carry on without us. They would find us waiting for them on their way back. Gérard shrugged his shoulders as much as to say, 'What's the problem this time?'

Cassie was still lying face down where she had fallen, her thin shoulders shaking with sobs, her eyes pink and swollen. I knew we had to have a talk.

I picked her up and wiped her knees clean with some tissues from my handbag. Spreading out my skirt so that she could sit on it too – those frail little legs would have found the ground very prickly – we settled on the dry bracken in the shade of a tree.

'Cassie,' I began. 'Do your knees hurt very much?'

'It's not *that*, Mummy. *Why* do I keep falling over?'

I took a deep breath. 'Your legs are not strong because you were in such a hurry to be born that you came out of Mummy's tummy too soon. Before you were really finished.'

Silence. She was thinking it over, trying to understand. Because she was so thin, her eyes seemed enormous.

'Other children who were ready when they were born can walk easily and not fall over. But for you it is more difficult. You have to try very hard to walk the same as the others.'

The expression on her face was one of puzzlement and relief. Relief at being told, at last, the truth. At being given the respect of an explanation instead of the evasive reassurances I had tried to soothe her with in the past.

'Your left leg and your left arm are not so strong as your right, you see, so it's better if you use your right leg – this one – to start off when you want to go upstairs or run or jump. That's why you spill your milk if you pick it up with your left hand.'

'Do I have to go into hospital and have something done?' She spoke in a very grown-up way.

'No, my love. *You* are the only one who can do something. Because it's not really your leg or your arm that is weak. It is the little part of your brain which tells your leg or arm what to do. So it can't ever get better. But what you *can* do is to learn to do things *your* way. If you try, you can do the same things as everyone else, you just have to do them *differently* or do them with the other arm or leg. I will help you. We have to do exercises, especially for your left ankle, to stretch the muscle. And if we do them every morning and every evening, we will give Lucienne a nice surprise.'

'Hmm.'

She sat still for a while, thinking. We were side by side, leaning back against the trunk of the tree and all round us the ground was alive with crickets and ants.

From that moment, everything changed. We worked together, Cassie co-operated and we no longer had to use the machine when we went to visit Lucienne.

Mary-Ann was in love. She had been over to England for her sister's wedding and had fallen in love with an attractive cousin of the bridegroom. We knew the romance was flourishing because the postman brought so many letters from England. Sure enough, one day she announced that she would be leaving to be married. When the time came, we tearfully drove to the airport to see her off. She had been part of our lives for so many years.

But I knew how I would replace Mary-Ann. Fortunately I was earning well and could afford to hire a physiotherapist full-time. My sister-in-law told me about her cousin in New Zealand, Margo, a young, fully-qualified physiotherapist who wanted to travel in Europe for a year or two before joining a practice back home. She was due to arrive in Europe in a few weeks. I telephoned her and she was delighted. It was all arranged. She would spend a year with us.

Margo was a very sensible, down-to-earth young woman and we took an instant liking to one another. She came with us to our sessions with Lucienne and later drove Cassie there in my car when I was away. Every morning and evening in the warm bathwater she helped Cassie with her exercises, adapting them to fit in with nursery rhymes and songs we could all sing. When she left after a year, I was able to take over, having watched so often, and as Cassie sat cross-legged on the carpet, I pushed down each knee in turn as we sang to the rhyme.

One urgent problem we had to deal with, because it was so noticeable, was her eyes. She seemed to lose control of her left eye and it wandered at random if she tried looking sideways. Her father was impatient and would shout: 'Don't look at me like that! You're going cross-eyed. I can't sit at the table with you looking at me like that.' Obediently she would get down from her chair and disappear until he had finished.

I discovered that if she looked straight ahead her eyes were fine, and taught her to turn her head and not her eyes, so that she was always looking straight ahead.

The following year the orthopaedist suggested surgery to improve the elasticity of the tendons in her left ankle by cutting little windows in them. I discussed this with Lucienne and Margo as well as with Cassandre herself. Instead of surgery we decided to concentrate on improving the use of her left ankle for a while and spent patient hours teaching her to climb a wall and go up and down stairs using her left foot as much as possible, also hopping with both feet together.

Lucienne was amazed at Cassie's progress. She had never seen such achievements and was so stunned when she looked at the soles of Cassie's shoes that she asked if she could take a photograph of them to put in her files and perhaps use in a medical paper. (The wear on the soles showed that she was walking almost normally.)

When Cassie was five, Gérard surprised us all by announcing one day that the mechanics who worked for him had made a trampoline for Cassandre. In 1968, trampolines were very rare, almost unheard of. We had discussed different ways of making her use her left leg and ankle without realising it and agreed she should ride a bicycle as soon as possible and that a trampoline would be a good idea if only we could find one.

It was a very exciting day when the trampoline arrived. In no time at all we had all the children from the neighbourhood jumping on it. Gérard and I tried it out, so did Marc and Steffi. Cassie soon became an expert.

She also loved climbing her cherry tree, which was doing its best to catch up with the other two. Sometimes she filled a bag with peanuts, sweets and biscuits and climbed to the top where she perched herself happily, enjoying her picnic and supervising what was going on in the house and passers by along the road outside the tall hedge.

Cassie rode to a nearby international school on her bicycle – I never used the special disability certificate which would have entitled her to go to a special school for the disabled. Nor did she go on the 'skiing for the disabled' holidays to which she was entitled. We took her to the mountains with us; she went to normal ski-school and was soon skiing more or less like all the other children. She even got her bronze medal.

On Mothers' Day Cassie wrote me a poem which, after singing my praises for two verses, ended with the punch line: 'I understand why you have so many lovers.' By 'lovers' she meant 'people who love you'. The fault is with the English language.

When she was seven, Cassie announced that she was inviting me out to dinner for my birthday. I chose my favourite Chinese restaurant. We dressed in our best and off we went. She was the perfect hostess, insisting I try this and that on the menu. She had emptied her money-box before leaving home and all her savings went to pay the bill. The waiter was amused to be paid in small coins by a beribboned, long-plaited schoolgirl.

At nine, she went on a week's school skiing holiday and broke her leg. I was in great anguish and didn't dare ask over the phone which leg had been broken. When I got there I was relieved to discover it was her good leg, so all was well. When she was ten, Cassie also got her silver medal for skiing.

At the age of eleven, a big decision had to be taken. The difference in length between her left and right legs was five centimetres. Our orthopaedist wanted to operate on her right leg to staple the bone at its growing points and prevent it from growing any more, so that the shorter leg could catch up. This surgery had been performed successfully in America and he wanted to be the first to do it in Switzerland. He seemed to think it was a foregone conclusion and all we had to do was set the date. Cassie and I were still in shock as we left the doctor's surgery, saying we would think it over and call him back.

We went into Movenpick Café and had tea (for me) and ice cream (for Cassie) to talk it over between us.

'He's going to ruin my good leg!' Cassie cried, letting the tears flow. 'There'll be scars all up my good leg! I want them to leave my good leg alone!'

Later I went for a walk along by the stream in the Versoix woods to think it over further. I believed in the body's ability to adjust. I had noticed during her examination, that the difference in length was apparent only when Cassie was lying down. When she stood up, her body adapted: the left side of her body adjusted, her left-side ribs spread a little more, she looked straight.

So we telephoned the orthopaedist and told him we had decided not to have the surgery. He was angry and I knew he thought I was a bad mother, not taking my responsibility seriously. She would never be able to have babies because she would not be straight, she would be crooked, he said. Since the muscles on her left side did not work properly, she would not be able to give birth normally in any case.

But, I thought, adapting is what life is about. Cassandre had adapted to her situation and seemed to have no problem walking or running. She was an excellent skier and horse-rider and later became a very keen dancer. Some years later she even won first prize in a disco-dancing competition and when the time came she gave birth normally to three healthy, beautiful children.

In 1969 Gérard was doing well on the stock exchange and bought himself a new sports car. He came home jubilant.

'Come on, we'll go out for a drive!'

I was glad we had left the children at home with the maid. Gérard had always been a fast driver but when he was feeling good his driving was hair-raising. When we drove straight through some red lights without stopping I couldn't repress a gasp.

'If you go fast enough it's not dangerous,' Gérard protested. 'It's slow drivers who are dangerous, they are the ones who cause accidents. I'm too fast to hit another car or be seen by a police-man. No-one can read my number-plates at this speed. Speed is definitely the answer.'

I was glad when we got home safely. There was something frightening about him when he was in high spirits.

Needless to say, there came the day when a letter arrived from the head office of the *Gendarmerie*. He opened it, then looked up:

'I have the maximum number of fines. Next time my driving licence will be taken away.'

He sighed, then his eyes fell on Marc.

'Marc, come here and talk to your Papa. You're a slim, agile, clever boy. Perhaps you could do something for me.'

Marc looked up, eager to please.

'What would you buy if you had a thousand Swiss francs?' he asked.

Marc hesitated. 'A motorised bicycle, a moped. Or perhaps a record-player. It would be difficult to choose.'

'Supposing I tell you a way to earn a thousand francs, would you do it?'

Marc could hardly believe his ears. He drew up a pouffe in a businesslike, manly way and sat at his father's feet.

'All I need is a piece of paper. It's in a file with my name on. You'd have to find the drawer marked 'B' for 'Baumier', then look in there under 'G' for 'Gérard'. Just one piece of paper. That would be worth a thousand francs, wouldn't it?'

Marc got a pencil and paper. He was taking the matter seriously.

'There's a narrow window under the ceiling in the room of the central police station where the files are kept. I could go there once or twice and then draw you a map of the place. I think you could get in through the little window. We would do it at night, preferably on a Sunday. I'll drive you there and wait for you. Just think of all you could get with a thousand francs.'

I listened disbelievingly. Then I jumped to my feet.

'I hope this is a joke!' I exclaimed.

'You keep out of this. This is between men, isn't it Marc? We don't want women getting involved. This is a business deal. Serious business.'

I was furious. 'For heaven's sake! What a way to bring up children!'

'Don't interfere, it's between my son and me. We don't want to know what you think.' He started hitting out at me and his glasses fell off. I grabbed them. He couldn't see to look for them. Why hadn't I thought of that before?

Marc disappeared into his room. Gérard thundered after me, but without his glasses he didn't stand a chance.

Gérard lost his driving licence. Of course it was all my fault because I had not allowed Marc to get the piece of paper through the *Gendarmerie* window. He found an excuse to dismiss his secretary (who was on the brink of a nervous breakdown anyway) and recruited another who lived near us and drove a car. One of her tasks was to drive him to and from work each day.

When finally Gérard got his licence back after six months, I heard him banging about one evening in the garage. He was exchanging the numberplates on our cars.

Everywhere I went after that, I was followed by police cars. They would pull me over to tell me they had been checking whether I had waited the required number of minutes at the 'Stop' sign. I had, but they wanted to warn me that they were checking. They pulled me up to say I had not exceeded the speed limit but I was close – they just wanted to warn me. When I drove into France, I was followed by a police car right up to the frontier control. The policeman came across to say that my tyres were all right now but would soon need changing. I also kept getting phone calls from irate people saying I'd squeezed them up on to the pavement in the rush-hour or overtaken them going round a corner and had to explain that it wasn't me. In the end I confronted Gérard and made him put our numberplates back as they had been.

Gérard's undeniable charm often got him out of trouble. A policeman always stood on traffic duty at Geneva's busiest intersection in the centre of town. To ensure he was visible, in addition to his white gloves and white baton, the policeman stood on a small round white platform. Every morning Gérard and a friend of his, who lived on the other side of town, timed their drives to work and compared notes when they got there. One morning, Gérard was in such a hurry, the stopwatch ticking away, that he not only knocked the policeman off his little white stand, he also drove across the intersection with the policeman on the bonnet of his car and then, when he fell off, ran over his toes. The policeman was taken to hospital. Gérard and his friend got together to decide what to do. It was bound to mean a big fine. That wouldn't be too bad; what would be more serious would be if Gérard lost his driving licence again. They came to the conclusion the only thing to do was to butter up the policeman. So Gérard went to visit him in hospital and took him some flowers. The following day he took him a bottle of wine. Amazingly it worked. He did not lose his licence. In the end all he had to do was pay the fine. The policeman was most apologetic about the fine.

In the early years of my marriage I couldn't bring myself to confide in friends. Perhaps it was a matter of pride. I once over-heard a colleague complaining, 'Valerie has it all – a charming husband, children, a nice home, a brilliant career. If anyone has to work on Saturday it should be her, not me; I don't have any of those things. It isn't fair . . .' The others murmured their agreement. *Little do they know*, I thought. I would have hated to disillusion them. But later, when I knew many of my friends had seen Gérard in town with his mistresses, I probably bored them to death with my marital problems. Talking them through helped enormously. My friend Christiane had endless patience, kindness and understanding. Over a glass of red wine one evening I was telling her about Gérard's latest scheme: 'Now he's decided the left side of his car needs re-painting so he's trying to get it done at the expense of an insurance company. If he sees a woman driver or an elderly man at the wheel of the car in front of him, he tries to manoeuvre so the cars touch and the damage is their fault. Last night he said, "I just missed getting a free re-spray for my car tonight. Only just missed! But I'll keep trying!" '

'Why don't you leave him?' she said thoughtfully, rubbing one finger round the rim of her glass.

'I couldn't uproot the children. It wouldn't be fair to them.'

'Marcus Aurelius said, "Oh Lord, grant me the serenity to accept the things I cannot change; the courage to change the things I can, and the wisdom to know the difference." You could each be happy with someone else. That makes four people who could be happy, apart from the children.'

'We've been playing games all these years. Take away the games and there'd be nothing left.'

But I never forgot that conversation. The words remained in the back of my mind, slowly germinating.

Chapter 15

The speakers at international conferences come from a range of countries and are there because they are at the forefront of their field. Working as a simultaneous interpreter, I was in contact with the frontline of new ideas and the latest research in many diverse fields. Often a meeting would be held on the last day to decide what to tell the public and I felt very privileged to know the whole story, even though I was bound by my oath of secrecy and could tell no-one.

I soon discovered the champagne of simultaneous interpreting. You feel on the crest of a wave when, on a good day, you are working well and finding expressions in utter freedom with no-one to contradict you or suggest alternatives. Sometimes, your eyes on the speaker; you feel you are deep in his thought processes, immersed in his speech. Your spirit is lifting you ever up, you are using words you haven't heard for years: specialised words that have risen from the dark depths of your mind, words you didn't know were there yet now when you need them you hear yourself pronouncing them.

Row upon row of listeners are hanging on your every word; pausing with you when you take a breath, following your every intonation. It is heady, it is stimulating, it is intoxicating.

In the course of my work I encountered many famous people: presidents, prime ministers, foreign affairs bigwigs and I even once met a king, Don Juan of Spain. There were eminent scientists and professors, astronomers, brilliant philosophers, businessmen–millionaires, well-known ambassadors and diplomats. I remember sitting on a sofa in someone's drawing room talking with thin, pink-faced Oppenheimer and being dazzled by his bright blue eyes. I recall the gentleness of Pandit Nehru and the intensity of Indira Gandhi, Marshal Tito's fatherly ways and the kindness of Fidel Castro. I interpreted for them during meetings and sometimes sat next to them later at dinner or chatted with them over cocktails. I even danced with some of them. Sometimes we would meet in airports and talk over a drink in the transit lounge. I once sat next to Cambodian prime minister Hun Sen in an aircraft on the way to a conference; he was an engaging companion and his conversation helped while away the hours.

I was working with Eric Simla, a permanent WHO interpreter, in the English booth in 1967 when Dr Christian Barnard came to Geneva for a Round Table on heart transplants and gave a commentary on the film of his first such surgical procedure.

Eric was a delight to work with and knew the names and symptoms of all the diseases in his three languages, as well as the names of all the vectors, symptoms, treatment and remedies. There were heart specialists and surgeons from all round the world at the table, including several who spoke French or Spanish and one or two Russians as well. The interpreters' task was complicated by the fact that, as this type of procedure was new, there were no documents to study ahead of time and the names of the immuno-suppressants had not yet been published. All we could do beforehand was study the anatomy of the heart.

But somehow Eric and I managed and, summoning all my willpower, I was able to continue interpreting in spite of feeling faint from the sight of so much blood on the screen. I had never witnessed surgery before and the initial incision by the gloved hand and the bleeding took me by surprise. When I left the meeting for a few moments to go down the corridor to the toilet, leaving Eric alone, I got another shock. Most of the offices I passed had loudspeakers on the wall so the staff could listen in. I had no idea people outside the conference room could also hear us.

The only glimmer of memory I have about that Round Table is that while all the other countries were very enthusiastic about what Dr Barnard was advocating, the USSR delegation was opposed to transplanting human organs and preferred to research the creation of artificial hearts.

After the 1973 Yom Kippur War, I interpreted for the English-speaking Israelis and the French-speaking Arabs. This was the first time they had agreed to meet with one another and talk. It had to be a circular table so that the question of 'head of the table' and precedence didn't arise. And the room had to have two entrances so each delegation had its own. It was an interesting meeting. One accused the other of not telling the truth.

'Are you accusing us of lying?'

'No, of course not. We would not do that. We are merely stating that you are not telling the truth.'

This went on for some time. I thought of Bertrand Russell's words: 'It is better for countries to fight with words rather than with weapons.' At least they were talking to one another, which was, I supposed, a step forward.

It was in December of the same year that Henry Kissinger came to Geneva to attend the Middle East Peace Conference and the

Swiss army was out in full force to protect him. There were tanks in all the streets surrounding the Palais des Nations and the nearby Hotel Intercontinental where he was staying and wherever you looked, soldiers with guns could be seen. The Swiss had never seen anything like it. Normally very neutral, unemotional and down-to-earth, they were bursting with excitement.

The Swiss army has always taken itself very seriously. To start with, all eighteen-year-old young men had to do four months' basic training to become a soldier. After that and until the age of thirty-two, they had to do three weeks' very tough military service every year and then two weeks every second year until the age of forty-two; they kept their army rifle under their bed (to make sure it wasn't stolen) and polished it religiously every Sunday morning. Once a year they also had to go to shooting practice (*tirs obligatoires*), present their sealed box of ammunition and be given the necessary bullets for the shooting practice. These days military service is still compulsory in Switzerland for eighteen to forty-two year olds. Thus a Swiss army is constantly at the ready, even though they haven't actually been at war with anyone in well over a century.

Kissinger, his staff and bodyguards (*gorilles* is the rather endearing French term) occupied one whole floor of the Hotel Intercontinental. The floor beneath them was occupied by the Arab delegation.

It was just before Christmas and Kissinger presented his staff and bodyguards with a case of champagne. They had a wild party; at midnight they opened all the bottles at once. And, as the corks popped, the Arabs on the floor below thought they were hearing gunfire and that they were being attacked. The police were called and the army called out. There was great excitement in peaceful Geneva that night.

Before he became prime minister, Bob Hawke was the leader of the Australian delegation at the annual Labour Conference held every June in Geneva and I was often the interpreter he was listening to in the English booth. There were 151 member countries with 250 simultaneous interpreters and the languages were Japanese, Chinese, Arabic, Russian, German, Spanish, French and English.

They would talk of individual and collective bargaining, tripartite matters, guaranteed annual wage, grievance procedure, free riders, fringe benefits, escalator and escape clauses, employer's liability, dismissal compensation, disputes, dead time, bumping, stool pigeons, yellow dog contracts, wild-cat strikes, fellow-travellers, lock-outs and lay-offs, unified penal and common codes, indictment, subrogation, voluntary assignments, arbitration agreements, intellectual property laws and mandatory provisions – in all of those languages.

Before the plenary meeting began I had interpreted at a series of 'non-meetings' – as they were known – where various strategies had been discussed by the different parties. So I knew that if a particular statement was made by another party, the Australian delegation (most of them in shirtsleeves, unlike the other delegations wearing ties and jackets) would get up as one man and walk out. And this is exactly what happened. The whole Australian delegation rose to its feet and filed out of the room behind Mr Hawke.

Wisely, of course, they must have left someone behind to keep those now outside at the coffee bar informed. Clearly something came up that the Australian delegation wished to take part in because some fifteen minutes later, led by Mr Hawke, they suddenly all filed back in and resumed their seats.

The UK and Australia enjoyed exchanging banter whenever possible and the UK chairman had missed nothing.

'I thought the Australian delegation had left the room in a huff,' he commented.

'Not at all, Mr Chairman,' replied Mr Hawke. 'We all need to go sometimes.'

I remember a trip to the Philippines to interpret at a medical conference held in the then brand new Convention Centre in Metro–Manila. I received a message from Imelda Marcos to ask if I would consider setting up an interpreter training course for her new Convention Centre but when I discovered that Tagalog was to be the main language, I had to decline.

One afternoon Mrs Marcos hosted a *merienda* in the Mala-cañang Palace to which she invited the Heads of Delegations and their wives. In old Spain, the *merienda* was a sort of after-noon high tea with all sorts of delicacies: cold meats, sausages and egg dishes as well as cakes and biscuits, wine and coffee. A famous French doctor was invited as well as other eminent non-English-speakers so Mrs Marcos asked for an interpreter to stand beside her as she shook everyone's hand upon arrival, to interpret any exchange of courtesies there might be. That inter-preter was me.

About 250 guests queued up to greet their hostess and I did what was expected of me. Mrs Marcos's make-up smiled at each guest and at me. (But was she really smiling behind it?) Then we all filed into a huge hall hung with tapestries and red and gold silk draperies. Under the tapestries the walls were panelled with the most beautiful dark wood carvings and bas-reliefs. It was all polished to perfection; there were carved figures, rural scenes, animals, plants and trees all round us.

Round tables were set all over the room with handmade lace tablecloths, matching napkins and delicate china, and each place had a name-card and a small vase with a pale rose. Each woman had a delicate hand-made lace fan at her place, with '*Imelda*'

embroidered on it. There was a also a photograph of Imelda
Marcos on each guest's plate and a copy of the keynote address
she had delivered at the opening of the conference. At one end
of the hall, on a dais, was the head table decorated with white
flowers. Imelda Marcos was at the centre, smiling, and at either
side of her the President and Vice-Presidents of the Conference
were seated. Ferdinand Marcos appeared briefly on stage, smiled
and waved and everyone clapped. He then disappeared, Imelda
sat down and so did we. I noticed a brigade of doormen in gold-
braided uniforms enter the room, close all the heavy carved
doors and stand as if on guard. Finally a procession of waiters all
in immaculate white brought one dish of food after another and
the *merienda* got underway.

It was about half past five when we had finished eating and
I glanced at my watch. I had called a conference interpreters'
meeting for six, back in the Convention Centre. I guessed
we must have taken half an hour to drive to the Palace from
there, so it was about time I found out where I could get a taxi
back.

Imelda Marcos rose and announced that a concert would
now begin. A small, rather chubby, girl of about ten came up on
to the dais and started to sing while an elderly gentleman
accompanied her on the piano. She looked very much like
Shirley Temple at the same age: the same curls, the same short
dress. Unfortunately her singing voice was not as good, but we
all clapped politely and before I could call over a waiter, a little
boy of roughly the same age took her place. He played the
violin, rather badly. Politely we all clapped again. More and more
performing children followed. I was getting impatient. What
would the interpreters think? They would all have arrived by
now and I would not be there to greet them or chair the
meeting. I finally succeeded in attracting the attention of a
waiter but when I asked for the way out, and asked whether he

could call me a taxi, he looked horrified. 'No-one may rise until Madam Marcos gives the signal,' he hissed, and glided off.

The performance limped on. Another child sang slightly off-key, another pianist forgot the music and kept playing the beginning of the piece because that was all he could remember. Suddenly I could take no more. I rose to my feet. Consternation! Three waiters appeared and gently pushed me back into my seat, repeating that I could not stand until Madam Marcos rose. I had attracted enough attention as it was, I might as well make the most of it, I thought. Perhaps Imelda would think I had been taken ill. So, brushing waiters aside I dashed to the only open door I could see – which turned out to lead to the kitchen. Around me I heard gasps and waiters looked worried, as though my action might cost them their job. In the kitchen an urgent whispered conference took place in Tagalog. What could they do with me? I could hardly go back now and clearly I could not stay in the kitchen where the chefs and waiters were hurrying about their work. I asked an older man, who seemed to be the head of the kitchen staff, if he would help me find a taxi.

'Impossible,' he replied.

'Then will you please help me get out of the Palace?' I begged.

The kitchen staff was organised as in old Spain: the waiters brought out the food, but little boys, lower in the hierarchy, took away the dirty dishes. The rather superior, dignified head called over the youngest of the dirty-dishes boys and told him what to do. Nobody else moved. The child knew two or three words of English. 'Come,' he whispered, looking at me in awe as though I had committed a dreadful crime and he was afraid of what I might do next. 'Follow.'

So I did. Down a spiral staircase, through a few empty basement rooms, then down again into a damp tunnel. The little boy was ill at ease and almost ran. I followed as fast as I could in my high-heeled shoes. It was a long way. We hurried along for ten minutes or more. In spite of the semi-darkness I noticed along both sides of the tunnel there were chests, packing cases, stacked artwork, silverware and statues. I had once visited King Farouk's palace in Egypt and been very impressed by the tunnel underneath it, leading to a lake with a boat at the ready. On both sides of the tunnel there too had been packing cases and works of art, statues and paintings, ready to grab on the way out if necessary. Was this the same arrangement? I wondered.

Finally, light appeared. As we drew nearer, it was a relief to see the sun shining on trees and grass. The small boy touched his forehead and bowed slightly, then turned and ran back as fast as he could. I was alone on a country road. There were no buildings in sight, no people around, and no traffic. Getting more and more impatient, I waited until at last a car appeared and I managed to stop it. The driver took me back into town where I was able to catch a taxi back to the Convention Centre and my interpreters' meeting. Nobody would have believed my story so I didn't waste time telling it.

'Sorry I'm late,' was all I could find to say.

Many years later and over a period of about three years I worked in Bangkok and Jakarta for the Cambodian peace talks – a few days or a week at a time, depending on the mood of Prince Sihanouk. I would get a telephone call on a Monday, for example, asking whether I could be in Jakarta by Wednesday.

The meeting room was all crimson plush and gold. The tables, swathed in starched white tablecloths, had been set up in a square. There were always flower arrangements at intervals along them and one enormous floral display in a large shiny golden urn at the centre of the square. Our interpretation booths had been placed along the far wall and we too had flowers, bottles of mineral water, glasses and a bowl of peppermints.

I was told that sometimes Prince Sihanouk didn't like the colour of the flower arrangements and they had to be changed. At other times he was petulant and said he didn't feel like negotiating today – he would send his son instead. The other parties generally objected to that and said they preferred to wait for the prince himself so, with my colleagues, I would sit in the big wicker armchairs in front of the windows in the sunny lounge until we were summoned. We'd drink endless cups of tea and coffee and read all the newspapers available in the hotel and one evening I took a taxi into town and bought myself a big fat novel to read.

Some mornings the prince would be bright-eyed and enthusiastic and when we arrived in the anteroom where coffee was being served he would welcome us joyfully and announce, smiling at me, 'Now the interpreters are here, we can begin.' Once, with a mischievous sparkle in his eye, he came over to me as I sipped my coffee and told me that I was his English voice and he would not take part in any discussion unless he could see me there.

When the peace talks took place in Jakarta, I was accommodated in the secret wing of a famous hotel. I had a luxury bedroom, a sitting room and flowery balcony, with beautifully carved furniture and sumptuous wall hangings. Outside my door stood a bodyguard, gold braid on his shoulders, the whitest of white gloves on his hands, and a turban on his head; he was waiting to take orders for anything I might require. It was heady stuff, but even champagne and caviar get wearisome after a few days and you long for home, tea and toast.

Chapter 16

Travelling at a time when tourism hadn't yet taken off in many parts of the world, I visited some unusual places quite off the beaten track. In many, people were still living a traditional lifestyle largely untouched by contact with Westerners or the idea of tourism-based economies. In India and Africa, parliamentary conferences were held while local parliament was in recess so our accommodation was generally that normally provided for local members of parliament during sessions. This was far from luxurious and well do I remember the bathrooms with rough concrete flooring where you had to turn on the water full blast to wash cockroaches, scorpions and centipedes down the drain before you could take a shower. These minor inconveniences were, however, fully compensated by the warmth of the welcome we were given by the local conference staff, who invited us to their homes to meet their families and insisted on taking us out in the evenings and at weekends to show us the local beauty spots they were so proud of. We were invited to birthday parties, weddings and even, once, a funeral in India. They often gave us heartfelt parting gifts to remember them by when we left. Leaving Dahomey on one occasion I remember being given an enormous basket of mangoes at the airport. I soon learnt, too, to put a few toys and gifts in my suitcase when packing for conferences.

As a foreigner I was never regarded with suspicion but always treated as a guest and welcomed with open arms. When we were about to leave for poor countries we received official warnings about thieves and were told not to wear flashy jewellery or take expensive cameras, but I never had anything stolen from my room or any dangerous encounters even though I loved walking through the cool streets at night before going to bed. I refrained from taking photographs, telling myself my memory was better than a photograph. I knew that in some countries people believed that if you photographed them, you took away a piece of their soul. In any case taking pictures would turn me into a tourist.

I have only had one truly unpleasant experience and that was in a souk – it may have been in Kuwait – when I was spat upon by a passing group of chattering women – but that was my own fault. My ankles were visible beneath my burka.

Sometimes the most memorable part was the journey itself, not the destination. This was the case when I once went on a parliamentary trip to Belgrade.

It was winter and Geneva was white with snow. The airport runways were covered in ice and the airport closed. Europe was being battered and frozen by snowstorms and ice and most airports had been closed. Because of this a specially long train had been provided to make room for all those who were going from the UN to Belgrade.

There were six interpreters, all women. Waiting on the platform at Geneva station in our sheepskin coats and boots, long scarves blown about by the icy wind, we found and greeted one another. When the train finally arrived, late, we managed to get a compartment to ourselves. After removing our outer layers of clothing we struggled, puffing and blowing, to put our luggage up on the overhead racks and then, rubbing our hands together, sat huddled forward with our feet as close as possible to the heater underneath the upholstered seats.

Just as the train started to move a young woman with a small baby clambered on board. She must have been in her early twenties. We helped her up with the baby in a basket and an overflowing shoulderbag of clothes and nappies. Her clothes were not warm enough for the weather and she shivered as she sat down, rubbing her hands together. She had beautiful dark eyes and long curly black hair, knotted at the back. She smiled at us and we smiled back, squeezing up to make room and saying admiring things about the baby, but she did not seem to understand French or English. I tried my Russian on her but she appeared not to understand that either. So we contented ourselves with smiles. The baby cried a little, but eventually slept. So did we all – it was to be a long journey and after the cold outside, the warmth and the motion of the train soon lulled us to sleep.

I think I was the first to wake. Looking around me in the semi-darkness I noticed the baby asleep in its basket on the seat opposite me. No sign of the young mother. She must have gone to the toilet, I thought vaguely. I dozed off again for a while, but when I opened my eyes a second time, the mother had still not come back. Strange. I sat up and so did one or two of the others. 'The mother is a long time going to the toilet,' I said. 'I'll have a look in the corridor, perhaps she is talking to someone or having a smoke.' But there was no sign of her. The corridor was deserted. In the other compartments everyone seemed to be asleep or reading quietly. There appeared to be no 'wagon-restaurant'. I walked the whole length of our carriage and then tried those on either side but there was no sign of the young mother. Doubts started creeping into my mind.

We had all heard of young mothers deserting their babies, especially if they were poor. Yugoslavia was suffering the coldest winter for years; perhaps the young woman felt we were better able to look after her baby than she was. She must have noticed we were all well dressed and obviously had more money than she did. The train had stopped at several stations already. Now we were all awake, whispering our fears, leaning forward in our seats, anxious not to wake the baby.

But it wasn't long before the baby did wake and start to cry. Then the cries turned to screams and the baby's face turned red. Astrid had another try at finding the mother while I took the baby out of the basket and rubbed its back, making soothing sounds. 'I think it's hungry' I said finally. 'I wonder if there's a bottle.' It felt wrong to look in someone else's bag, but I swallowed my scruples and hunted until I found a bottle. It was almost warm, so I installed the baby on my lap, loosened its clothing, and started to feed it. 'Perhaps there's some contraband in the baby's basket,' Elisabeth said. 'I've heard that's where people hide drugs. No customs officer would look underneath a sleeping baby. Perhaps that's why she went away – to get us to take the stuff through Customs. She'll probably reappear and claim the baby afterwards.'

I concentrated on keeping the baby happy, putting it on my shoulder and rubbing its back until it brought up its wind. 'I think its nappy needs changing' said Elsa, sniffing the air. 'You're more experienced at that than I am,' she added hastily. So I changed the nappy (establishing in the process that it was a girl), the baby went back to sleep and we took it in turns to keep an eye on her and watch out for her mother.

A few hours later, we were in anxious whispered consultation again. We had been awoken by shadowy customs officials asking to see our passports but they paid no attention to the sleeping baby. The more we thought about it, the more likely it seemed that the young mother had deliberately planned to leave the baby with us. The overflowing navy blue bag was full of baby clothes, enough for months, surely. What should we do when we arrived in Belgrade? We could hardly turn up at the conference with a baby! Obviously, we should hand her over to the station-master at Belgrade upon arrival.

Then Elisabeth started dreaming aloud: 'What if I kept her? I could give her a good home. I would love a little girl to bring up. My mother would look after her while I'm at work.'

'No, no, it would be better for *me* to have her,' said Elsa. 'I have a husband and a normal family life, it's not good for a child to be brought up by a single parent.'

'I think Val should keep her,' declared Astrid. 'She's already got a family and the baby would be much happier with other children.'

I didn't know what to say. I was picturing Gérard's reaction – probably explosive – if I came back from the Belgrade conference with a baby in my arms.

Gradually we worked out a fairly plausible plan for the conference. We would hide the baby just outside the interpretation booths and work out a roster so each one of us looked after her in turn. There was no need to tell anyone about it. As soon as the train arrived at the station, Elsa would go off and buy formula for a three-month-old baby. The passport authorities would probably let her through as she was so young and I had my children listed in my passport. We were getting quite excited now and laughed happily at the new turn our lives had taken. With six of us to share expenses we would be able to afford to keep her quite easily. Eventually we would have to make formal arrangements for adoption but in the meantime we would share her, take her on holidays with our families. She would have a lovely life; we would probably spoil her. We all wanted to buy her pretty clothes and presents. Perhaps one day we would all club together to buy her a pony. We would form a committee to decide on serious things like her name, her christening and later her schooling. We would be like a benevolent six-headed fairy godmother.

One after the other we crept over to admire her as she slept while the others dreamed tender, maternal dreams. Our baby, pink, warm and well fed, cosy in her clean nappy, smiled too in her sleep.

The train slowed down, jerked a bit and finally pulled into Belgrade station very slowly. We were a long way down the extra-long train; there would be quite a walk along the train tracks to get to the platform and the snow outside was deep. Who would carry our baby? 'I'll carry her, if someone will carry my luggage for me,' said Astrid, gently but firmly. She was the tallest and most athletic of us all. Coats, gloves and scarves on, we were at last organised and about to step down from the train when the young mother burst into the compartment, looking rather dishevelled. With a bright 'thank you' smile she picked up the baby in her basket in one hand, her navy blue bag in the other, and jumped down the steps in front of us.

'My man train guard. I sleep with him,' she said with an enchanting Slav accent.

When I first arrived in Madagascar for a six-week conference, looking out of the taxi window as we drove from the airport to my hotel I noticed whitewashed tombs surrounded by bougainvillea and hibiscus in the front gardens of the houses.

A printed sign by the taxi meter caught my attention as we drove along: *Pour les défunts, prix à discuter* (For the deceased, price to be negotiated). I was puzzled but felt it might be impolite for a foreign visitor to go into such a delicate subject, especially immediately upon arrival. In the course of my stay, I noticed all the taxis carried this notice.

I enjoyed Madagascar: the brilliant flowers, the Botanic Gardens, the lemurs, and especially the fact that there seemed to be music and people singing everywhere, just like the south of Italy. The Malagasies broke into song at the drop of a hat. I particularly loved the bright colours and smiling faces at the Sunday market, the Zoma, and the wonderful display of hand-crafted raffia baskets of all sizes. There were also beautifully woven rush mats. I couldn't resist a large raffia wall hanging of intricate design and a strange bird-creature rather like an emu, made of straw, with a long beak, that stood over a metre tall.

Walking from my hotel to the conference venue each morning, I puffed as I climbed a steep path through the leafy park, stopping to admire the enormous travellers palms, the leaves of which formed great fans; the stems always full of water. Often lemurs played like children on fallen tree trunks or darted from tree to tree, excitedly screeching. Imagine a round, fluffy white face surrounded by a stiff whitish fringe of hair like the whiskers of a Dickensian gentleman, large round shiny impertinent amber eyes and a black pointed fox-like nose. As they swung from one tree to another, they grabbed fruit, taking a bite in mid air.

The lemur was named by Linnaeus from the Latin *Lemures*, meaning 'spirits of the dead', or ghosts, because of their spectre-like faces. The name may also be linked with their cries and the story of the lovesick souls trapped in purgatory, whose ghostly calls can be heard by the living.

The people of Madagascar have their own legends about the larger lemurs, called indri. They tell of the boy from the honey-collecting tribe who climbed up a tree to gather honey and was attacked by bees; he was so stunned he was unable to climb down again. An indri realised his plight and came swinging to his rescue, carrying him back to the ground.

The cry of the indri is impossible to describe. You have to hear it for yourself. It is a haunting rainforest lament that takes you by surprise, chills your blood and paralyses you. The most common cry is a territorial wail that carries two to three kilometres through dense forest to warn other indri to keep away. If you're standing anywhere near a group of howling lemurs, the noise is so deafening it is almost unbearable.

The indri is the largest surviving lemur and the patriarch of the prosimian family that is the ancestor of monkeys, apes and us. It has been more or less wiped out by its more highly evolved descendants everywhere in the world except Madagascar. The villagers view the indri as the ancestor figure for specific highland clans and for this reason it is revered. It is taboo for Malagasies to eat them.

One hot day I wore a cool white cotton dress to work and noticed that the local staff looked at me strangely. At lunchtime I took a taxi into town. The kindly, grey-bearded driver turned round with a friendly smile and, patting me on the shoulder in a fatherly way, said: 'Be careful when you wear white. It is the colour of death. Do not go out after the sun has gone down or people will think you are a ghost.'

From conversations with friendly locals like the taxi driver I soon learnt that ghosts were very real to the Malagasies. The white tombs I'd noticed in every garden held the bones of grandparents and great-grandparents wrapped in silk and laid out on stone slabs. If they were not treated as they wished, the ghosts of these ancestors would haunt their families and make everyone unhappy. It was indeed not a good idea to wear white.

I made friends with a Canadian couple, both doctors, who lived with their family in a luxurious condominium just outside town. We spent many pleasant evenings sitting talking on their verandah in the cool after the heat of the day, and one evening

I asked them about the taxi fare for the defunct. They told me how, soon after their arrival, their houseboy had asked if he could have the following day off and borrow their car. He said he would need it from early morning and for the whole day. When pressed, he explained the first of November was the Day of the Dead. He had to take his great-grandparents and grand-father to the family celebration.

'You are lucky they are still alive.'

'Oh no, they will be in baskets.'

This is how they learnt about the ceremony of *Famadihana* (the turning of the bones), when the tombs are opened and the bones of the ancestors brought out.

While the ancestors are out of the tomb there is much singing and dancing. Their descendants talk to them, telling them what's been happening in the family, even give them a little rum. The ceremony is a festive affair.

If the tomb isn't in the family's garden, the bones are placed in baskets and taken to the family gathering

Next time I took a taxi I questioned the driver about the notice. He explained that the reason you need to discuss the price for the defunct in the baskets is because the 'dryer' the ancestors are, the less space they take up and therefore the cheaper it is to transport them.

You can fit quite a few baskets in the back of a car. It is important not to forget anyone.

Packing my bags at the end of the conference, I once again realised I had bought too many presents and the rush wall hanging, raffia lampshades and long-legged bird-creature with the big beak would not fit into my suitcase. I asked the hotel concierge for advice and he gave me an old sheet, a needle and thread. So I rolled the bird and lampshades up inside the wall-hanging and stitched them all into the sheet. The concierge gave me a strap to make it easier to carry.

When I checked in at the airport, the customs official tapped the sheet and asked suspiciously, 'What's in here?'

It dawned on me that the lampshade looked like a head at one end, and the bird's feet at the other were quite obvious.

'My grandmother,' I replied.

He smiled and waved me through.

One visit I made to Kuwait for a medical conference was memorable for something wonderful that happened while I was there.

Kuwait was once nothing but undulating sandy plains and merciless heat; the only vegetation was along the coast and that was limited to a few straggly salt-tolerant plants. Then in the 1930s the discovery of oil brought unexpected prosperity and when I visited the capital city for the first time in the '60s the airport was like a freezing cold, air-conditioned cathedral. Cold was a luxury the Kuwaitis had just discovered, thanks to their newfound wealth, and they couldn't get enough of it.

Our flight had arrived at about 2 a.m. 'my' time, and I could hardly keep awake. As we stepped off the plane my only thought was to find my suitcase as soon as possible, jump into a taxi and get to my hotel and bed. Unfortunately, there was a reception committee waiting for us, even though it was the middle of the night for them too. The Kuwaitis were so incredibly polite. Later, at cocktail parties and receptions I noticed that although they were extremely solicitous as far as we, their guests, were concerned, constantly passing us food and drink (mainly strong mint tea), they never ate or drank anything in our presence.

Together with a group of portly middle-aged ministers of health from various countries, I was shown into the VIP lounge of the airport which was even colder, if possible, than the airport hall. Comfortable sofas were pointed out to us but I preferred to remain standing in the hope they would understand I wanted to leave as soon as possible. Servants then brought in decorative trays of small hand-painted glasses. I accepted one and sipped cautiously: it contained tea flavoured with cardamom. The tea was so strong and so bitter, I found it difficult to swallow.

Our hosts were dressed from head to toe in flowing white. Beneath their cool headdresses they were bearded and sun-tanned and very handsome with dazzling smiles. In an effort to be as polite as my hosts, I struggled through my glass of strong tea and finished the last drop with relief. The servant hurried to refill it. I smiled 'No, thank you,' but he bowed and refilled my glass anyway. By the third glass I was desperately wondering how long this would go on. I was the only woman there and the only interpreter. I seemed to be the last one still drinking the bitter tea.

A gesture made earlier by one of our Arab hosts, tall and magnificent in his immaculate gown and headwear, had caught my attention. He had raised his right hand to shoulder height, extended the thumb and the little finger outwards, and waved the hand sideways. In desperation I decided to try it the next time the waiter appeared with more tea. It worked wonders. The waiter bowed with a smile and went away without refilling my glass. At last we were led out to the waiting black stretch limousines and driven to our hotel.

Air-conditioning being such a luxury in the desert, our hosts were particularly proud of it – to them it represented success. So it was always turned up to the maximum. The hotel windows were all fixtures and could not be opened. I was so cold that night I had to ask for an extra blanket before I could sleep. The breakfast room was freezing too. Luckily I had flown to Kuwait straight from a skiing holiday with the children in Verbier so I had a thick skiing jumper in my case which I wore down to breakfast.

Next day the Kuwaiti Ministry of Health took us on a tour

of the city. There was just the one main street lined with jewellery shops. Their windows were packed with gold trinkets and precious stones: gold Swiss watches, gold chains, necklaces and bracelets. In the distance stood the circular Emir's palace – the windows of the 365 rooms belonging to his wives were pointed out. We were also taken to see the miracle of the desert: the enormous modern seawater desalination plant. I saw no small cars – only luxury American air-conditioned limousines, mostly of the stretch variety. Everyone I saw, including our driver, wore an impressive gold watch.

The medical conference was held in the exemplary, brand-new hospital complex. We were taken on a tour of the hospital and it was like Utopia. Everywhere was the very latest and most expensive equipment, including an enormous maternity ward with rows and rows of empty incubators and shiny new equipment for the care of premature babies. My guide explained that all medical and dental care was free of charge, as were all telephone calls within Kuwait and education, including university. Food, water, electricity and transport were all subsidised. The Kuwaitis had everything it seemed – except birds.

During my breaks I went searching for windows to see what I could see. All round the hospital, set in the sand, were very new-looking strips of bright green, manicured lawn with low fences to protect them. Irrigation sprays were sending out a fine mist of water, making it all look fresh and cool, an oasis in the desert. There were even beds full of brightly-coloured flowers. And a few trees: young, rather spindly trees, carefully staked and obviously nurtured – they all had fresh green leaves and looked healthy. Some trees had grown quite tall.

Towards the end of the conference, as I watched from the window one morning I heard an unusual sound. The twittering of birds. An amazing thing had happened. Some migrant birds had found the trees. The first birds had arrived.

At the end of the conference, the Kuwaiti Minister of Health, surrounded by his staff, was waiting for us at the airport. With a bow and a smile we were each handed a small box. The women were given a silk jewel box containing a tiny watch with a choice of five different silk straps and three different jewelled surrounds into which the watch fitted snugly. The men received a simple, plain gold watch. (I would have preferred that as I could have given it to Gérard.) We all felt obliged to accept these gifts even though we knew we shouldn't – it would have been extremely rude to refuse them.

In the early 1970s I accepted a contract for a six-week conference in Málaga-Torremolinos at the time of the summer school holidays. Marc and Steffi were both away now at university. I loved Spain so much, I wanted Cassie to discover it too. I rented a flat for three months and took her, our cocker spaniel Rouquine (which means 'red head') and our maid at the time, an English girl called Jackie. We packed ourselves and our cases into my turquoise Fiat and drove south.

It turned out to a delightful third-floor flat. From my deckchair on the balcony overlooking the swimming pool, I could watch Cassie, who was now about ten years old, swimming or playing in the garden.

She soon made friends. There was a group of seven or eight children about the same age and after a few days she was speaking Spanish like a native. Jackie, who was pretty and dainty with long black hair, was a very keen horserider. We had a stream of Spanish boyfriends at the door to take her riding and to parties in the evenings. In the afternoons they sometimes took Cassie riding with them; she became an excellent horserider, and all in Spanish.

I was still a very keen flamenco dancer. The first night I persuaded some colleagues to come with me to a flamenco club to see if I knew any of the dancers. I did and was flattered that they hadn't forgotten me – they called out to me as they danced, as flamenco dancers do: '*¡Hola!* Haven't seen you for a while. Where have you been? Come to El Cortijillo tonight!'

Flamenco dancers and musicians often meet after the tourist shows are over, at about 3 a.m., to dance 'for real' and the place where they meet is often called 'El Cortijillo'. At this particular El Cortijillo there were wooden chairs and tables, a few people drinking wine or sherry and someone strumming a guitar. Feeling inspired, someone would suddenly start to sing *cante jondo*, softly at first, until a guitar picked it up and then it filled the room. *Cante jondo* are songs that are not written down but passed from father to son. They tell earthy stories of peasant life, family tragedies, miners at work, people working hard in the fields, their horses and sometimes of unrequited love. I would quietly take my castanets out of my handbag and play them, softly at first until my turn came, then I would play louder, louder until the rhythm commanded me to stand and dance. For a while I would tell my story in movement then, hot and exhausted, I would sit down to get my breath back and the singer would take over. On a good, inspired night, we would continue making music right through to five or even six in the morning – until the voice of reason became too insistent. I knew I had to be in the booth at the conference at nine o'clock, feeling alert and capable. Fortunately the Spanish custom of the siesta applied to conferences held in Spain then.

In fact, dancing flamenco actually seemed to improve my alertness. I never felt jaded or tired when arriving in the booth the following morning; on the contrary, thanks to flamenco, I felt particularly alive and vital.

I took Cassandre with me several times to flamenco per-formances, on the condition she slept the following day and she too became enthusiastic about it. I bought her a three-quarter size guitar and arranged for a guitar teacher to give her lessons in the afternoons while I was at work. She took to the guitar like a duck to water and learnt to play beautifully, even though she had difficulty controlling her left hand and arm and had to lean her chin on her left hand to keep the fingers in place. She also had some lessons in Spanish dancing and soon we could dance the *Sevillanas* together. Back in Geneva, Cassie continued her guitar lessons at the Geneva Conservatorium and I bought her a full-size guitar a few years later.

It was not just flamenco, although that was my grand passion – I adored any kind of dancing and took every opportunity to indulge.

A six-week Plenipotentiary Conference, held in Mar del Plata, a summer resort town in Argentina, was one such time. It was off-season so we more or less had the place to ourselves. You could see Uruguay across the silvery-grey waters of the river Plata. Every morning two of our colleagues could be seen performing yoga on the beach at dawn – one of them has since become an orange person and stopped interpreting altogether. We had the most wonderful meat I had ever tasted (*el bife*) and conference receptions galore with *asado* in which the whole beast is roasted over glowing coals. The coffee (*cafecito*) was also the best I had ever tasted – it came from Brazil.

We often danced the tango in the evenings but my partners were generally elderly British delegates with large paunches, which meant that we demurely kept our distance.

One of the Russian-booth interpreters, tall, dark and bearded, fell in love with a beautiful tall, slim Argentinian blonde in Document Distribution. Each time she came into the plenary hall to distribute a document, the flow from the Russian booth microphone faltered or took on a dreamy, faraway tone. She distributed her documents round the room without looking where she was going – her eyes were on the Russian booth. We were all carried away by the romance in the air.

Argentinian presidents, it seems, rarely look at their watches and we often had to work well beyond the normal closing time. By the end of the day, our stamina began to fade and every minute past closing time was an effort. I was struggling to con-centrate about forty-five minutes past normal closing time one evening, leaning forward in my chair, talking as if in my sleep. The delegates could not see that in actual fact behind the 'modesty panel' which went from the document bench to the floor of the booth, I had my legs up on my colleague's chair because my booth-mate had gone out to stretch his legs and try to revive himself with a breath of fresh air.

I was concentrating so hard that I did not notice Eric going past on his way back to the Russian booth. He happened to have some string in his pocket and silently and deftly tied my ankles together, to the back of the chair.

When my half-hour was over and my booth-mate returned, I tried to remove my legs from his chair quickly, surreptitiously, but alas alack! Luckily the microphone was not turned on or the crash when the chair fell over might have woken the delegates too.

After the Mar del Plata conference I was envious of my colleagues, Toni and Madeleine, who went off on a trip down the Amazon in a boat. I spent a few days in Santiago de Chile, visiting friends and enjoying wonderful Chilean ice cream with the locals on Sunday afternoon. With my Chilean friends I climbed the St Christopher mountain which was covered with yellow flowers. Then I went to Buenos Aires for a few days and had tea with friends of friends in the elegant tea-rooms in Calle Florida, before catching the flight back to Geneva via Rio de Janeiro.

The loudspeaker announced that we were beginning our

descent to Rio, where we would have a one-and-a-half-hour refuelling stop. I sat back in my seat, enjoying the warmth of the sun coming through the window. I had just had a satisfying lunch with Argentine beef, Chilean wine and Brazilian coffee. Suddenly I sat up as a thought struck me. How could I spend just one and a half hours in Rio? I might never get another chance to visit Brazil. It would be crazy. Gérard was in Germany on a business trip, probably with Monique or Ilse (another girlfriend), and the children were fine with their nanny – I had spoken to them just before leaving Buenos Aires. I could telephone them from Rio and keep in touch as often as necessary. I summoned an air hostess. 'Where do you stay when you are in Rio?' I asked her. 'What do you recommend?'

I soon had a group of them round me, with maps of the city, and a list of hotels and places to visit. 'What is your particular interest in Rio?' they asked.

'I have never been able to be in Brazil for the *Carnaval*. They must be preparing for it now. What I would like to do is go to a samba school rehearsing for the *Carnaval*.'

'Phone from the airport to book a hotel room,' they advised.

And that is how I spent a week in Copacabana and danced with the *escola da samba* called *Bafo da Onca* (The Breath of the Tiger).

It was a bit of a scramble getting my luggage off the plane in time, but sitting back in the taxi heading for Copacabana I felt I had accomplished the almost impossible. The sandy beach was covered with paper bird-kites of all colours, the young salesmen, some still children, squatting beside them, keeping an alert eye out for possible customers. Sugarloaf Mountain was magnificent in the sunshine, the gigantic statue of Christ looked benevolently down on the city. Whoever said 'God made the world in six days – the seventh he devoted to Rio' was absolutely right.

On my first day, I joined an excursion to visit the rainforests.

Walking ahead of the group, fascinated by the lush vegetation all around me, I heard a stifled gasp behind me. Looking round, I saw I was being followed by the biggest, hairiest black spider I had ever seen – as big as my hand. Nobody dared say anything for fear of galvanising the spider into action: we were all paralysed. I felt rather silly in my shorts and open sandals. Taking a deep breath, I carefully stepped over the spider which was walking along the path quite slowly, and went back to the group. After that I stayed close to them.

I wasn't sure how to contact a samba school but one morning I caught the bright-eyed young man who had helped me with my luggage when I arrived practising his samba steps in the luggage-room. He told me he was rehearsing for the *Carnaval*, and that there would be a practice that night. I asked if I could go along too.

The people there were obviously very poor, their clothes were ragged but clean. They told me they lived in one-room shacks with no running water, but, they declared, they forgot all their cares when they were dancing the samba. Their whole life seemed to centre round the *Carnaval*. In a sort of hangar we found musicians practising, women sitting at tables sewing sequins on dresses, dancers limbering up. In the corner stood a silky, glittering banner with *Bafo da Onca* written in sequins. After that I spent my evenings dancing with them.

Except the last evening, when I persuaded my samba-dancing friend from the hotel to take me out to Macumba to experience voodoo. (Tourists were not generally allowed.)

I was shown into a large whitewashed cave, which seemed to be carved out of the rocks, and ushered to a seat. On the back wall were framed portraits of Joan of Arc, Victor Hugo and Jesus Christ, with candles in front of each. The people had added Christianity to their ancient beliefs in a most user-friendly way when conquered by the Catholic Portuguese and now addressed their prayers to Joan of Arc and Victor Hugo as well as Christ. The women wore crosses on chains round their necks together with voodoo charms and dangling crosses for earrings. There were flickering candles everywhere; the air was heavy with incense. On both sides of the cave sat the drummers, repeating the same rhythm endlessly, producing a strange, hypnotic effect. Frail, wrinkled, shrunken old women, their almost bald heads partly hidden in their shawls, toothless jaws protruding, sat on a row of low chairs against a wall, muttering and crossing themselves. They were speaking with the dead. Others, younger, wore high white turbans and long white dresses. The men were also dressed in white and stood in groups, leaning against the walls, puffing out smoke from strong-smelling cigars. All were barefoot.

Everywhere people were chanting words I could not understand; the same words, over and over again, on their faces an expression of beatitude. The drum beat seemed to get louder and louder. One by one the women stood and started to dance, though it wasn't so much a dance as a whirling round and round, arms flailing. Sometimes they uttered little cries and their eyes glazed and turned upwards, as if they were in a trance. There was often an expression of ecstasy on their faces; sometimes one collapsed and fainted, and had to be brought round by an old woman with much face-slapping and some water.

I was greatly tempted to get up from my chair and join in. As the temptation grew stronger, I gripped the sides of the thatched seat and, looking up, I caught the eye of my friend, standing by the door. He came over and helped me to my feet, guiding me towards the exit.

Outside in the fresh evening air was a different world. As we drove back to the hotel, he explained that, according to voodoo, disease is due to neglect of spirituality. 'Voodoo' means spirit or life and is a 'way of being' in relationship with plants, trees and animals, a tradition the voodoo people want to keep for future generations. If I had stayed and joined in the dance, my soul would have gone to the sacred island under the sea where the souls of the dead go.

He also told me about zombification, which is the voodoo form of justice for wrongdoing. A bonfire is lit and special herbs are burnt to induce a sort of trance which turns into paralysis. Everyone wears a mask except for the man who has committed a violent crime. Soon he collapses, unconscious. He is then buried alive and everyone goes home. Except for the voodoo priest who, after a while, digs him up again. He is still alive but the lack of oxygen to his brain has turned him into a zombie. He no longer has any aggression or even willpower and is quite harmless.

When I walked in the front door of my home in Switzerland, the sun was shining, the children had come home a few hours before and, to give me a surprise, had already laid out the teacups; a home-made 'welcome home' iced sponge-cake was in the centre of the table. Rio and the world of voodoo seemed far away.

But that was not my only experience of the occult. And one of them, an encounter in India with a soothsayer all dressed in white, still lay ahead of me.

Chapter 17

I had no idea that the 1977 conference in India would play such an important part in my life. It was a meeting of the Non-Aligned Movement in Delhi (countries like India and Yugoslavia which were not part of the main blocs).

Our hotel had a superb swimming pool where we all congregated at lunchtime for a refreshing dip, the inevitable chicken sandwich and a cool fruit drink. At twenty to two we would dash up to our rooms for a shower, get dressed and be back in our booths by two, cool and refreshed. It was a good life.

During our free weekend, I took the plane to Khajuraho with a couple of colleagues. We landed in a grassy area which could hardly be called an airport; once again the pilot proceeded to remove whatever could be removed for safe keeping, explaining that people would even take the wheels of the plane if they could.

The thousand-year-old temples were covered with delicate, amorous scenes. Thirty temples were all that remained of what had been, in the tenth century, the capital of the Kingdom of Jahoti. They were in groups, some taller than others, all the same strange squat shape.

I was in medieval India. The grass was fresh and green, the bougainvillea coral-red and purple; the temple carvings were of tall protective gods and beautiful, graceful, grapefruit-breasted godesses with wasp waists, carved in flesh-coloured sandstone. Temples of different faiths were side by side, all to the glory of physical love. Traces could be found of Buddhism, Jainism, sun-worship, animism and various other cults like the esoteric Tantric – testimony to the remarkable eclecticism of the Chandella kings.

There were amorous couples in all positions in pairs and in groups; gods and goddesses in fond embrace. All around me was a hymn to the glory of love and the union of the phallus and the yoni. Shiva and Parvati, heaven and earth, day and night, man and woman: two into one. The male represented the passive aspect – the impassive male god, eternity – while the female was active energy, the dynamism of time – the goddess embracing her lover and trying to melt into him, uniting their opposite natures into one. Together they were divine. Sexual rapture was a way of reaching heaven, the gods, and spiritual understanding.

Just looking at the graceful wasp-waisted goddesses made me feel voluptuous. I thought of Janek and felt grateful to him for giving me an understanding of sexual fulfilment. How could I bear to continue living with someone so insensitive and lacking in sensuality as Gérard ? I had to take a decision and find a way to leave him. I had to summon the courage to change my life as well as that of Gérard and the children. But the thought of the upheaval it would cause was daunting, and I postponed thinking about it.

On the last day of the conference. Reka, Maria-Cristina, Silvia and I were relaxing by the hotel pool, making the most of the warm Indian sunshine because next day we would be flying home to cold Geneva in time for Easter.

'I'm glad it's almost over,' said Silvia. 'We've had too many night meetings. There's only one thing I regret and that's not having my fortune told while I was here. I thought there would be fortune-tellers all over the place. Does anybody have the address of a fortune-teller I could go to? This is my last chance.'

'You met a fortune-teller when we were here last time, didn't you?' said Reka, looking at me. 'Have you still got his address?'

'I'm sorry. He didn't give me his address,' I replied. 'He came to me, I didn't go to him.'

I told them the strange story. In 1961 a seer dressed in white had stopped me in the street and told me my past, my present and the future. I had immediately written all he said down in shorthand, to be sure to remember. And it had all come true. He had even predicted the birth of my third child, Cassandre. I remember smiling cynically at the time because my husband and I were hardly on speaking terms then. But Cassie had been born the following year after our vain attempt at reconciliation. The fortune-teller had also said I would inherit some money: 'Thirty-three somethings – whatever money you have where you live, not Indian rupees,' he said. That had come true too. I had inherited 33 000 French francs. He had foretold all that would happen during the following ten years or so, but no-one could say I had co-operated or he had read my mind because I hadn't believed a single word at the time.

'How much did it cost?' asked Silvia.

'He refused any payment at all. In fact, he said that on the contrary he wanted *me* to accept something from *him* and he gave me a talisman that he said I must keep with me always. It was a strange stone, black with a white spiral through it. He said it would bring me luck but I was not to show it to people. Afterwards I would have thought I had imagined the whole thing if it weren't for the strange stone in my pocket and the pages of shorthand notes in my handbag.'

'You *are* lucky!' said Sylvia. 'I wish something like that would happen to me.'

Suddenly Monique and Colette appeared with the news that the afternoon plenary wouldn't be starting at two as planned because the texts of the resolutions weren't ready yet in all languages. No need to rush back. The closing plenary wouldn't start now until four o'clock.

I grabbed my things and hurried up to my room. Two hours would give me time to go to the airline office and change my return ticket to fly back to Nice instead of Geneva. We generally went to Nice for Easter to stay with Papa in his villa on boulevard de Cimiez. Gérard would drive there with Cassandre and meet me at the airport. All I would still have to do was telephone him to confirm my time of arrival in Nice.

It was all done in no time. As I came out of the air-conditioned Air-India office, the warm afternoon air felt pleasant on my face. I started to walk back along Janpath in the direction of the Vigyan Bhavan, where the conference was being held. There was no need to take a taxi or a bicycle-rickshaw. I had plenty of time. I would enjoy the walk, breathing in the sights, sounds and smells of India for the last time before the hassle of packing, taxi, luggage and airport. I could 'switch off' for a while.

The moment I stopped hurrying, the thought that was always there in the back of my mind came to the fore again. It was the first thought that assailed me each morning the moment I awoke. What am I going to do about divorcing Gérard? It had to be done but I dreaded it. We had been married for twenty-six years and built a solid framework of habit, routine, ways of dealing with one another, of coping.

I picked my way through the dubious puddles and litter on the dusty footpath, smiling a 'no thank you' at the incense-stick vendors and the child holding up ivory bracelets. Along the kerb were dilapidated metal stalls. Meat cakes were frying in spitting oil and I was offered glasses of brightly-coloured syrup drinks and newspaper cornets of seeds to chew. A one-legged lottery-ticket seller pulled my sleeve, a blind trinket vendor chanted his wares. Three little boys with shaved heads and matchstick legs (reminding me of Cassie's), selling jasmine flowers threaded onto cotton intended to adorn Indian women's hair, put a few jasmine flowers that were left over into my hand as I passed them.

Suddenly I was aware of a tall figure dressed in dazzling white in the far distance, walking towards me. He must have been a Sikh with his white turban and flowing white robes. He was dark-skinned and had a black beard.

It was as if a spotlight had been turned on him. The people around us seemed to fade into the shadows, the Tibetan market vendors' cries grew weaker, the blind beggars, the boys selling cigarettes, matches and cola leaves, the graceful women with baskets on their heads all seemed unreal. All that mattered was the tall figure coming gradually closer. His burning brown eyes shone intently into mine. I felt almost as if we were being carried towards one another a few inches above the ground.

As he came up to me, he touched me lightly on the elbow and said in a kindly voice: 'I have a message for you.'

'Oh, thank you, I am so relieved,' I heard my voice say. I was not taken aback. It seemed perfectly normal.

'Let us go somewhere quiet,' he said, leading me by the elbow through tall white gates into the gardens of the Imperial Hotel.

We sat in the grass in the shade of a group of palm trees which seemed to be waiting for us. My messenger sat opposite me and smiled. I noticed that his feet were dirty.

'I was hoping you would come,' I heard myself say.

'My message is threefold,' he said.

'Do you mind if I write it down?' I asked. 'It is very important and I am afraid I might forget something.'

'If you like, but you must concentrate on what I say and write afterwards.' His English was educated yet stilted. He continued: 'To give you proof, I shall write some names and dates on this piece of paper, but you must not look at them until I have finished.'

He took a stub of pencil from a fold in his robe and a torn grubby slip of paper. Having written on it, awkwardly, he folded it in half, then closed my fingers over it.

He spoke so quietly I had to strain forward to catch every word.

'Before I give you your message, I want to tell you some things about yourself. You will be lucky once in a lottery or a gambling game. You will win some money. But only once.'

He took a deep breath, leant back and looked at me intently.

'You have had much unhappiness in the past,' he said. 'But your life will change and you will have many years of day-to-day peace and happiness. You will live in a smaller house with a small garden and fruit trees. You will not be rich. You will not have great money as in the past. But you will have enough. In the past, much money has gone through your hands. You have received a lot. You have spent a lot. Mostly, you have given a lot and spent a lot on your family. Not on yourself, so it will not be very different for you in the future.'

He paused.

'There are two men in your life. One is on his way out, the other is on his way in.'

'The message?'

'The message is threefold. First,' he said, so quietly I could hardly hear him, 'do not worry about "when". The day will come and you will know. Soon, but not before July. So you have some time to think about it. Until July. Just think about it until then.'

I felt great relief at his words.

'Second, do not be angry. Let him say what he will. Be calm, knowing you are waiting until July.

'Third, do not give him money when he asks. Do not lend

him money. Keep what you have. You will need it for yourself. Remember my words.'

I was so amazed by the relevance of what he said that at first I forgot to take notes. I found it difficult to take my eyes away from his. Finally, I pulled myself together, took a pen and notepad from my handbag and wrote down in shorthand everything he had said. I still have the piece of paper.

'Do you have any questions?'

This time I was ready, having thought over my earlier experience at lunchtime.

'Yes. Why did you come to me?'

'Your aura. I saw it from afar. You are a very happy, lucky person, within yourself.'

'Are you the same person who spoke to me here in 1961?'

He smiled and shrugged as though he hadn't understood my question or couldn't answer it. I decided to let it drop. There were more important things to think about. I rose to my feet, unscrewing the crumpled paper in my hand, and found my mother's date of birth and death, with her initial, N. Underneath was a 'V' with the date of my birth, a 'G and V' with the date of our marriage, and the dates of birth of my three children preceded by their initials, written in a strange hand that seemed unused to the English alphabet. I must have gasped. There was a short silence.

'How much do I owe you?' I asked, trying to bring myself back into reality.

He smiled enigmatically. 'It is *I* who want *you* to accept something,' he said.

He held out to me a small squarish stone, red on one side and black on the other.

'This is from Hanuman, the monkey-god,' he said. 'You must always carry it with you, wherever you go, but show it to no-one.'

I couldn't believe this was happening again.

'Will you tell me why?'

He thought for a moment.

'Up there,' he said, raising his eyes to the sky, 'is – you may call him God. I may call him something else. But whoever it is, he give you good. You therefore lucky, happy person. If I give you talisman, perhaps some of your luck and happiness come to me if you keep it always with you.' He rubbed the strange square object, held it in his closed hand for a minute, and then put it in mine.

'Do you have any dreams you would like to tell me?' he asked.

Suddenly I felt weak. As though I might collapse. I could take no more. It was as if he had exhausted my life-force. I felt like a rag doll.

'No more, no more,' I murmured weakly and turned away.

'Come back to India with your new husband some day when you are in your new life,' he said when I said 'Goodbye'. Though the words were not spoken, it was as if he had added: 'I shall see you then.'

I managed to get back to the conference building but once inside my legs gave way and I collapsed on the floor of the entrance hall.

When I came to, I was lying on a couch and being given tea. Someone was saying: 'She has been working too hard. All those night meetings.'

As with the first encounter, I might have thought it had all been a dream, were it not for the pages of shorthand and the strange black and red talisman in the outer pocket of my handbag.

At Nice airport I was going through Customs when I saw Cassie's excited face and waving hand through the window. The moment the first passenger went out, Gérard squeezed himself through the glass doors. He took my case and, bending down, offered a cool cheek to be kissed.

'I hope they paid you,' he said in a confidential tone. 'I haven't got any money to pay for anything while we're here in Nice. I spent all I had on the petrol to get down here. We are counting on you.'

I lied to him for the first time in my life. 'I haven't received the cheque yet,' I said, looking away.

School broke up at the end of June, and I put Cassandre on the plane to England. My father would meet her at the other end and drive her down to the New Forest for a horse-trekking holiday. I had arranged her holiday to fit in with mine in Greece but no sooner had she left than I received a telephone call from my friend to say she could no longer manage it. Her mother had had a serious car crash and she had to stay to look after her. We cancelled our hotel bookings and I resigned myself to a three-week holiday on my own, at home. (By then, Gérard was spending most of his time with girlfriends.)

'I shall read all the books I've always wanted to read, sleep when I am tired and eat when I am hungry,' I promised myself. 'I'll turn off the alarm clock and put my watch out of sight in a drawer. Sometimes I'll walk down to the lake and have coffee in the sunshine with the tourists.'

It was a pleasant way to live. The summer was at its height, the days hot and clear, the garden green and in the distance, behind the deep blue lake dotted with sailing boats, the snow-capped Mont Blanc glistened against the blue sky. I felt that if I stood on tiptoe on the terrace and leaned forward with a very long-handled ice-cream spoon, I should be able to take the top off. It would taste creamy and cool and delicious.

One morning I awoke early to the sound of the birds singing in the trees. It was dawn and a delightful warm feeling spread over me as I stretched out in bed knowing that another perfect day lay ahead. Suddenly a thought struck me. It was my birthday! The seventh of July. What would I do to celebrate? I would give myself a present. Something I really wanted, something to remember. Then the date flashed across my mind. The seventh day of the seventh month and the year was 1977. That was a very rare date. An historical occasion. It was a very special day. Then I understood. It was The Day.

I was completely on my own. All my friends thought I was in Greece. There would be no distractions. I would plan everything, think it all out carefully, take my time and make no mistakes. I prepared myself a breakfast tray which I took out into the garden and, swinging back and forth on the red fringed swing, I munched and thought and jotted down notes on the lined notepad I had put on the tray. Then I telephoned Gérard at work to arrange to have dinner at a restaurant that evening. The wheels had begun to turn.

I had no time for lunch. I telephoned the solicitor a friend had recommended as the best in Geneva; he said he could see me briefly during his lunchtime since it was so urgent. I also made an official appointment with him for a few days later for Gérard and myself. I arranged for an expert to call that afternoon to value the house.

I kept adding to my notes. I also prepared a card like the one I took into the booth on an interpreting assignment, with basic essentials, entitled 'Things I must not forget to say'. Cassandra's school fees to be paid by him. No allowance for me – I was too proud.

Just in case he took umbrage and marched out of the restaurant in the middle of dinner, leaving me to pay the bill, as he had done in the past, I stuffed a handful of his visiting cards into my silver evening bag. This time, if necessary, I would leave a trail of them and sail out of the restaurant behind him.

Having typed slogans like: 'You do not have to apologise', 'No need to feel guilty', 'You are a person too', 'Don't play his games any more', 'Fifty is a good age to start living', I placed them all over the house wherever my eye would catch them.

Then I got down to the serious business of getting ready. A leisurely bath. I poured half a bottle of expensive scent into it and a glassful of sherry into myself. This was an important, unique occasion. I tried in vain to keep calm in spite of the excitement mounting inside me.

A new hairstyle, that was what I needed. You were only fifty once. I washed and dried my hair and installed myself in front of the mirror with hairbrush and comb, hair lacquer, hairclips and some dainty silver hairpins with little silver bells on them that I had brought back from India. After a while, I proudly inspected my creation from all angles, thanks to an array of mirrors and it wasn't at all bad! Just the thing for a woman of fifty. Not too young and frivolous but not too grandmotherly. Quite elegant. I tried it with earrings and liked the result.

At last I was ready. I arrived at the restaurant with ten minutes to spare. I parked the car and waited until he arrived.

'Would you care to choose a table, Madame?' asked the head waiter.

There was one set apart in the garden, in an alcove formed by trees, a table for lovers with a vase of roses and three candles flickering. The waiter smiled knowingly.

'An anniversary?' he murmured, drawing the chair out for me.

I decided to wait until Gérard had a mouthful of food before starting on my speech. He would be less likely to walk out.

It was a pleasant summer's evening. The details of the shrubs, trees and flowers around us are imprinted on my memory. I savoured the scene for a moment, then took my notes out of my handbag and propped them on my lap so I could see them easily, the basic essentials card on top. I took a deep breath and began:

'We have been married twenty-six years.'

He looked at me coldly, politely, self-assuredly. His suspicions were confirmed: I was about to say, 'Let's make a fresh start . . .'

'Twenty-six years is a long time. Too long. It's time to end it like a business contract, unemotionally, without fuss or senti-mentality.'

His fork dropped with a clatter onto his plate. His mouth fell open. He ran one hand through his hair and there was some-thing pathetic in the gesture. I almost put out a hand to clasp his wrist and say 'It was only a joke. Forget it. I didn't mean it . . .' But my glance fell on the notes on my lap under the table and instead I said calmly, 'The children are old enough to look after themselves now. Marc is earning his living and is quite independent. Stephanie finishes university soon; she is inde-pendent too. Cassandre is fifteen and old enough to understand. The time has come for us to go separate ways. Let us share what we possess without drama and end our marriage. No need to fight and make our lawyers rich. I have prepared a memoran-dum of understanding for us both to sign, with two carbon copies – one for each of us and one for the solicitor. And here is a list of our assets and an inventory of the contents of the house, also in triplicate. All we have to do now is go back to the house after dinner, go through the inventory and agree on who keeps what.'

Speechless, he stared at me disbelievingly. For the first time ever he was actually listening to me.

Once I had started it was easier than I had thought. I realised then that many things which seem impossible are really easier than you think, provided you know what you want. That is the key: to know what you want. Once you know that, the rest fits snugly round it. It had taken me some time but I had at last understood that my 'happy-ever-after' depended not on Gérard or Janek or anyone else – but on me.

The solicitor said it was the quickest and most painless divorce, and the least costly, he had ever known. There was no acrimony. I think Gérard was still too dazed to argue – it was certainly out of character.

After the court case, we took our solicitor out for a celebratory coffee and croissant. It was a crisp sunny autumn morning in the old part of Geneva town and the cobbled streets and ancient stone buildings all looked new and fresh to me.

That afternoon I bought myself a divorce dress – a flimsy affair I had been admiring in a shop window for some time. Then I went home and telephoned a local nursery. 'I would like a tall lime tree to be planted by the terrace as soon as possible,' I said.

The next thing to organise was my divorce party. An official piece of paper from the court and a bill from the solicitor were not enough. Our wedding had had a lot of 'tra-la-la'. In order to feel free, I also needed a tra-la-la, pomp and ceremony divorce.

All my friends were invited and all those who had seen me cry. This put my hairdresser at the top of the list. She had always pretended not to notice the tears as I sat cooking under the dryer. It was a pity I had lost touch with Miranda, who had warned me against Gérard so dramatically on the eve of my marriage. I would have liked to have had her at my divorce party.

There were over a hundred guests and a five-piece jazz band, the Vieux Carré, all of whom were old friends.

It was December, and outside everything was covered by a thick carpet of snow. As the guests arrived and were shown into the cloakroom to remove their snowboots, fur hat, coat and gloves, I whispered, 'Have you ever been divorced?'

If the reply was in the affirmative I pinned a red carnation in their hair. I had prepared a tray beforehand with red carnations and hairpins. The men looked very jazzy with a red carnation over one ear. Most of the musicians wore a carnation – the drummer wore two. An American woman was wearing three. I hadn't dared ask my question of an old friend who was constantly talking about her husband and the long, happy years they had spent together, but to my surprise I noticed later in the evening that she too was wearing a carnation in her hair.

'The carnations are only for those who have been divorced,' I explained.

'I know,' came the wry answer.

During the evening we put our boots and coats on again and all went out into the garden for a fireworks display. Somehow the secret had got out that there would be fireworks and many of the guests had brought their own.

My children had spent that morning pumping balloons with helium. The balloons floated now above the heads of the dancers, just under the ceiling. At midnight the music stopped, glasses of champagne were handed round and each man stretched up to catch the string of a balloon for his partner and one for himself.

I opened the French windows. It was full moon. The lime tree (the divorce tree, as I thought of it) was heavy with snow. We all stepped out on to the terrace and released the balloons. I watched them rise into the sky; suddenly the air was filled with coloured balloons. They were caught in the rafters of the overhanging roof, caught in the surrounding fir trees, the sky was a blaze of colour. Then they grew smaller and smaller and disappeared into the dark blue night sky. I was free.

Now the 'happily-ever-after' could really begin.

Acknowledgements

I wish to express my thanks to Katie Stackhouse whose patience, perseverance and encouragement truly made this book possible.

Also available from Bantam

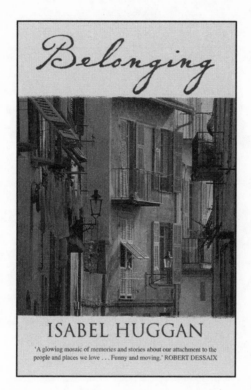

Belonging

ISABEL HUGGAN

'A glowing mosaic of memories and stories about our attachment to the people and places we love . . . Funny and moving.' ROBERT DESSAIX

Also available from Bantam

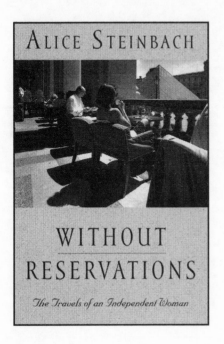